Praise for *Beyond Behaviors*

"*Beyond Behaviors* provides the basis for a paradigm shift in understanding and treating children with disruptive behaviors. Historically, educational and therapeutic models treat anti-social and asocial behavior as motivated and incentivized. In this accessible and beautifully written volume, Dr. Delahooke pulls the veil off this myth and replaces it with a neurobiologically-informed treatment model that provides insightful directives leading to effective outcomes."

—**Stephen W. Porges, PhD**,
Distinguished University Scientist, Indiana University,
Professor of Psychiatry, University of North Carolina, and
author of *The Pocket Guide to the Polyvagal Theory:
The Transformative Power of Feeling Safe*

"As a developmental psychologist, compassion teacher, and autism mom, I can whole-heartedly say this book is brilliant. Traditional methods of 'shaping' children's behaviors typically ignore children's emotional state, at great cost to the child's ability to learn, develop, and form secure relationships. This book provides concrete ways to help understand safety as the foundation for children's learning, working with rather than against natural brain functions to maximize learning potential."

—**Kristin Neff, PhD**,
Associate Professor, Department of Educational Psychology,
University of Texas at Austin, and author of *Self-Compassion:
The Proven Power of Being Kind to Yourself*

"I love this book. It will be one I give and recommend over and over. *Beyond Behaviors* is succinct, accessible, practical, science-based. And it's a game changer. My hope is that not only parents, educators, clinicians, and all helping professionals read it, but that it becomes required reading for professionals in training. It's time for us to use science-informed approaches to go beyond mere behaviors to support children and their caregivers, and this is the book to light the way."

—**Tina Payne Bryson, PhD, LCSW**,
Executive Director of The Center for Connection and
co-author of *New York Times* bestsellers *The Whole-Brain Child* and *No-Drama Discipline*

"This book will embrace every parent and professional puzzling over behavioral challenges and make you question the assumptions about their meaning and re-evaluate how to help. Dr. Delahooke reframes our understanding by integrating perspectives from development, brain science, mental health, and child and parent experiences using example after example to guide you towards insight and compassionate approaches that are respectful of neurodiversity. *Beyond Behaviors* will help every child and family progress, feel safe, enjoy relationships, and develop to their fullest."

—**Serena Wieder, PhD**,
Clinical Director, Profectum Foundation, co-creator of the DIR Model and
co-author of *The Child with Special Needs* and *Engaging Autism*

"Dr. Mona Delahooke is a child psychologist with over 30 years of experience working with children who have behavioral challenges, including those who are neurodiverse and/or have experienced early trauma. In this easily readable book, Dr. Delahooke encourages professionals and families to see concerning behaviors as the tip of an iceberg that obscures early embedded feelings of danger or life threat. With compassion and insight, she guides us toward creating healing environments of safety and security."

—**Marilyn R. Sanders, MD, FAAP**,
Attending Neonatologist, Connecticut Children's Medical Center and
Professor of Pediatrics, University of Connecticut School of Medicine

"I love *Beyond Behaviors* for a whole lot of reasons. First, I think, is the message of compassionate non-judgment. Mona Delahooke shows how important it is that parents be compassionate with themselves, and practice good self-care techniques as necessary prerequisites for intelligent responding to their challenging children. One of the best features of this book are the practical, empowering, step-by-step ideas for finding the calm self-acceptance necessary for building a healing, supportive relationship with even the most challenging and frightened child."

—**Dona Matthews, PhD**,
Developmental Psychologist and co-author of
Beyond Intelligence: Secrets for Raising Happily Productive Kids

"This book should be required reading for frustrated parents and those of us in a position of diagnosing or creating behavior plans for children. Imagine the amazing outcomes if we followed Mona Delahooke's guide to empower and support children through their big feelings and behaviors, rather than focusing only on the tip of the iceberg."

—**Nicole Schwarz, MA, LMFT**,
Parent Coach

"In *Beyond Behaviors*, Mona Delahooke, PhD, applies the Polyvagal theory developed by Stephen Porges to children, convincingly making the case that many children who can't seem to behave themselves simply don't have that developmental capacity yet, and giving us a social-emotional roadmap for how children learn to self-regulate. Delahooke guides us to the realization that children act out when they feel stressed, so the most important tool in our toolbox is always our connection with the child, which restores safety. This break-through book reframes children who exhibit "problem" behavior and challenges us as therapists, teachers and parents to shift our own paradigm so that we can help them. Highly recommended."

—**Dr. Laura Markham**,
author of *Peaceful Parent, Happy Kids*

Beyond Behaviors

Using Brain Science and Compassion to Understand and Solve Children's Behavioral Challenges

Mona Delahooke, PhD

Published by
PESI Publishing & Media
PESI, Inc.
3839 White Ave
Eau Claire, WI 54703

Cover: Amy Rubenzer
Editing: Tom Fields-Meyer, Jenessa Jackson PhD, Tara Miner
Layout: Bookmasters & Amy Rubenzer

ISBN: 9781683731191

PESI Publishing
pesipublishing.com

About the Author

Mona Delahooke, PhD, is a licensed clinical psychologist with more than 30 years of experience caring for children and their families. She is a senior faculty member of the Profectum Foundation, an organization dedicated to supporting families of neurodiverse children, adolescents and adults. She is a trainer for the Los Angeles County Department of Mental Health.

Dr. Delahooke holds the highest level of endorsement in the field of infant and toddler mental health in California, as a Reflective Practice Mentor (RPM). She is a frequent speaker, trainer, and consultant to parents, organizations, schools, and public agencies. Dr. Delahooke has dedicated her career to promoting compassionate, relationship-based, neurodevelopmental interventions for children with developmental, behavioral, emotional, and learning differences.

She is the author of *Social and Emotional Development in Early Intervention: A Skills Guide for Working with Children* (PESI, 2017).

Dedication

To Scott, my husband and partner on this joyous journey.
Your life embodies compassion for others,
and I am forever grateful for your love and support.

Acknowledgments

I extend my sincere gratitude to the following people, who made this book possible:

Tom Fields-Meyer, for his insight, wisdom, and editing talent, which give flight to my ideas and words.

Stephen Porges, PhD, whose life's work provides me and millions of others a new lens to view behavioral challenges and new ways to help children and trauma survivors with compassion and understanding.

Serena Wieder, PhD, for her mentorship, voluminous body of work, and for cocreating a paradigm that respected neurodiversity before it was a movement.

Karsyn Morse, my editor at PESI Publishing and Media, for her unwavering support.

Connie Lillas, PhD, for reading the manuscript and for all I have learned from her through the years.

Doreen S. Oleson, EdD, for inspiring generations of school leaders to value diversity, community service, and the power of relationships.

Jenessa Jackson, PhD, for meticulously organizing my ever-changing reference list and chapter notes.

Table of Contents

Part Three:
Neurodiversity, Trauma, and Looking to the Future

Introduction

A kindergartner whose father pinches her on the arm at night—once for every time her teacher wrote the girl's name on the behavior chart at school that day.

A three-year-old in foster care who was found sitting in a car by the side of the road with his mother, who was passed out at the wheel. His daycare-center teacher sends him to a time-out room for "challenging behaviors."

A ten-year-old diagnosed with Oppositional Defiant Disorder. His teachers say he is chronically disruptive, always seeking attention. His problematic behaviors began after his family relocated to a new state.

Practically every day, I encounter teachers, professionals, and parents who are desperately seeking answers for how to help children like these when traditional strategies have failed them. I hear from them in my practice as a child psychologist and speaker, on my blog, over social media, and in emails.

This book is my answer. I invite you to join me on a journey, one that forced me to question everything that I was taught about how to manage challenging behaviors. Over time, I came to a new understanding, far from the narrow understanding I acquired in graduate school. I wanted to know: Why are we failing to help children with the most seriously challenging behaviors?

My search brought me to the deepest regions of the brain, where a visionary neuroscientist finally provided answers.

Too many books about children's challenging behaviors take a one-size-fits-all approach, without consideration for the autonomic state—the brain/body connection. They also fail to consider children's individual differences—their unique strengths and challenges. And most approaches to challenging behaviors fail to examine those challenges in the context of a child's social and emotional development. As a result, many treatment approaches fall short because they simply lack a cohesive rationale or guiding principle.

This book aims to provide a new context to understand behavioral challenges and offer a roadmap for making decisions based on each child's brain and body. While research and knowledge about the brain has progressed exponentially over the past three decades, we have barely begun to translate this understanding into practical use. In my experience, the neuroscientist Dr. Stephen Porges's work—his Polyvagal Theory, and specifically the concept of neuroception—offers the best new way to view and support behaviorally challenged children and their families.[1]

Several years ago, when I couldn't find a simple primer to recommend to childhood professionals across different fields, I decided to write a book on social-emotional development: *Social and Emotional Development in Early Intervention: A Skills Guide for Working with Children*. One of its chapters covered challenging behaviors. The interest that chapter and my other writings on the topic generated inspired this book, a deeper dive into the topic.

Over the years I have sat with parents, teachers, therapists, administrators, and others in countless settings—in my office, at public and private mental health agencies, and in schools—discussing how to help children with challenging behaviors. Inevitably, the well-intentioned professionals move the conversation quickly toward techniques, behavior plans, and reinforcement contingencies. But these plans should come only after we ask a fundamental and vital question: Are the child's brain and body experiencing safety? And if not, how do we first help the child to feel safe?

Three sources inform my answers. The first is the visionary work of Dr. Porges, work that demonstrates that safety is the foundation upon which children build the many skills of emotional and behavioral self-control.[2] I am deeply grateful to Dr. Porges, whose support for clinicians like me is enabling the practical application of the Polyvagal perspective in childhood mental health and allied fields. Of particular importance is his concept of neuroception, "the process by which our nervous system evaluates risk without requiring awareness."[3] This idea provides the brain-science rationale to help us tailor our approaches to the unique needs of each child's nervous system.

Secondly, I am indebted to the psychologist Dr. Serena Wieder, my mentor and a pioneer of child development and symbolic play. Along with Dr. Stanley Greenspan, Dr. Wieder developed a model known as DIR® (Developmental, Individual-differences and Relationship-based) after conducting research in the late 1970s on infants at high risk for developmental challenges.[4] Their work led to a new and revolutionary approach to working with children and families, introducing a new conceptualization of the developmental stages of social and emotional development. It also helped explain the critical need to gauge support for each child and family by respecting the wide range of individual differences inherent in every human being.[5]

The third factor influencing my approach is a recognition of the importance of how we take in information through our sensory systems. Too many professionals and educators don't appreciate the significance of our sensory systems and fail to integrate this important factor into mental health, medicine, or education. The truth is that sensory systems form basic substrates underlying all human behaviors. My colleagues in the field of occupational therapy taught me that analyzing a child's sensory systems and preferences offers a practical perspective on how we understand and support children when they exhibit challenging behaviors.[6]

I have worked with parents, professionals, and educators to understand children's problematic, challenging, or confusing behaviors for two and a half decades as a clinical psychologist. We all struggle with how to ascribe meaning to these behaviors. Many current treatment paradigms focus on what are considered common causes for behavioral challenges: attention-seeking, noncompliance, manipulation, and avoidance of nonpreferred activities. In contrast, this book lays out a developmental and relationship-based approach, one that views behavior problems from a different perspective. As we shall see, many persistent and concerning behaviors are manifestations of physiological stress responses that occur when a child experiences a neuroception of threat. When I came to view problematic behaviors *as adaptive responses* and not *purposeful misbehavior* I shifted nearly all of my beliefs about how to help children and families.

In my clinical work, I have found that perpetual challenging behaviors are rarely caused by intentional, willful defiance, avoidance, or manipulation. Yet many treatment approaches for severe behavioral problems are based on the assumption that they are. Often, methods to help children follow the Premack principle: behaviors with a higher level of intrinsic reinforcement can be used as rewards or reinforcements for less preferred behaviors.[7] In other words, positive reinforcement or negative consequences improve compliance and reduce problematic behaviors. But persistent and seriously challenging behaviors in children are often impervious to reinforcement schedules, punishments, time-outs, and other such techniques.

Many professionals believe that problematic behaviors represent a child's efforts to *get something* or to *get out of something*. We often blame a child's behavior challenges on "lax" parenting, or a diagnosis. Too often, we assume that what a child or teen needs is better behavioral management, more consistent parenting, or better medication. Current neuroscience, though, reveals a more complex reality: many problematic behaviors reflect how the child's brain and body perceive stress.

The new approach I describe in this book moves away from simply blaming children or parents. A recent poll by the Zero to Three Foundation found that 90 percent of parents feel judged "most of the time."[8] In a poll of parents of children with behavior challenges, the percentage would probably be closer to 100. Too often, we blame children or parents for a child's behavior.

Further, we tend to believe that children can overcome their challenges *if only they put their minds to it*. We become cheerleaders, hoping to help children "will themselves" into better behavior. And we feel disappointed in them (and in ourselves) when the behaviors continue despite our best efforts. We falsely assume that children of a certain age have volitional control over their emotions and behaviors. That assumption is the main reason that many techniques to help children with behavioral challenges fail, taking a heavy toll on relationships.

The book's three sections show how to deconstruct behavior challenges to discover their causes and triggers for each child. Part One (Chapters 1–3) defines the problem and issues to be aware of in order to help children. **Part Two** (Chapters 4–6) describes what we do with this knowledge and how to apply it. **Part Three** focuses on particular populations. Chapter 7 explains how to apply this approach to redefine the meaning of challenging behaviors in children diagnosed with autism and other forms of neurodiversity. Chapter 8 covers ways to support children who have been exposed to toxic stress and trauma and who display behavioral challenges. Chapter 9 explains what we can do to help children and families build positive experiences to counteract the stress and pressure felt when working with a child who has behavioral challenges.

Brain science is exceedingly complex. I have greatly simplified the information about the brain to make it accessible. I am a clinician (and mother) in mind and heart. Translating neuroscience concepts can be humbling and often daunting. My presentation of the underlying neuroscience is by choice reductionistic in order to maximize its utility for practical application to a wide audience. It seems appropriate to invoke Pope's adage: "A little learning is a dangerous thing; Drink deep, or taste not the Pierian spring."[9] While it is a reach for a clinician to oversimplify how the brain works, I feel qualified to take this leap of faith in my translational applications because I have seen them work in my clinical experiences over many years. I am also indebted to Dr. Porges for generously taking the time to read some of my clinical translations of the Polyvagal Theory over the past several years to ensure that my version reflects an accurate understanding of the concept of neuroception.

A word in the spirit of collaboration and relationship-building: This book is not intended as an indictment or criticism of dedicated colleagues working with children using more traditional methods in their respective fields—or of the way you might be raising your own child. Rather, I hope it will serve as an additional lens through which to see current approaches, across the parenting, educational, developmental, juvenile justice, social work, and mental health communities—to bring into focus basic concepts that we can all embrace to support children who struggle.

This book is not a substitute for professional advice or support for each child. If you are a parent, you should seek appropriate support from a variety of professionals you trust as you navigate your child's challenges. And if you feel that your own mental health is fragile, it's important to seek support and find opportunities for self-care. Valuing your own mental health and ability to feel emotionally stable is the best thing you can do for your child and the children you care for.

A final word of caution: This book includes many activities for personal reflection. As with all psychological methods, unexpected reactions can occur. If any of the exercises I describe cause distress for you or the child you are working with, simply discontinue the exercise.

I am happy to share this exciting information and hope you will enjoy discovering its hopeful message: that a new comprehension of behaviors has the potential to change lives for the better, resulting in a more humane way of understanding, teaching, treating, and supporting children who are struggling.

PART ONE
Understanding Behaviors

1.
Revealing the Hidden, Adaptive Benefits of Behaviors

> *"One looks back with appreciation to the brilliant teachers, but with gratitude to those who touched our human feeling."*
>
> **Carl Jung**

By the time Stuart hit second grade, his teachers had pegged him as a "problem child." They knew he came from a loving home and could discern right from wrong, but he frequently started fights and had outbursts that caused classroom disruptions. Stuart had a number of professionals in his life trying to help him, including school counselors, a private therapist, and a developmental pediatrician.

His parents and team were relieved when Stuart controlled his behaviors, sometimes for days, or even weeks, but then—seemingly out of nowhere—he would explode with anger at a peer, sibling, teacher, or one of his parents. His difficulties only deepened with time and eventually a psychiatrist offered a diagnosis: Oppositional Defiant Disorder. His parents sent him to a series of special schools and even residential treatment centers, but despite elaborate efforts by many people, he made only modest progress.

In my work as a child psychologist, I encounter "Stuarts" all the time, young people whom adults have diagnosed with disorders, disciplined for misbehaving, or judged for making bad choices. Parents and others send them to mental health professionals like me in the hope that we will help "cure" their problematic behaviors. What I have observed and experienced over many years is that all of us—parents, teachers, and other professionals—use a wide range of techniques and approaches that sometimes conflict with each other and often prove ineffective, leaving us frustrated and confused.

But there is hope. This book will present a new way of understanding behaviors and new and helpful approaches based on that understanding. Whether you are a therapist, an educator, a paraprofessional, or a parent, you will gain a new perspective on what behaviors are and why they arise. And I'll offer tools you can utilize to improve the lives of children and their families. In this chapter, we'll start by examining what's wrong with the status quo. We'll look at the three most common mistakes we all make in treating and managing behaviors. Then, once we have established the limitations of our current approaches, we'll discuss a new way of framing and understanding behaviors and begin to lay out a helpful and enlightened approach based on current neuroscience.

What's Wrong With the Status Quo?

Before we launch into our examination of a new approach to behavioral challenges, it's important to understand why we fall short in the way we currently comprehend, evaluate, and treat them. Again and again, we make three significant mistakes: (1) we don't pinpoint the behavior's correct etiology before we address it; (2) we use one-size-fits-all approaches instead of tailoring the treatment to the individual; and (3) we fail to use a developmental roadmap to ensure we're using the right approach at the right time. Let's examine each of these three shortcomings.

We Fail to Determine the Etiology of Behaviors Before We Try to Change Them

Timmy spent his early years in the foster care system and by the time he turned four he had been diagnosed with multiple psychiatric disorders. Prone to disagreeing, running away, and physically striking others, he had been placed in three different foster homes within a single year. His meltdowns would appear suddenly and seemingly without warning. At age eight, Timmy was so upset to learn that a beloved PE teacher had transferred to another campus that he refused all classwork, and then when a teacher asked him to line up for lunch, Timmy toppled a heavy desk.

His teachers tried to deal with these incidents with detailed behavior plans designed to reward appropriate behaviors and offer consequences (such as withholding screen time) for maladaptive behaviors. But these efforts proved ineffective. Why? *Because the plans were based on the assumption that Timmy had volitional control of his actions.* He didn't. His behaviors resulted from the difficulty he had staying emotionally regulated. At that stage, he simply wasn't capable of changing his behavior to earn a reward. Far from improving his behavior, the plans only served to frustrate Timmy and negatively influence his emerging self-image.

What happened? Timmy's teachers decided what to do about his behaviors before they fully understood what caused them. In our cognitive-centric environment, we often assume that a child has deliberately chosen how to behave—or misbehave. This reflects a predominant cultural bias that values punishment when children exhibit a certain range of "atypical" behaviors.

Case in point: The Center for American Progress analyzed data from the 2016 National Survey of Children's Health (NSCH) and found that an estimated fifty thousand preschoolers were suspended from school at least once and seventeen thousand were estimated to have been expelled.[1] The other cultural bias (sometimes referred to as implicit bias) that emerged from the survey is that male children of color were consistently over-represented in these expulsion and suspension rates. *These high numbers indicate a fundamental misunderstanding of the meanings of childhood challenging behaviors and solutions for them, as well as the continuing effects of racial bias on how we identify them.*

What causes these misreadings? *When we fail to recognize that many behaviors represent the body's response to stress, not intentional misbehavior, we expend effort on techniques designed to help children logically connect their thoughts, emotions, and behaviors when they simply can't—yet.* As we'll discuss later, in addressing behaviors, sometimes we aim too high and sometimes too low. We aim too high when we assume that a child's behavior is the result of thoughtful intent when it's actually a response to stress. We aim too low when we assume a child *lacks* certain abilities he actually does have. For example, neurodiverse children with sensory/movement differences might have complex thoughts and ideas they are unable to express or behaviors they are unable to inhibit because of the way their brains are wired.

> ## When we see a behavior that is problematic or confusing, the first question we should ask isn't "How do we get rid of it?" but rather "What is this telling us about the child?"

The answer will provide valuable clues about what to do next. In Chapter 2, we will learn how to determine whether a behavior is top down (controllable, intentional, or planned) or bottom up (reflexive, automatic, or a stress response), and what the implications of the answer are for our interactions, treatment tools, and techniques.

We Use One-Size-Fits-All Approaches

Anna, a fifth grader, struggled to get through nearly every school day. She often refused to go to school, and her father had to physically help her into the car and the classroom. Anxious and preoccupied, she bit her nails and picked at her skin until it bled. In response, her teacher developed a support plan. When the teacher noticed Anna picking at her skin, she would ask Anna to take a "sensory break," when she was to walk around the periphery of the room in an effort to calm herself and shift to more positive behaviors. The teacher had found this to be an effective strategy for a previous student who had behavioral challenges.

But the strategy proved ineffective for Anna. When the teacher told her it was a good time for a sensory break, Anna felt that the teacher was singling her out and blaming her; she felt self-conscious walking around while her classmates watched. Anna was deeply embarrassed and confused about her own behaviors.

The teacher's idea of a sensory break to help her relax certainly had merit—*but not for this specific child*. Why? Because it didn't take into consideration Anna's perception of the intervention and, further, it didn't address the multiple underlying reasons for Anna's emotional distress. In short, the plan failed to accurately and comprehensively address Anna's *individual differences*.

That's the problem with many paradigms and programs intended to help children with problematic behaviors: they utilize principles that are based on *general* notions about child development. *Sometimes these programs are successful, but often they fail because they are not tailored to the unique needs of each child.* Just as dishwashers have adjustable settings for temperature and time, each child has her own "settings," the sensory, emotional, cognitive, and learning "settings" to which she responds best. It takes effort, but it's important to discover which settings work best for each child, developing an appreciation for his or her individual differences.

Individual differences in this context include anything that affects how a person perceives the world through his or her body and mind.[2] That includes everything we feel on a conscious or subconscious level—such as bodily and other sensations, thoughts, and feelings.[3] These differences dynamically influence the relationship between children and caregivers, deeply affecting social and emotional development and the child's behaviors, emotional regulation, and behavioral control. The key is for caregivers and providers to understand each child's individual differences, including the child's underlying needs, preferences, and inborn traits.[4] Providing generic techniques, even if they are helpful to some children, is often insufficient for children who have difficulties with emotional and behavioral regulation, as it was for Anna. Decades ago, Drs. Stanley Greenspan and Serena Wieder proposed the thoughtful consideration of individual differences in child development and infant mental health treatment.[5] When I studied their perspective in the 1990s, it transformed the way I practiced psychology (and parented my own children).

Understanding each child's individual differences helps us tailor our relational and therapeutic approaches. Too often, we make assumptions about supportive techniques and environments without asking if they are tailored to the specific needs of the child. This idea of personalizing approaches is now popular in the medical field, and specifically in *precision medicine*, "an emerging approach for disease treatment and prevention that takes into account individual variability in genes, environment, and lifestyle for each person."[6] We can apply the principles of precision medicine to address the limitations inherent in one-size-fits all approaches. This complex approach can make all the difference in how we support children. In fact, the word that best describes the human brain/body connection is *complex*. If we don't embrace this complexity, we can miss essential opportunities to help children where they need it the most.

> ## *Understanding each child's individual differences helps us tailor our relational and therapeutic approaches.*

Parenting and behavior-support books are full of useful, general suggestions, but most neglect to specify how to tailor them to each child's unique needs. Parents know this. A large study recently found that 63 percent of parents feel "skeptical of people who give parenting advice and recommendations if they don't know my child and my situation specifically."[7] We need to customize the way we communicate with children, making sure we do so in ways that are *effective for each child's mind and body*—that is, how each child processes information through her body, emotional system, senses, and thoughts. In Chapter 3 and throughout the book, we will explore how to go beyond one-size-fits-all approaches and tailor our interactions and approaches to the needs of each child.

We Don't Use a Developmental Roadmap to Understand the Optimal Times for Each Approach

Liam was six when he transferred into a charter school that his parents and school district team hoped would meet his needs. Considered "twice exceptional," Liam was intellectually inquisitive, scoring above grade level academically. But he also had challenges in emotional regulation and expressive language that caused him to experience frequent meltdowns in class. Things had reached a breaking point at his previous school when a classroom aide asked him to put away a book on his favorite topic—animals of the Arctic—and get ready for lunch. Instead of complying, he kicked the aide in the shin.

At his new school, his teacher, trying to be sensitive, ordered a beautiful picture book for Liam, with a personalized title: "Liam's Calm-Down Book." The text offered detailed suggestions for what Liam could do when he felt upset. His parents and team had high hopes that in this new and supportive environment, Liam's behavioral outbursts would subside. They did for a few days until he kicked someone again—this time a peer, who had grabbed a ball from him on the playground.

Why did the plan fail to curb Liam's behaviors? In part because it wasn't tailored to Liam's developmental level. The "Calm-Down Book," a great idea, might well have benefited a child with more advanced social-emotional capacities. *But the book required top-down processing to stop bottom-up behavioral and emotional reactions.* Liam simply didn't have the developmental capacity that would have made the book an appropriate tool—yet.

A developmental roadmap helps us know which behaviors are top down and which are bottom up. Only when we know where behaviors fit in the child's larger developmental picture can we help the child to express needs and to communicate distress, thereby preventing behavioral challenges. Of course, this is much easier said than done. We can't simply ask a child to calm down and use her words unless the child has the developmental capacity to do so. Sometimes, we expect children to be able to do something (like control their impulsive behaviors) that is outside their developmental, or "in the moment" ability, leading to confusion and frustration for all.

Many of our approaches falsely assume that children can self-regulate their emotions and behaviors when in reality, they do not yet have that ability.

For example, one reason parents can feel so frustrated about a toddler's behavior is the "expectation gap."[8] Many parents assume that tots are capable—or should be capable—of doing things that their brains simply aren't ready to do yet.

A large study by the Zero to Three organization dedicated to infant and toddler well-being revealed that 56 percent of parents believe that children have the impulse control to resist the desire to do something forbidden before age three. And of those parents, 36 percent believe that children under age two can do so. The truth: toddlers don't start developing these abilities until age three and a half or four at the *earliest*.[9] The same survey found that 43 percent of parents think children can reliably share and take turns with other children before age two. In reality, this skill develops between three to four years as well.[10]

Children develop the ability to use top-down thinking to control their behaviors through brain development and active engagement with caregivers—engagement that increases in complexity as the child grows. Understanding how children develop the skills for self-control helps us learn where to focus our efforts to support each child.

Drs. Greenspan and Wieder introduced a developmental roadmap that provides an elegant conceptual approach to understanding a child's social and emotional milestones.[11] Without such a guide, we lack the *context* for utilizing our tools and techniques. This is one reason we often fall short in supporting vulnerable children's behavioral and emotional challenges. In Chapter 2, we will look at social-emotional development and how we can use it as a roadmap to decide if (and when) a child is using top-down or bottom-up processing. Placing the child's behaviors in the context of his or her social and emotional processes will help to guide our decisions about what to say (or do) or not say (and not do) when a child experiences behavioral disruptions.

Many parenting and behavior experts emphasize teaching children about how to behave better. Teaching is great when a child is neurodevelopmentally ready to be taught, but the foundation for helping children is built through the experience of love, safety, and connection in relationships. Emotional co-regulation with caring adults leads to successful self-regulation. As we proceed through the book, this distinction will become very clear. We need to know when to use bottom-up approaches first if the problem is bottom up. Too often we rely solely on top-down approaches for bottom-up problems, leading to frustration for all involved.

A New Way of Understanding Behaviors

Now that we have discussed the most significant mistakes we make in dealing with behaviors, let's begin to explore a new way of framing and understanding them—a view that will inform a more effective and successful approach to dealing with behavioral challenges.

What Is Behavior?

Let's begin by considering what a behavior is: the observable response to our internal and external experiences.[12] This broad definition suggests that behaviors are outward manifestations of a person's internal bodily processes, perceptions (how one processes information from the environment), emotions, thoughts, and intentions. Too often, though, we build our recommendations, treatment plans, and techniques based on what we see, without adequately considering what lies beneath.

Instead, we should consider another approach, a way of taking into account the many factors that are less obvious and less visible. That is to think of behaviors as the tip of an iceberg—that part of an individual that we readily see or know. The tip reveals answers to "what" questions about a person. The tip reveals answers to "what" questions about a person. Just as we can see only the tip of an iceberg, while most of it remains hidden underwater, we can observe childhood behaviors with the understanding that the many factors that contribute to them are hidden from view.[13]

*As with an iceberg, below the surface
is a much larger piece, concealed from view,
but far more significant. Hidden here is the valuable
information that can help us understand the "why"
of a child's behaviors, including the rich clues about
possible causes and triggers.*

Another benefit to looking below the tip of the iceberg is that it helps us to determine which behaviors we should leave well enough alone. Many children have behaviors, including different ways they move their bodies in order to concentrate or feel comfortable, that teachers or parents target for change because these adults view the behaviors from a deficit-based rather than a strength-based perspective. For example, many children diagnosed with autism have behavior plans aimed at eliminating motion/movement differences before anyone performs a thorough evaluation of the benefits or adaptive purpose these movements serve for the child. We will discuss the need to proceed with caution when we support children diagnosed with autism in Chapter 7. When we take a closer look, we can gain an appreciation for all behaviors as we more thoughtfully determine what to do (or not do) about them.

Too often, we are so focused on what is visible that we don't take the time to look under the surface.

Developmental Iceberg

What's going on?
Behavioral challenges

Why is it happening?
Internal bodily processes

Sensations processed
in the brain/body

Emotions

Developmental capacities
and processes

Ability to plan and
execute actions

Memories

Thoughts

Ideas

One reason it's so difficult to change persistent behavioral challenges is that we focus on the wrong targets. When we focus on the observable behaviors alone, we're missing the bigger and more complete picture. What can we do to see the bigger picture? *We can look at each child through a new lens, and without automatically blaming that child.* This intentional shift in targets isn't a systematic part of training across childhood professions and education. For example, Joe Federaro and Sandra Bloom, leaders in trauma-informed care and cofounders of the Sanctuary Programs, suggest that we need to "deliberately shift attitudes, to move the fundamental question that we pose when we confront a troubled or troubling person from 'What's wrong with you?' to 'What's happened to you?' and 'How can we help?'"[14]

As we look beneath the iceberg's tip we can also shift from the assumption of something wrong with the child by asking another question: "What is this child experiencing at this moment in body and mind?"

The most effective way to help children is by looking above *and* below the surface. Why don't we routinely do this? Why do we judge a child's behaviors as "good" or "bad" without fully understanding their underlying causes? In part it's because we who love and work with children—parents, teachers, foster parents, caregivers, extended family, and paraprofessionals—lack a common base of knowledge that encompasses this contemporary perspective, which acknowledges the complexity of the body-brain-mind connection.[15]

That's where this book comes in. It will describe the benefits of viewing behavior challenges through a new and expanded lens, a perspective informed by a dynamic synthesis of three areas: (1) neuroscience via the Polyvagal Theory of Dr. Stephen Porges and specifically the guiding principle of neuroception; (2) social-emotional development; and (3) an appreciation for individual differences.

In Part One of the book, we'll examine the first area—a clinical application of the Polyvagal Theory—in this chapter and then discuss social-emotional development in Chapter 2 and individual differences in Chapter 3. We will then move to Part Two and the remainder of the book for practical applications of this knowledge and how we use it.

The Polyvagal Theory: New Light on Understanding Behaviors

Dr. Stephen Porges is a scientist on the faculties of both the Kinsey Institute at Indiana University and the University of North Carolina at Chapel Hill. His Polyvagal Theory offers a remarkable explanation of how the brain and body work together in a bidirectional fashion to help human beings survive and thrive.[16] This complex perspective gave me a newfound appreciation for the adaptive role that challenging behaviors serve for children. The Polyvagal Theory also provided the neuroscience information that enabled me to build new and more effective strategies for helping children and families than I had been taught in graduate school.

As Dr. Porges explains it, behavioral responses represent how a person's nervous system is constantly regulating the body's response to stress.[17] So when a child experiences persistent behavioral challenges, it's an indication that the child's nervous system is automatically adjusting and responding to these various forms of stress.

Informed by the Polyvagal perspective, we see behaviors as *adaptive* responses to an individual's ever-changing nervous system as a demonstration of phylogenetic competence, that is, the human drive from our evolutionary history to survive and thrive.[18]

> *As human beings we start out grounded in our biological survival instincts—those processes that help us stay alive—and our "psychology" is built upon how our caregivers meet our biological perceptions of the environment.*[19]

These survival instincts still live, as Dr. Porges explains, in three underlying neurophysiological states: social engagement, defense (fight or flight), or life threat (shut down). Even though the social engagement system is, phylogenetically speaking, the newest and most adaptive, all three states are adaptive because they are driven by our survival instincts to move our body into a safe place when we don't feel safe.[20] Essentially, the visceral state (our body's physiological state) influences children's behaviors and reactions to help children cope with their unique experience of being in the world.[21]

Viewing behaviors as adaptations changed the way I view, diagnose, and support children with behavioral, emotional, and developmental differences and their families. It is a radical shift from the way I was trained to view and treat children with behavior challenges. In that *medical model,* I learned to focus on observable behaviors and to view symptom clusters as disorders to be treated. In this new approach, we focus instead on the *underlying processes* that *cause* the behaviors.[22] This understanding offers us a more comprehensive way to support children who display persistent behavioral challenges.

*In paradigms that focus solely on behaviors,
the question generally is: What is the child getting
out of the behavior? (Attention? Control?)
In this new paradigm, the question is different: What
are behaviors telling us about the child's underlying
neurophysiological processes?*

Neuroception: A Guiding Principle

A concept devised by Dr. Porges, neuroception, provides a key to understanding behaviors as adaptations. Dr. Porges introduced this term in 2004 to denote the brain's and body's ongoing subconscious surveillance of safety and threat in the environment.[23] Sometimes a person's body and brain detect threat when the person is actually safe, or alternatively, detects safety when actually at risk. Dr. Porges calls this *faulty neuroception*, and in his view, it lies at the core of many psychiatric labels and disorders.[24]

It also probably underlies many behavioral challenges. In other words, serious and persistently challenging behaviors are responses to a child's subconscious perception of risk in the physical or relational environment. When a child is acting defensively, (fighting, fleeing, or shutting down) the child's body is involved in a process aimed at basic survival. These internal processes are invisible and below the surface; what we observe are the challenging behaviors that result.

What causes faulty neuroception? Sometimes children overreact or underreact in their evaluations of situations or the environment. A child with a vulnerable nervous system or a trauma history can mistakenly detect threat in the environment even when that child is safe, triggering defensive reactions, hence faulty neuroception. Throughout the book, we will discuss examples of how an understanding of neuroception can help us deconstruct the causes of behavioral challenges.[25]

In my view, neuroception is the single most unifying concept to guide the treatment of children across parenting, mental health, early intervention, education, and all childhood professions. Its elegance is that the construct accounts for all dimensions of behaviors, and it speaks to the human condition. Additionally, when we examine the impact of safety on human behaviors, a child's (and caregiver's) subconscious perception of safety regulates *physiological state*, which becomes an important intervening variable—that is, one that influences the space in between a stimulus and a response.[26]

As we will see in Chapter 4, the concept of neuroception shifts the way we respond to behaviors.[27]

Instead of focusing on **what we do to** *children,*
we prioritize *how we are with them. Instead of focusing
on eliminating behaviors, we need to provide children with
signals of safety (personalized to their nervous systems) that
allow social-engagement behaviors to emerge spontaneously.*

This idea—that human beings need to feel safe in order to make use of their thinking brain—is a common denominator in the field of neuroscience. Dr. Bruce Perry's Neurosequential Model of Therapy (NMT), for example, stipulates that in order to have effective engagement with children, we need to first *regulate,* in order to *relate*, and only then can we *reason* with the child.[28] Dan Siegel and Tina Bryson echo this idea in the "Whole-Brain" parenting strategy called Connect and Redirect, with interpersonal connection leading the way *in all of our interactions with children.*[29] In short, the first step in helping children with challenges is to build a secure relationship with them.

Wait, What About Diagnoses?

When I was in graduate school decades ago, we studied the *Diagnostic and Statistical Manual (DSM)* of the American Psychiatric Association to diagnose and treat individuals with emotional, behavioral, developmental, and psychiatric conditions.[30] At the time, the *DSM* was considered progressive, a tool to guide clinicians to help people feel better and reduce suffering. Things have changed. While the *DSM* is still an important and necessary diagnostic tool (and integral to decisions about insurance coverage and public assistance), we can improve outcomes with a more informed approach that focuses not on diagnostic labels but on underlying causality.

Knowledge from many fields—including affective and cognitive neuroscience—is shedding new light on the causes of human behaviors, the role of emotions, and how human beings adapt to challenges in their minds and bodies. As we learn more about the value of focusing on these causes, *labels become less significant* and *determining underlying causality becomes more significant.*

This transformation is reflected even in the policies of the National Institutes of Mental Health (NIMH). In 2013, the NIMH shifted funding away from research based solely on *DSM* criteria.[31] Why? Because leaders in the field agreed that it is more important to identify underlying causes that cut across diagnostic categories than symptom checklists such as the *DSM-5*. The NIMH is addressing this change by funding research into *underlying processes* that are relevant to a range of human behaviors and conditions.[32]

Stuart — **Underlying Causes**

Given what we have learned in this chapter about behaviors, let's take another look at Stuart, the young man who had such difficulty controlling his explosive outbursts. From the time he was adopted as a toddler, Stuart seemed to overreact to everyday experiences. Oftentimes, what appeared to be a mild trigger—such as a stranger who looked or sounded a certain way—could set him off. As a small child he frequently ran away from large groups of people or refused to converse with others at gatherings. Later, he habitually refused simple requests from his parents or preschool teachers. By elementary school, that apparent disobedience became a pattern of defiance and lying about behaviors.

The problem was that too many people in his life focused on his *observable behaviors*—the visible tip of his developmental iceberg—instead of making the effort to understand the causes hiding beneath the surface.

When doctors prescribed treatments and medications for his "oppositional defiance," they helped for a few weeks at a time, but his defiant behaviors persisted year after year. Why did Stuart continue to struggle? Because his treatments were aimed at the wrong target. They focused on the *visible* behaviors instead of the *underlying* causes.

What finally did help was a multidisciplinary team—including his parents, teachers, therapists, and physicians—that considered his entire iceberg from different perspectives and in its various dimensions. Surveying his social and emotional development, the team learned that from the time he was a toddler, Stuart had experienced difficulty with one foundational milestone: maintaining a calm state in his body. This caused him to experience many everyday activities and sensations as stressful.

In short, he suffered from faulty neuroception. Why? Stuart experienced emotional difficulties at the most basic level from the time his parents adopted him, despite their best efforts to help him. But it had gone undetected for years. That was why everyday events and particular individuals' voices could set him off: he perceived ordinary phenomena as threatening. As he got older, those experiences lingered as memory fragments that influenced his perceptions and behaviors. Fragments such as these form *implicit memories*, powerful forces shaped by past experiences that one doesn't consciously remember.

Early in Stuart's life, a provider had told his parents that the boy's behaviors were likely learned responses that were reinforced by attention. In other words, the way the parents and others reacted to Stuart reinforced or triggered more behaviors. But that wasn't accurate. Stuart's diagnosis of ODD—Oppositional Defiant Disorder—gave him a label but not much help. What did help was when his team looked at his behaviors from a treatment approach grounded in relational safety with a respect for his individual differences. When they understood that his behavior actually stemmed from a false sense of danger, they were able to react appropriately, and, at last, Stuart began to heal.

Stuart's Iceberg

Behavioral outbursts

Oppositional defiance

DSM-5 Diagnosis (ODD)

Prenatal and perinatal toxic stress

Faulty neuroception (sensing threat in the environment when it was safe)

Challenges in emotional and behavioral regulation

Auditory hypersensitivity

Implicit memories triggering uncontrolled behaviors

Learning from Behaviors

As we saw in Stuart's story, challenging behaviors offer a paradox. Parents, educators, and professionals often view them as a scourge, a source of concern and conflict. Yet at the same time, behaviors provide a clear benefit, and they are a tribute to the brilliance of human survival. *A child who seems to be misbehaving is, in the process, adapting and surviving. Instead of viewing behaviors purely as difficulties we need to get rid of, it's helpful to see them as forming an instructional manual for how to support each child's nervous system.*

> ***When we view behaviors comprehensively and in a holistic brain/body paradigm, we will come to understand the difference between emphasizing behavioral compliance and building the capacity for emotional regulation that underlies behavioral control.***

Using this new lens and viewing behaviors as adaptations, we will move from making *behavioral compliance* the goal, to prioritizing *emotional and relational safety* in an individualized fashion, thereby creating an optimal state for a child to eventually develop self-regulation and intentional control of behaviors.

Now that we have examined some of the neuroscience that helps explain behaviors as adaptations, it's important to see how they fit into the larger picture of a child's social-emotional development. That's the subject of Chapter 2.

Main Points —

- Three main limitations of traditional approaches to helping children with behavioral challenges are: (1) not determining the etiology of behaviors before we try to change them; (2) using one-size-fits-all approaches; and (3) failing to use a developmental roadmap to insure we're using the right approach at the right time.

- Neuroception, a concept developed by Dr. Porges, is the brain's and body's ongoing subconscious surveillance of safety and threat in the environment.

- Children's mental health is influenced by how caregivers meet their child's neuroception of the relational and physical environments.

- We need to understand the difference between an intentional misbehavior and a stress response.

- Our approaches/parenting methods will all benefit when we prioritize relational safety as a frontline intervention.

2.
Top Down or Bottom Up?
Before We Respond to Behavior, We Need to Understand Its Origin

> *"Social behavior and the capacity to manage challenge are dependent on the neural regulation of physiological state."*
>
> **Dr. Stephen Porges**

From the time Rinaldo started kindergarten, he struggled with behavioral challenges. Early in his second-grade year, his teacher observed that he was unable to follow instructions, and he frequently struck peers or grabbed toys and other objects from them, even after she repeatedly asked him to stop. When a team met to formulate his individualized educational plan (IEP) they addressed this issue with a primary goal: that Rinaldo would "use his words or tell others what he needs or how he is feeling instead of using physical behaviors."

If only he could have. Despite repeated admonitions, Rinaldo's impulsive, disruptive behavior continued, unabated. His teachers and parents reminded him repeatedly, and he made earnest attempts to comply, but he simply wasn't able to use language to solve his problems with any consistency. Each year, the IEP team kicked the behavior goal forward to the next school year. What they didn't do was ask a simple question: "*Why* isn't Rinaldo able to use his words instead of acting out impulsively?"

The answer was that Rinaldo didn't yet have the developmental capacity to use words to represent sensations, ideas, or feelings. Children don't acquire that ability by a specific age. It surfaces only after they acquire the many other skills that lead up to it. The adults in his life assumed Rinaldo had the core ability to talk about his feelings instead of acting them out, but even by age nine, he simply didn't. This ability must be nurtured and tailored according to each child's growing body and mind, and for vulnerable children it can take time.

Why do well-intentioned goals often fail for children with persistent behavioral difficulties? *Because they are not customized to the child's social and emotional development.*

Here's another way to look at it. When we encounter challenging behaviors in a child, the first question to ask is: Is the behavior's etiology top down, or bottom up?

In other words, is this purposeful, intentional misbehavior? Or does the behavior represent the child's developmental challenges and/or reflexive responses to perceived threat—or a combination of both? You cannot determine the best way to respond to a behavior until you have those answers. I came to understand the importance of looking at behaviors from this new perspective as I completed post-doctoral training in the field of infant mental health and child development. I was fortunate to learn about Dr. Porges's work and the Polyvagal Theory during this time, but I didn't understand the impact it would have on my clinical work until I read his groundbreaking article "Neuroception: A subconscious system for detecting threats and safety" in an infant mental-health journal.[1]

After reading that article, I never looked at challenging behaviors in the same way. In my clinical work in school systems, I grew increasingly uncomfortable as I observed children being subjected to negative consequences for behaviors that I now saw as stress responses. As I began to use the Polyvagal Theory as an organizing principle for my psychology practice, **I found that the strategies I designed based on a child's neuroception were far more effective than those I was taught in graduate school and those that schools and agencies were (and still are) using to manage children's challenging behaviors.**

So in order to answer that question—is this behavior top down or bottom up?—we need to perceive a child in two ways: **(1) we need to understand the child's social-emotional development; and (2) we need to be able to read a child's cues *in the moment* that help reveal what underlies the behavior.**

In this chapter, we'll learn how to do that. First, we will take a close look at social-emotional development, giving you the tools to recognize the impact of the child's developmental processes on the behaviors you are witnessing. Then we'll examine a technique for analyzing behavior in the moment: a color system to help determine what the behaviors tell you about the child's autonomic state and stress levels. With this perspective and these tools in hand, we'll be able to move forward in later chapters with strategies for addressing these behaviors. But first, it's essential to be able to answer that question: top down or bottom up?

Top-Down Behaviors: Intentionality and Planning

Some behaviors are the result of thoughtful intent, an individual's willful ability to take a particular action. Goleman and Davison describe top-down processing as "brain activity that reflects our conscious mind and its 'mental doings.'"[2] Dan Siegel and Tina Bryson write about top-down thinking as mental processes occurring in the "upstairs" brain, the part of the brain known as the cerebral cortex.[3] Top-down thinking develops over time, with connections in the prefrontal cortex, the region known as the brain's "executive center." The prefrontal cortex is essential to plan and direct motor, cognitive, affective, and social behavior.[4] Even though most children begin to have "effortful control" of their attention, impulses and behaviors by three-and-a-half to four years of age, it can take many more years for these abilities to fully develop, and the process continues into early adulthood.[5] Eventually, brain growth supported by nurturing and attentive relationships allows us to develop intentional control, learn, reflect, plan, and pursue long-term goals.[6]

Consider the way preschoolers experiment with the intoxicating power they feel as they realize they have the ability to control their bodies and have their own ideas. (This phase can be less enjoyable for their parents, who have to set limits and teach children that there are boundaries!) This is the beginning of the development of top-down mental processing, which involves *conscious effort, intentionality, and thinking.* Efficient top-down thinking can take many years to develop, depending on each individual's development, and can be hijacked at any moment by the lower, survival-based instinctual brain when one experiences threat or danger, as we discovered in the previous chapter.

Bottom-Up Behaviors: Stress Responses

Before any of us develops efficient top-down thinking, however, we rely solely on *bottom-up behaviors*. We are born with bottom-up abilities, and they help us to stay alive. This second category of behaviors emerges not from intention but subconsciously. These reflexive, automatic responses are known as bottom-up behaviors and do not involve conscious thought.[7] As discussed in Chapter 1, the subconscious perception of safety and threat underlies these behaviors, which are adaptive and emerge from the instinctive drive towards self-protection. Siegel and Bryson describe the area of the brain associated with bottom-up reactions as the "downstairs" brain, with activation in the area of the brain known as the limbic system, including the amygdala.[8]

Too often, caregivers, teachers, providers, and parents assume that a child is acting deliberately, when in fact a behavior is actually a stress response, precipitated by the neuroception of threat. As Goleman and Davison put it, "a surprising amount of what we think is top-down is actually bottom-up."[9]

When we make incorrect assumptions about the root of behaviors, we can end up with ineffective ways to respond to them, as we saw with Rinaldo's IEP behavior goals. *That's why it's essential to pinpoint whether we're primarily witnessing a top-down behavior or one that's bottom up, or body up.* (I use the terms "bottom up" and "body up" interchangeably in this book.)

Of course, describing behaviors as top down *or* bottom up is an oversimplification of the complex brain/body connection, because our body, brain, and mind are inextricably linked in a feedback loop. The vast "information highway" in our brains and bodies includes the dynamic influences of the central and peripheral nervous systems.[10] But I have found this simplification useful in conceptualizing a new approach to understanding behavioral challenges in my efforts to support children and families.

In this book I describe behavioral challenges through the lens of the Polyvagal Theory, which focuses on the autonomic nervous system, and its practical and effective applications for all of us who parent and work with children. I will not describe the neuroscience in depth, however, and I urge you to learn more about the Polyvagal Theory and the brain/body connection if you have interest. (See page 267, for a resource list.)

The mind/body dualism (separation of brain and body) in our professional training programs is one of the reasons we don't use a common neurodevelopmental roadmap across our disciplines. This dualism comes at a cost for all of us who parent and work with children, however. In the words of Dr. Porges: "This dynamic, bidirectional communication between brain structures and bodily organs influences mental state, biases perception of the environment, prepares the individual to be either welcoming or defensive of others."[11]

We need to understand children's behaviors from both directions, from the body up *and* the brain down, and understand where to aim our intervention efforts in order to truly support children and families. How do we do this? I'm a clinician and not a neuroscientist, so I will break this down into simple chunks by describing the differences between bottom-up and top-down processes and what it means for our treatment and support strategies. In order to understand the journey human beings travel to develop top-down thinking, let's begin by first looking at the larger scheme of the child's arc of social-emotional development.

Newborn to Communicator: Social-Emotional Development in a Nutshell

As much as we would like our children to be able to "use their words" and exert control over their own behavior, none of us is born with that ability. The capacity to act with intention and to communicate one's needs emerges through an extended process of development nurtured by attuned relationships.

To understand that process, let's start with a quick overview:[12]

When a baby is born, its first act is taking a breath outside of the mother's body. At that moment, everyone pauses, looks at the baby, and waits for that breath—and the cry that often accompanies it and signals the baby's healthy arrival.

In order to survive, the baby needs to breathe, and in short order, instinctively coordinate how to suck, swallow, and breathe at the same time. If the baby is healthy, these three things happen quite naturally.

In the hours, days, weeks, and months that follow, if these basic abilities develop properly—and if her needs are properly met by an attentive caregiver—the baby experiences a sense of calm, alert attention to the world around her. (Infants who are premature or struggle with any of these basics may reach this point later.) She enjoys gazing into her parents' eyes—indeed, human babies are hardwired to do so. With physical abilities and relational support in place, the child is launched into the first process of social and emotional development: **regulation and attention.**

A newborn whose body is regulated has remarkable abilities for **engagement,** the next process of development, which spontaneously emerges from feelings of safety sensed deep within the body/brain. Within months, she is smiling and connecting with her caregivers as they smile back with delight. **Engagement and connection** emerge out of a physiologically regulated system between baby and caregiver.

This connection, the ability to touch the heart of another, is reciprocal. As the baby smiles and coos and her caregiver mirrors her sounds and actions, what happens is not caregiving, but *care-sharing.*[13] It's an instinctive dance that human babies and parents do with each other in a shared, reciprocal relationship. This constitutes the third process of social and emotional development: **the ability to communicate in a back-and-forth way.** The baby smiles, and mom smiles. The baby arches her back and lifts her arms, and dad picks her up. Eventually, over the course of the first year, the baby gains the motor control to point or gesture at something or someone, and hopefully, care-sharers pick up the signal and look in the direction of baby's point, or otherwise respond to the baby's emergent social communication.

Throughout her first year, the baby enjoys the power of increased motor control fueled by motivation. By her second year, she can point or gesture, and suddenly, let care-sharers know that she wants out of the crib, into her shoes, and outside for a walk. She can go back and forth to communicate her needs and understand what someone else is communicating back to her, all through facial and body gestures, and emotion-driven behaviors. Now the child has reached another process of development: **shared social problem solving.**

This capacity opens the child to new possibilities: she can ask, tell, show, and direct others as to her needs, ideas, and feelings—all without spoken language. Next comes a process that makes communication even more efficient: **the use of words or symbols.** No longer limited to using her body to gesture (or if her body can't, using pictures, pointing, or using technology), now she can use a word to stand in for physical actions. Instead of having to lead mom by the hand from room to room to get to the kitchen, now the child can simply say, "cookie." Imagine how much easier (and fun) life is when you can use symbols to stand in for physical actions!

Over the next several years, or more, depending on the child's unique development, using words to describe objects grows into using words to describe how the child feels. The child acquires an ability that will serve her for the rest of her life: she can begin to **describe her feelings and her internal life and share her experiences with others**.

This ability to use symbols leads to yet another pinnacle of human development: **building bridges with other people.** We learn how to empathize with others and realize that others don't always feel the same way we do and may have different opinions from ours. Now an individual can engage in debates and articulates opinions, entering a phase that allows her to navigate the many complexities of the social environment.

Through these dynamic processes, children eventually develop the ability to control their impulses, emotions, and behaviors. The ability to do this—talk about their needs, internal life, struggles, fears, and emotions without having to act on them behaviorally—continues to develop through adolescence and even into adulthood. The process varies from one person to another, depending on the child's relationships, experiences, early environment, constitution, and brain wiring.

Functional Emotional Development

The developmental trajectory that I have just described is based on research conducted in the 1970s by Greenspan and Wieder, who created a roadmap describing social-emotional development.[14] The capacities they described are known as Functional Emotional Developmental Levels (FEDLs), and they describe how a child uses relationships in a developmental hierarchy:

- **Functional** refers to how the individual takes in the world and comprehends it.
- **Emotional** denotes the role of feelings at each level and the way that feelings alter the meaning and understanding of experiences.
- **Developmental** indicates the pattern of growth through the milestones.
- The **Levels** are the experiences necessary for social-emotional maturity at various phases as children grow.

Children cycle through capabilities in these processes through the complex interaction between their emotional and physiological regulation and their interaction with the relational and physical environment.

Dr. Wieder now describes the levels as *processes* rather than milestones or phases.[15] They are nonlinear in nature because they are dynamic, and can shift depending on many variables that we will discuss in the next chapter. Children cycle through capabilities in these processes through the complex interaction between their emotional and physiological regulation and their interaction with the relational and physical environment. All children develop at their own pace. These processes will look different depending on the particular child's unique brain/body connection. We should expect variations on the theme of each process according to the child's individual differences, early environment, and unique brain wiring and not apply a neurotypical filter to these processes. Our task and challenge as parents and providers is to properly read a child's behaviors and interpret what they mean for that child.

The abilities of your child (or the child you are working with) may not fit neatly into these descriptions of social-emotional development. Still, we can use them to provide direction when we are struggling to understand and support children's behavioral challenges.

Building the House: The Processes of Social-Emotional Development

As we have seen, none of us is born with the ability to control our behavior and to regulate the way our bodies react to our emotions. Rather, it is an ability we acquire over time and through attuned relationships. To understand how the process plays out, it's useful to think of the way a house is built. Each distinct phase of building a house contributes to the final structure. The same applies to the process of human development: each phase contributes toward how the child develops increasing abilities for emotional regulation and intentional behavioral control.

And just as in building a house, circumstances and factors arise that make each process unique. A contractor who has built many houses knows that sometimes there's a plywood shortage and other times the electrician's crew is busy with another project when they're needed, so you have to do things in a different order. In the same way, each child encounters the same developmental process, but they are influenced by many other processes. That's why it's important to track the child's progress in real time so we can pinpoint the best way to support the child. And since relationships are the driving force of a child's social and emotional development, adults need to track our own progress as well.

Why is this relevant to our understanding of how to respond to children's behaviors? **The reasons for the challenging behaviors often diminish when we are properly addressing the child's physiological and emotional needs.** This understanding helps move from a sole focus on behavior management to supporting children's emotional regulation first. So, to gain a better understanding of how to support children's emotional regulation, let's examine the six stages of "building the house" of social-emotional development.[16]

The Foundation of the House

Process One: Regulation and Attention

The first developmental process is gaining the ability to be calm and alert. When a child is calm and alert, he can focus and attend to the world around him. Think of this capacity as the foundation of the house of social and emotional development. A house built on a strong foundation is best equipped for the storms it will face. If a child has a solid foundation of calm attention to her world and to the people around her, she will have a strong base for all future development.

The foundation is the most important part of the house. The foundation of a child's social-emotional house can be solid, flimsy, or something in between. And it's always changing as the child reacts to the demands of the environment.

Regulation and Attention

- ☐ Calm and alert

- ☐ Regulated physiological state

- ☐ Ability to attend to the relational and physical environment

- ☐ Neuroception of safety

Framing the House

Process Two: Engagement and Relating

Once a building has a foundation, workers carefully create a frame for the structure that is to become the house. This frame defines all that the house will contain, and without it, the rest of the house cannot be built. The same applies to the second social-emotional process: experiencing and engaging in warmly connected relationships. Think of loving relationships as the house's frame, within which growth happens. Along with the solid foundation of calm attention achieved in Process One, relationships provide the support for growth according to each child's unique potential.

Engagement and Relating

- ☐ Engaging with others

- ☐ Smiling, noticing, looking, laughing

- ☐ Mutual enjoyment and pleasure

- ☐ Other signs of connection according to the child's individual differences

The Electrical Wiring

Process Three: Purposeful Emotional Interactions

Once a person feels comfortable, alert, and safe, she begins communicating with others. If the capacity for engaged, loving relationships symbolizes the house's framing, think of communication as the electrical wiring for the house. Just as household wiring allows electricity to flow to various parts of the house, gestures—including facial expressions and body posture—allow communication to flow between people.

Purposeful Emotional Interactions

☐ Rhythm and flow

☐ Back and forth communication

☐ Reading each other's body language and gestures

☐ Giving and receiving verbal or nonverbal signals

The Rooms of the House

Process Four: Shared Social Problem Solving

Think of this process as the rooms and hallways of the house. Aided by the two-way flow of communication in Process Three, a child can now explore all the rooms in the house through social problem solving. Motivated by an idea, he can provide his caregivers with a series of nonverbal clues in order to reach his goal. The child uses a range of back-and-forth interactions to show, tell, ask, or otherwise communicate with others.

Social Problem Solving

☐ The child's ability to communicate nonverbally

☐ Piecing together multiple back-and-forth interactions

☐ Asking, showing, telling

☐ Using gestures, words, or a combination

Decorating the House

Process Five: Creating Symbols and Using Words and Ideas

The foundation, framing, and wiring all support the child's ability to explore the rooms of the house. These abilities now propel the child to do something that truly opens up the world of creativity: use words and symbols. Think of this process as decorating the house. The child has new abilities that allow for adorning his world with words, descriptions, opinions, and pretend play. Now, instead of grabbing a parent's hand to get what she wants, a child can express her desire in a word or point to a picture to stand in for an idea. Now the child is able to use words, ideas, and his own awareness to describe and ultimately control his behaviors. When a child has a top-down structure to understand a bottom-up reaction, he can create meaning out of chaos. *The child is now beginning to connect internal sensations, feelings, thoughts, and emotions to words. This leads to the ability to understand one's own behaviors through top-down thinking.*

Symbols, Words, and Ideas

- ☐ Child no longer tied to physical gestures to communicate

- ☐ Can use words, or symbols, technology, art, etc., to communicate ideas

- ☐ Can now link a feeling/bodily state or idea to a symbol (word, picture, or another object)

- ☐ Top-down processing emerges

The Driveway to the World

Process Six: Emotional Thinking and Building Bridges Between Ideas

When a child can translate ideas and thoughts into words or symbols, she is ready for this important process. She can now begin to share her understanding of her own behaviors and motivations with others. Now she can organize her thoughts and emotions, resulting in the ability to think logically and build bridges between her own ideas and those of others.

Think of this new capacity as a driveway leading out from the house to the outer world. When the child develops the ability to answer both "how" and "wh" questions (when, what, why, where), she has developed the capacity to reflect simultaneously on her own opinion and somebody else's. Now a child can express opinions, engage in debates, and understand that others can have different opinions and thoughts.

Where Does the Child Stand?

How do you know where a child stands in regard to the house of social-emotional development? The key is to survey where the child is in the house's creation or construction at a given time. The questions on page 46 are a shorthand version of the phases.

Building Bridges Between Ideas

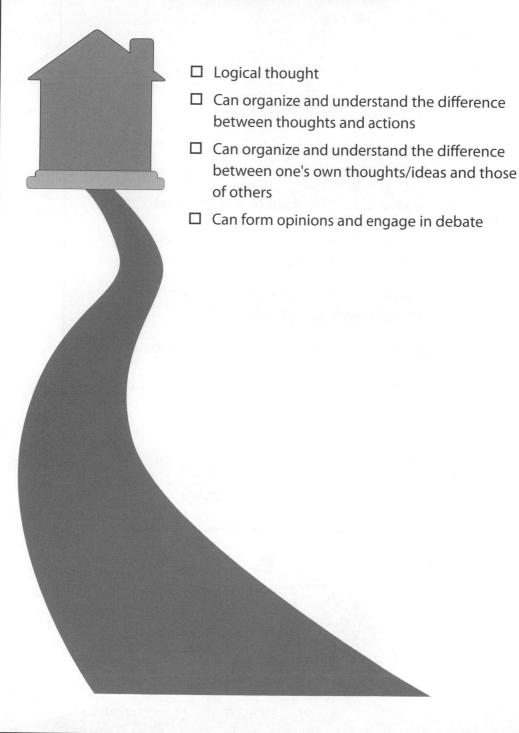

- ☐ Logical thought
- ☐ Can organize and understand the difference between thoughts and actions
- ☐ Can organize and understand the difference between one's own thoughts/ideas and those of others
- ☐ Can form opinions and engage in debate

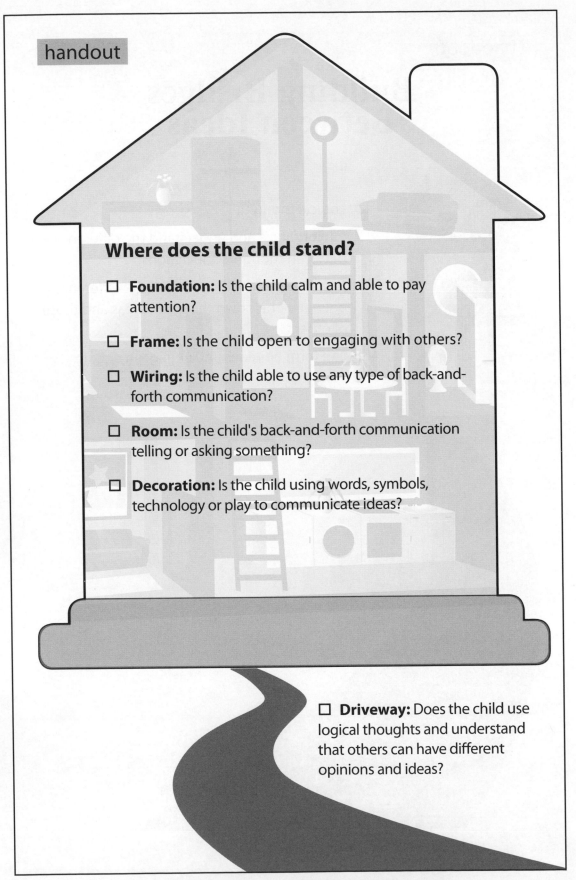

Where does the child stand?

☐ **Foundation:** Is the child calm and able to pay attention?

☐ **Frame:** Is the child open to engaging with others?

☐ **Wiring:** Is the child able to use any type of back-and-forth communication?

☐ **Room:** Is the child's back-and-forth communication telling or asking something?

☐ **Decoration:** Is the child using words, symbols, technology or play to communicate ideas?

☐ **Driveway:** Does the child use logical thoughts and understand that others can have different opinions and ideas?

Is the child:

- ☐ **C**alm—foundation
- ☐ **C**onnected—frame
- ☐ **C**ommunicating through back-and-forth rhythms
- ☐ **C**ommunicating through gestures (or technology if gestures aren't available)
- ☐ **C**onnecting words/symbols to thoughts and ideas
- ☐ **C**rossing ideas and thoughts with others

Back to the Question: Top Down or Bottom Up?

We started with the question of how to determine what underlies a behavior and where to focus our support: is it top down or bottom up? We know that *all* of a baby's abilities (and behaviors) are bottom up, because the brain circuitry that supports higher-level thinking is still developing. When we're born, our brain's threat detection system is fully operational. *But the parts of the brain that help us plan, think, learn, and calm ourselves require neural connections, built over time, that eventually support the ability for top-down control.*

How can we use our understanding of the house of social-emotional development to pinpoint whether a behavior is top down or bottom up? Think of it this way: of the processes we discussed, the *first four* denote predominant bottom-up functioning and the *last two* represent the emergence of top-down processing.

It's important to remember that these processes are dynamic and can shift according to what the child is experiencing. At any moment, different parts of a child's social-emotional house—or an adult's, for that matter—can be undergoing remodeling. *The key is to survey where the child is in real time and always attend to the earliest area of challenge, starting from the foundation.*

My own children were in elementary school when I first learned about the idea of focusing on the foundation first, and it was liberating. As a child psychologist, I never learned about social-emotional development in this way. My education and training focused on the importance of secure attachments with one's child, along with a separate understanding of cognitive-behavioral approaches, but not the overlay of how the brain and body work together to form experience. Therefore, I often fell into the trap of believing that my children were purposefully choosing to misbehave, when in actuality, many times they were experiencing bottom-up responses to stress.

One day shortly after I came home from a conference, my daughter was having a particularly difficult day and refusing to do her homework. I decided to try a new approach and rather than problem solve with her right away, I simply sat on the floor of her room and shifted my awareness, assuming a spirit of newfound compassion. I realized that my absence had likely added to her stress load at the beginning of a school year and quickly wiped a tear from my eye when I realized that she was suffering, and not intentionally trying to make my life difficult through her challenging behaviors. She looked at me quizzically, as if to ask, "What are you doing here in my room?" I told her I wanted to sit with her because I had missed her while I was away at the conference.

After about thirty minutes, she looked up and started talking to me about a difficulty she was having at school with a peer, and we sat and talked for an hour. Before this personal paradigm shift, what I thought was the most important issue (confronting her on homework avoidance) turned out to be the tip of the iceberg, with her stress and need for connection and warmth from me below the waterline.

This fuller understanding of social and emotional development, mostly relegated to the field of infant mental health and early interventions (and not my own field of psychology), truly changed the way I interacted with my own children as well as my patients and their families. Once I understood the pathways of social and emotional development, it became clear to me that I needed to know more about stress responses in human beings and how easily stress can derail our top-down capacities.

Porges's Polyvagal Theory, and specifically the concept of neuroception, and Greenspan and Wieder's developmental stages formed a strand that bridged social and emotional development and the workings of the autonomic nervous system. In order for a parent, teacher, or provider to support a child's house of development, I realized that we need to have a basic comprehension of both. So I began a practical study of the autonomic nervous system, the body and brain's incredible threat detection system and the gateway to supporting behavioral challenges.

The Pathways of the Autonomic Nervous System

Many professionals use color systems to teach individuals how to develop self-regulation and emotional control.[17] I use colors in a much different way; not to teach children, but for *adults* to learn about the child's (and their own) autonomic state in real time. In other words, I use colors as a guide that informs us how to gauge our interactions with children to foster physiological and emotional co-regulation.

The following color charts are adapted from the work of Lillas and Turnbull, in which behaviors and their associated colors represent *features of the autonomic nervous system and various levels of stress responses, or calm, alert attention.*[18]

The colors represent the activation of three autonomic pathways of responses defined by the Polyvagal Theory. The oldest pathway is the primitive *dorsal vagal system*, which helps us protect ourselves against life threat by immobilizing and shutting down.[19] The second pathway is the *sympathetic nervous system*, which supports survival through mobilization, commonly known as the "fight or flight" response.[20] The newest pathway, the *ventral vagal system*, supports social engagement and connection under the condition of safety.[21] In this book, I will describe these three primary pathways with the colors blue, red, and green, respectively.

I use a simple color chart as shorthand for these complicated brain terms. It provides an easy way to codify a child's (or our own) state of arousal. When children are in the **green (ventral vagal) pathway**, they can communicate, play, and learn. As therapist Deb Dana puts it, "When we are firmly grounded in our ventral vagal pathway, we feel safe and connected, calm and social."[22]

In the **red (sympathetic) pathway** of the autonomic nervous system, an individual may experience a racing heart, sweating, and other signs of activation. In the red pathway, a child is adaptively mobilizing to counteract the neuroception of threat.[23]

In the **blue (dorsal vagal) pathway**, one's body is responding to cues of extreme danger.[24] Here one can experience deceleration in heart and breathing rate, with a sluggish body. The individual is in an adaptive state of energy conservation or withdrawal in the service of survival. We sometimes overlook children in the blue pathway because they do not exhibit overt behavioral difficulties. But these children are vulnerable and at high risk, so we must pay close attention to children who don't necessarily display what we typically consider behavioral challenges.

Three ways of categorizing the autonomic pathways—represented by the colors—correspond with certain behaviors. We look for clues by observing characteristics of the child's eyes, face, voice, body, and rate and rhythm of movement.

These pathways become our basic radar, alerting us where a child needs help. As discussed in the previous chapter, *using the child's physiological state, described by these autonomic pathways, is a far more effective guide for our interactions than a DSM diagnosis or simply tracking behaviors without an understanding of their adaptive meaning in each child's nervous system.*

Why is a child's autonomic pathway important? *Because the green pathway is the pathway that leads to healthy social and emotional development.* On the red or blue pathways, the brain is focused on basic survival, not human engagement and connection. As we will see in the stories throughout the book, without this understanding, our tools and techniques, when applied to a child outside of the green pathway, will be less effective.

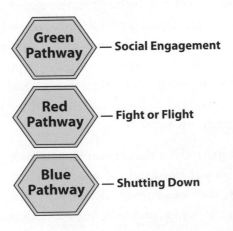

Green Pathway — Social Engagement

Eyes

- ☐ Bright, shiny eyes
- ☐ Looks directly at people, objects
- ☐ Looks away for breaks, then returns to eye contact
- ☐ Seems alert, takes in information

Body

- ☐ Relaxed with good muscle tone
- ☐ Stable, balanced and coordinated movements
- ☐ Infant moves arms and legs toward center of the body
- ☐ Infant molds body into a caregiver when held
- ☐ Moves faster or slower depending on environment

Face

- ☐ Smiles, shows joy
- ☐ Neutral
- ☐ Can express all emotions

Voice

- ☐ Laughing
- ☐ Tone changes

Rhythm/Rate of Movement

- ☐ Changes smoothly to respond to the environment
- ☐ Movements not too fast or too slow

Red Pathway — Fight or Flight

Eyes

- ☐ Open, squinted or closed eyes
- ☐ May have direct, intense eye contact
- ☐ Eyes roll upward
- ☐ Eyes look quickly around the room

Body

- ☐ Fingers spread out
- ☐ Arched back, tense body position
- ☐ Constant motion
- ☐ Demands space by pushing, shoving, and getting into other's space
- ☐ Biting, hitting, kicking, jumping, throwing
- ☐ Bumps into things, falls
- ☐ Threatening gestures (shakes finger or fist)

Face

- ☐ Wide, open mouth
- ☐ Anger, disgust
- ☐ Frown, grimace
- ☐ Fake, forced smile
- ☐ Clenched jaw or teeth

Rhythm/Rate of Movement

- ☐ Fast movements
- ☐ Impulsive movements

Voice

- ☐ High-pitched crying, yelling or screaming
- ☐ Loud
- ☐ Hostile or grumpy
- ☐ Sarcastic
- ☐ Out of control laughing

Blue Pathway — Shutting Down

Eyes

☐ Glazed-glassy eyes (looks through rather than at)

☐ Looks away for a long time, looks down

☐ Seems drowsy/tired

☐ Does not look around the room for interesting items

☐ Looks at things more than people

Face

☐ Flat/blank

☐ Mouth turned down, sad

Voice

☐ Flat

☐ Makes few to no sounds

☐ Sounds cold, soft, sad, too quiet

Rhythm/Rate of Movement

☐ Slow movements

☐ Slow to start moving

Body

☐ Slumped/slouching

☐ Low muscle tone

☐ Little or no exploring play or curiosity

☐ Wanders

☐ Frozen or slow-moving

Adapted from *Infant/Child Mental Health, Early Intervention, and Relationship-Based Therapies: A Neurorelational Framework for Interdisciplinary Practice*, by Connie Lillas and Janiece Turnbull. Copyright © 2009 by Interdisciplinary Training Institute LLC and Janiece Turnbull. Used by permission of W.W. Norton & Company, Inc.

Of course, each child is unique and has her own thresholds and preferences, but these colors represent behavioral patterns that signal various states of physiological responses in human beings and are useful indicators for most children. One limitation of using observable behaviors is that we are dependent on just that: what we can observe. Some individuals—including many on the autism spectrum—have differences in the body/brain connection that affect their facial and body movements. (In other words, their face, gestures, or body language may not accurately reflect the level of internal autonomic arousal). In Chapter 8, I will explain this in detail, and Chapter 9 will describe promising "sense" technology that provides a potential "work around" for movement differences.

Children cycle through gradations of the various pathways on a regular basis. *The key is that they don't stay in the red or blue pathways too long or with too much intensity.*[25] When we adapt to stress in a healthy manner, we can recover and get ourselves back to the green pathway according to the demands of the situations we face. If we can't, and the stress lasts too long, we can end up in a toxic stress pattern.[26]

Why is all of this important? Too often we react to a child's behaviors and decide on a response before we understand the basis of the behavior. Instead, we need to pause and ask: *Is this top down or bottom up? Is this a developmental challenge, a stress response, or a conscious, intentional action?*

Answering these questions with care and accuracy is the key to determining the most effective and helpful response.

A Success Story: Using Developmental Levels as a Guide to Therapy

What happens when we are able to read a child's developmental level accurately and respond appropriately? Consider the case of Kira, a spirited child who experienced a rough start in kindergarten. When her parents would drop her off at school, she frequently cried and then kept to herself most of the day, avoiding interactions with her peers.

When a school team did an evaluation, they discovered that Kira had a mild speech delay and difficulties with "social skills." The school placed her in a speech-and-language class, a program that aimed to teach children about feelings and communication through activities such as using flash cards to learn to recognize facial expressions. But participating in the group didn't improve Kira's behaviors. In fact, it exacerbated her problems because she so feared the speech therapist calling on her that her anxiety and hypervigilance increased.

The following summer, Kira started to see a developmental speech and language therapist who offered a different approach. The therapist started by assessing Kira's autonomic regulation (the color pathways) and her developmental processes (her developmental house) to see how they were affecting her challenges. In other words, she began with this question: What was holding Kira back from engagement with peers in the green pathway? Her evaluation answered this question. Even though Kira could use words to communicate basic needs, the *underpinnings* of her social communication (developmental processes one through four) were actually still under construction.

So the therapist focused on helping her mother build up Kira's green pathway as the first step to supporting her development. Her main goal: helping them feel safe and have fun together. She supported Kira and her mom engaging in a comfortable back-and-forth rhythm based on the pleasure of interactive play rather than *teaching* or *requiring* anything of Kira. The point was for mother and daughter to experience joyful interactions and have fun together, exercising Kira's weak muscles of social-emotional development.

By the end of the summer, Kira's demeanor changed. She began approaching other children at the local playground and spontaneously playing with them. Her previously immature social problem-solving abilities now began to resemble those of her peers. The therapist's plan worked. She used a developmental and relationship-based approach rather than the generic approach that attempted to "teach" Kira social skills. Under conditions of relational safety, Kira's social engagement behaviors emerged spontaneously. In time, the concerning behaviors—school refusal, avoiding peers, and lack of play—all resolved.

In this chapter we have discussed how children like Kira benefit when we assess their developmental level—and whether a behavior is top down or bottom up—in combination with an appraisal of their autonomic state, before we decide how to respond and set goals. With that understanding, we can move forward and learn, once we have answers, how to maximally support each child.

Sometimes, a child needs support for his thinking, top-down mind, and sometimes a child will need support from the body up first. Sometimes, we will be supporting both at the same time. Remember that we always survey the child's autonomic pathways first. It's complicated, yet elegantly simple, once we put all the pieces together. Knowing which approach to use in a given situation greatly enhances our ability to help children with behavioral challenges. This wisdom allows us to begin to "retune" a child's nervous system through the process of social engagement.[27]

House and Pathways for Child and Adult

What is your role?

Parent/Caregiver_____Teacher_____Therapist_____
Practitioner/Provider_____ Other_____

☐ **Foundation:** Ask what pathway is the child in?
Green__Red__Blue__

☐ **Frame:** Are you and the child warmly engaged?

☐ **Wiring:** Are you and the child communicating back and forth?

☐ **Rooms:** Is the communication fruitful?

☐ **Decoration:** Is the child able to describe feelings, concerns, or define the problem?

☐ **Driveway:** Are we building bridges towards a solution?

Now that we have discussed the basics of a developmental social and emotional roadmap as well as ways to discover whether a behavior is top down or bottom up, let's turn to the third area as we improve our understanding of how to support children's behavioral challenges: an appreciation of individual differences.

Main Points —

- When we encounter challenging behaviors in a child, we need to know: Is this behavior's etiology top down or bottom up?

- Bottom-up or body-up behaviors are reflexive, self-protective, automatic responses and do not involve conscious thought.

- Top-down thinking develops over time and allows us to eventually develop intentional control over behaviors and impulses, to learn and reflect on our actions, and to pursue long-term goals.

- Even though most children begin to have "effortful control" of their behaviors, attention, and impulses at three-and-a-half to four years old, it can take many more years for these abilities to fully develop.

- Six processes of social-emotional development illustrate how children develop effortful control of behaviors through social engagement with caring adults, over time.

- Three pathways, of different colors, represent the three primary states of autonomic arousal described by the Polyvagal Theory: the older *dorsal vagal* (blue) pathway involves immobilization and conservation of energy, the *sympathetic* (red) pathway activates fight or flight behaviors, and the *ventral vagal* (green) pathway supports social engagement and connection.

3.
Individual Differences

> *"Always remember that you are absolutely unique. Just like everybody else."*
>
> **Margaret Mead**

Acknowledging each individual's uniqueness helps us understand the critical difference between intentional misbehavior and a child's adaptations to her body's signals. It also moves us away from building explanations—and solutions—based on our own personal biases or our limited scopes of subspecialization. Further, an appreciation of individual differences explains why two children may react differently to the same situation.[1] When we understand individual differences for what they are, we gain the information necessary to customize and personalize our treatment, educational, and parenting approaches.

In this chapter I will describe various examples of individual differences that I have found contribute to emotional and behavioral challenges. The vignettes in this chapter are illustrations of four main categories of individual differences and are not meant to be comprehensive treatment examples. In this chapter I will highlight *salient features* of each category as we construct each child's developmental iceberg and discover how better to understand challenging behaviors. We will discuss how to *apply* this knowledge in Part Two (Chapters 4, 5, and 6) of the book.

Bodily Processes, Sensations, Feelings, and Thoughts

What exactly is an "individual difference"? Individual differences are the characteristics and qualities that shape how we take in and respond to the world around us, and are influenced by our genetics and our environment. This includes the way we experience processes in the body, sensations, feelings, and thoughts.[2] In this chapter, we will see how children's individual differences contribute to behavioral challenges. We will discuss these general categories of individual differences in a neurodevelopmentally respectful order: from the body in general, to how sensations are processed, and finally to feelings and thoughts. So, to reinforce the importance of distinguishing body-up individual differences that impact behaviors (such as hunger, blood sugar levels, and illness) from top-down influences (such as a conscious thought or idea), let's begin our discussion about how the physical body influences children's behaviors.

Richie's story will help illustrate.

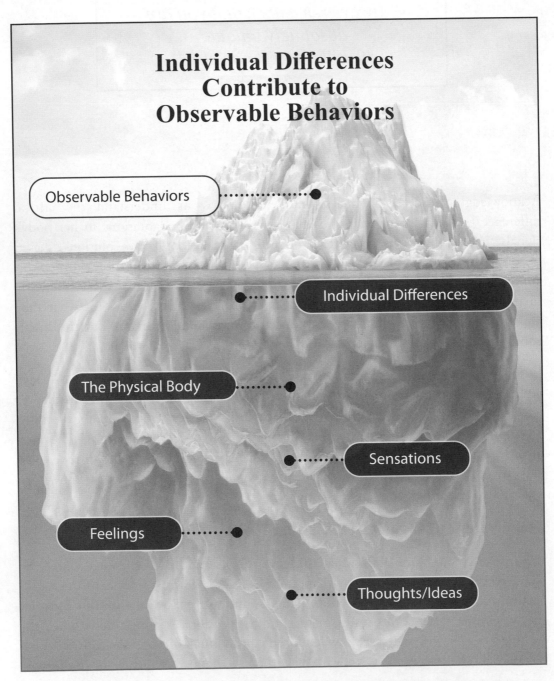

Richie — The Impact of Body Processes on Behavior

Richie's journey with his Type 1 diabetes sheds light on the relationship between the processes of the body and behaviors. Richie was seven years old when he suddenly experienced extreme thirst, lethargy, and frequent urination. Within weeks, a pediatrician diagnosed him with juvenile diabetes. His protective parents felt devastated and scared as they learned about this condition, which has no cure and which would change their son's and family's life forever. After the initial shock wore off, and they all learned about managing his condition, controlling the diabetes became a part of their daily lives.

When he was in third grade, Richie's parents noticed that he often became upset over homework, sometimes tearing up the page if he made a single mistake. He sometimes yelled at his mother while slamming a hand on the table over a simple task. Early on, Richie's nurse practitioner suggested that fluctuating blood glucose levels can cause mood changes, irritability, or even irrational behaviors, and that stress can also affect blood sugar levels. That proved true for Richie, whose rising blood glucose levels made him so upset that he often needed immediate interventions (skin pricks and medication adjustment) when he was already upset and uncooperative. The stress involved in helping Richie manage his condition affected the whole family.

When we met to discuss support strategies for Richie, a primary consideration was helping him manage and prevent blood sugar fluctuations. This was a sensitive and challenging prospect because Richie fought the blood glucose testing, finding it annoying because it took him away from his activities. When his parents used a daily journal to help analyze his behavior, it became clear that his blood glucose levels profoundly affected his emotional and behavioral regulation, and the vigilance around its management created its own stress between family members.

Eventually, Richie's parents designed ways to help their son engage in his own medical self-care. With his parents' permission, I spoke with his nurse practitioner so that I could learn more about his condition, and how to help empower Richie to become more proactive. His parents and I then met without Richie present, and they devised creative solutions to help their son better manage the many fluctuations he experienced.

Richie's parents allowed him to come up with creative rituals that gave him more control over his glucose testing, helping him feel more calm and cooperative. Since Richie liked "playing school" with them and enjoyed playing the role of teacher, they bought a large white board as a prop to play school at home. Richie found it useful to write reminders to himself on the white board, such as the early signs of both low blood sugar levels (hypoglycemia) and high levels (hyperglycemia), and what to do about either.

Richie volunteered to give his class a lesson on juvenile diabetes, empowering him to demystify it for himself and his friends. His lesson to the class had an added benefit: his classmates were intrigued and impressed with his bravery for the number of skin pricks he had to tolerate. They asked a lot of questions after his talk, and this made him feel important and proud of his knowledge.

With better management of his blood sugar fluctuations, and additional support for managing his stress levels, including attending a parent/child yoga class once a week, Richie's behavioral challenges decreased markedly. The key to helping Richie and his family was to help them understand the link between his behaviors and his diabetes.

Richie's Iceberg

Behavioral meltdowns

Diminished patience

Difficulty with homework

Difficulties with emotional control

Impact of juvenile diabetes

Fluctuations in blood glucose levels

Rapid neuroendocrine shifts

Leon — Emotional and Behavioral Challenges from Implicit Body Memories

Richie's story showed us how processes in the child's physical body can underlie behavioral challenges. Sometimes body sensations and resulting emotional coding happen early in life, as we find in Leon's story. Leon was born prematurely at thirty-three weeks' gestation. Though he weighed nearly four pounds, he had trouble breathing and maintaining an optimal body temperature. After he developed an infection, he spent weeks in the neonatal intensive care unit (NICU), his concerned parents at his side. Even though the hospital staff was friendly, the NICU environment was not parent-friendly. Still recovering from the shock of his early birth, his parents rotated sitting by his bedside while a stream of medical personnel monitored his body's fragile systems. His mother cried every time Leon had a blood draw from his tiny heel, wanting to protect her son from pain, but knowing that his life depended on the invasive procedures and medical plans to help him survive. She and his dad felt helpless as the days turned into a weeks-long effort to save their son's life.

Fortunately, Leon did survive, and after eight weeks his relieved parents finally brought him home from the hospital. One of the first things they noticed was how sensitive he was to the environment. If someone switched the lights on in his room, his whole body recoiled. On the other hand, he seemed to sleep better when there was a lot of background noise. Unfortunately, he was back in the hospital at six months for several weeks when he developed a bronchial infection. This created yet another traumatic disruption in what his parents described as the roller coaster ride of his first year of life.

At eighteen months old, Leon cried when he heard certain unexpected sounds such as a hair dryer or a toilet flushing. He also had a fear of places that resembled doctor's offices and panicked during his immunizations and routine well-child pediatric visits. When he was two, his parents found it so difficult to keep him calm in new places that they avoided taking him out in public at all. When they brought Leon, then three, to meet me, his parents described him as controlling, clingy, and prone to tantrums.

We surmised that the painful medical procedures he had experienced as an infant had sent his body onto a red pathway from which he could not escape, creating subconscious memories linked to certain sensations such as lights and noise. These early sensory experiences, along with his constitutional and genetic makeup, created a threat detection system that was all too easily triggered. As a result, the vulnerable toddler had difficulty tolerating many everyday sensations, including those in a busy preschool environment. The way he *adapted*—and strived to feel safe from the body up—was to control, cling, and protest.

Leon's team included a perceptive developmental pediatrician who referred the family to me during his difficult transition to preschool. In collaboration with his parents and teachers, we developed a plan to help Leon relax and feel safe in the classroom and at home. Through nurturing and attuned relationships, and with a developmental specialist addressing his environmental sensitivities, Leon eventually learned how to connect with an adult when he felt uncomfortable and to describe what he was feeling physically and emotionally. Leon learned that he could talk about things that bothered him. Over time, he used top-down thinking to overcome his body-up reactions and feelings, thereby illustrating the dictum of interpersonal neurobiology made famous by Tina Bryson and Dan Siegel: "If you can name it you can tame it."[3]

Leon's Iceberg

Controlling of environment

Clinging to parents

Crying

Difficulties in self-regulation

Lack of exploration/play at school

Faulty neuroception

Pain experienced during medical procedures

Challenges in physiological and emotional co-regulation

Implicit memories

Sensory over-reactivity to sounds/light

I have long observed that children with a history of invasive medical procedures, childhood trauma, or other circumstances involving physical or emotional pain beyond their control often experience greater vigilance in their nervous systems. This increased vigilance may result in separation fears, defiance, clinginess, or attempting to control people or aspects of the environment. It's helpful to remember that such behaviors are adaptations to situations over which the child originally lacked control. Later in the book I will explain how we can mitigate the effects of medical toxic stress or other disruptions in parent/child interactions by realizing how critical it is to creatively support a parent's ability to soothe and connect to their child during these disruptions. **It's good for growing the green pathway of parent and child, and should not be relegated to mental health, but rather considered as a part of comprehensive medical care for all children.**

The Physical Body and Behavioral Control

Many children have physical conditions that affect their ability to control their emotions and behaviors. These can include basic sensations such as hunger or thirst; chronic pain; genetic disorders; gut issues, including constipation and diarrhea; nutritional status (including blood glucose levels); sleep cycles; or physical illness. One form of illness—pediatric autoimmune neuropsychiatric disorders associated with streptococcal infections (known as PANDAS)—is thought to cause obsessive-compulsive behaviors, which often occur with a very sudden onset or worsening of symptoms. Other behaviors associated with PANDAS include:[4]

- ADHD symptoms (hyperactivity, inattention, being fidgety)

- Separation anxiety (child is clingy and has difficulty separating from his or her caregivers; for example, the child may not want to be in a different room in the house from his or her parents)

- Mood changes, such as irritability, sadness, emotional lability (tendency to laugh or cry unexpectedly at what might seem the wrong moment)

- Trouble sleeping; nighttime bedwetting, daytime frequent urination, or both

- Changes in motor skills (e.g., changes in handwriting)

- Tics

- Joint pain

It's important to share concerns about sudden, severe behavioral difficulties with a child's pediatrician or knowledgeable medical professional. If behavioral symptoms have a biological origin then the solutions need to address those origins and managing the child's behaviors in isolation of the biological triggers is inadequate.

We Understand the World Through Our Senses

Now let's explore how sensations at various levels influence childhood behaviors. But first, let me explain why, as a psychologist, I focus on sensory processing in a book on challenging behaviors.

I learned how much I had missed in my training and education as a licensed psychologist only after I decided to subspecialize in early development and infant mental health. My doctoral training included the cartesian split, also known as mind/body dualism—the belief that mental processes could be understood without a deeper consideration of the feedback from the body. This made my clinical conceptualizations reductionistic—they focused on observable behaviors, not underlying processes—and overly reliant on top-down thinking and the "processes of the mind."

I realized I needed additional training in order to truly understand the populations of children I sought to help: young children and those with developmental differences. Little did I know that what I was about to learn would also change the way I viewed myself, my own children, and the field of mental health in general. The first training program I attended, at a large, urban children's hospital, required active participation on a multidisciplinary team—that is, a team of professionals who evaluated a baby or toddler through different lenses, across different disciplines. One day, I heard several occupational therapists trained in sensory processing comment on a child, and I experienced a "light bulb moment." Suddenly, I realized that we couldn't understand a child's behaviors without understanding how the child understood the world through her sensory systems. To this day, my biggest criticism of mental health (and education) training programs is that they do not teach about the body/brain feedback loop and how this affects children's behaviors from the body up. This is one reason we often misunderstand behavioral challenges, and why I'm including the next section on how sensory processing should be considered within the range of individual differences.

Sensory Processing: How We Understand the World

Children (and all human beings) understand and interpret the world through our sensory systems. Sensory processing is critical to child development, yet its study is relegated to a subspecialty in the field of occupational therapy. **The role of sensory processing in children's overall development is not yet integrated into the fields of mental health, education, or social work in any comprehensive way, even though it is a foundational piece of the puzzle as we interpret children's behaviors and how to help them.** In other words, few people really talk about it, even though the research was solid enough for a sensory processing diagnosis to be strongly considered for the latest edition of the *DSM*, the *DSM-5*, narrowly missing inclusion in the final version.[5] Even though there's pushback from some in the medical and mental health communities, in my opinion, it's a matter of time before all pediatric professionals appreciate the implications of sensory processing differences on development and behaviors.

We need to understand a child's sensory systems in order to determine whether differences in sensory processing are contributing to emotional and behavioral challenges. This understanding is also important because it allows us to personalize bottom-up techniques to help children calm onto the green pathway, where learning, discovery, and growth happen.

As I explained in the last chapter, infants and toddlers operate from the bottom up because their cerebral cortex, the part of the brain associated with intentional control and mental activities, is still developing. Older children, teens, and adults can also operate from the bottom up when they are on the red or blue pathways. Our ability to understand sensory preferences helps us develop supportive approaches across the lifespan.

In order to utilize approaches that appeal to a child's thinking brain, we need to know how to support children from the body up so that they can access their top-down thinking brain. This provides us with tools other than simply talking to the child or asking for compliance. We will understand a child's sensory systems in two ways. In the following pages, I will describe what the sensory systems are and how a child's sensory over- or under-reactivity can contribute to emotional and behavioral dysregulation. In Chapter 4, we will discover how to use a child's sensory preferences to help us calm and deescalate when a child is on the red pathway and offer up-regulating support if the child is on the blue pathway.

Sensory-Based Memories

Five-year-old Lucas's parents found him unpredictable and bewildering. Some days he would wake up happy and energetic, but more often from the moment he opened his eyes, he was in a surly mood, protesting everything from brushing his teeth to wearing the clothes his parents suggested. Unless they gave Lucas his way, he would explode—crying, fussing, and pushing his little sister at the slightest provocation.

When I delved into his history, his parents revealed that at age two, Lucas had developed an unexplained skin rash all over his body. Though it resolved after a few weeks, the rash made Lucas so uncomfortable that he couldn't bear the feeling of clothing on his skin. From then on, he became, in his parents' words, "the boss of the house," refusing to wear anything but one of three soft t-shirts, and responding angrily when asked to wear anything else. Several months after the rash, Lucas's sister was born, adding an additional layer of stress for the toddler.

Since the behaviors arose so soon after the rash, I surmised that even though the intense itching had disappeared, Lucas retained strong "body memories" of the discomfort. His behaviors were likely reactions to how these painful sensory memories linked up with his life experiences at the time.

As Lucas's story illustrates, our minds pair the sensations we take from the environment with emotions, forming both conscious or subconscious memories of past experiences. This is known as the *dual-coding* of sensations with emotions.[6] It happens through bidirectional communication between the body and the brain. The brain easily "memorizes" a negative sensory experience, thereby protecting us from repeating the experience. But sometimes these subconscious memories cause hypervigilance, and a child responds to this hypervigilance by becoming overly controlling or striking out and landing on the red pathway. This is what happened to Lucas.

To use terms that were discussed in Chapter 2, I helped Lucas's parents understand the difference between "bottom-up" and "top-down" origins of behavior. This new sensory explanation of the bottom-up (below the surface) causes of his behaviors relieved his parents who had been blaming themselves and worrying about their son.

Occupational therapists taught me the powerful impact of sensory processing on behaviors. They keenly understood that "bottom-up" sensory processing influences how children respond and relate to the physical and social environment. This insight significantly enhanced my understanding of behaviors and my ability to help children. It also helped me see a significant limitation in my own field of psychology, which has a top-down bias, and often fails to recognize or appreciate the bottom-up influences on children's behavioral challenges.

Drs. Greenspan and Wieder considered early sensitivities to ordinary sensations "developmental pathways" to other conditions, such as anxiety.[7] They found that children with certain sensory profiles were more likely to have difficulty with emotional regulation, which, as we now know, is linked to behavioral control. In fact, research indicates that children with sensory over-reactivity are more likely to experience anxiety, and that their families experience distress and disruption as a result.[8] In my clinical practice, I have also found that these early sensitivities often co-occur in young children who present as anxious or controlling of their environments.

Parents, teachers, and mental health therapists are often not familiar with sensory processing and how it affects children's behaviors. Fortunately, organizations such as the Profectum Foundation, the Interdisciplinary Council on Development and Learning (ICDL), and the STAR Center in Denver are beginning to educate the public about the connection between the two, bringing hope (and less blame) when children have behavior challenges triggered by sensory challenges. (See page 267 for a list of these and other helpful organizations.)

What Is Sensory Processing?

Our sensory systems allow us to *hear, see, touch, smell, taste, and feel movement*, giving meaning to our experiences.[9] This happens automatically, without our consciously thinking about it. It's only when something goes wrong—when you experience a bad cold or allergies and find it difficult to hear or taste—that most of us pay attention to our sensory systems. Typically, though, our brains and bodies make sense of the world around us quickly and efficiently.

We all have some experiences we enjoy and prefer and others we dislike and avoid.[10] Sensory experiences can make us feel good or bad. They can help us function in our daily lives or make our lives more difficult. As adults, we are often aware of our sensory preferences, as reflected in the type (and volume) of music we listen to, the clothing we buy (with tags or tagless, polyester or cotton), the foods we eat, and the scents we wear. Though we might give these choices little thought, as adults we can opt for whatever brings us comfort—within the limits of our life and work environments, of course. Children don't usually have these options.

Understanding a child's sensory systems gives us a window into potential triggers as well as a helpful list of strategies to help children return to the green pathway when they're struggling. Let's review the major sensory systems before we explore how to better understand environmental triggers as well as how to use sensory experiences to help soothe children's distress.

We're all familiar with the body's five primary sense systems: hearing, sight, smell, taste, and touch. Lucy Jane Miller, PhD, an occupational therapist and preeminent researcher in the field of sensory processing disorders, teaches that humans have three additional sensory systems: the vestibular, proprioceptive, and interoceptive. Miller and Bialer describe the systems this way:[11]

> **Hearing**: The auditory system processes and interprets sound information. Auditory abilities enable us to discriminate between background and foreground sounds.

> **Seeing**: The visual system brings information from the environment into the brain through the eyes.

> **Smell**: The olfactory system driving our sense of smell is important to eating, enhancing the pleasure of taste and/or alerting you to what you should or should not eat.

> **Taste**: The gustatory system provides information regarding the nature of the foods and liquids we taste.

Touch: The tactile system, the largest sensory system, processes information gathered from sensory receptors on the skin.

Movement in space: The vestibular system provides information about the position and acceleration of the head and body and their relation to gravity.

Sensations in muscles and joints: The proprioceptive system processes sensations in the muscles and joints.

Internal sensations: The interoceptive system provides information about how body organs feel and sensations emanating from inside the body.

While we think about the role of various senses, we can ask these two questions:

- What factors are affecting a child's ability to have calm, focused, and alert attention in her body and mind?

- What impact does this have on his or her relationships and successful participation in daily activities at home and school?

Sometimes, behavioral challenges are a child's body's way of coping with sensory challenges. Understanding a child's sensory processing—how they interpret the world through their various senses—is an additional tool we can use to deconstruct the reasons for children's behaviors. Sometimes, over- or under-reactivity in one or more of the sensory channels contributes to a child's early behavioral and emotional disruption.

The following worksheets will help you consider whether or not a child has a tendency toward over-reactivity, under-reactivity, or craving various sensations. This initial exercise in developing questions is not a substitute for the advice of a qualified occupational therapist. If you feel that your child or a child you are working with falls within any of these categories of atypical sensory processing, it's worth consulting a qualified occupational therapist (or other professional) trained in the understanding of sensory processing.[12]

The sensations we experience influence our interactions with others. Over- or under-reactivity through one or more of the sensory channels can contribute to children's emotional and physiological regulation and sense of safety, creating a way to red- or blue-pathway behaviors.

Sensory Over-Responsive Checklist

Place a check mark next to the symptoms that your child exhibits:

Auditory/Sound

- ☐ Holds hands over ears to protect self from loud sounds
- ☐ Has difficulty completing work if background noise exists
- ☐ Is fearful of certain environmental sounds—toilet flushing, dogs barking, vacuuming, hair dryer
- ☐ Fears movie theaters or music concerts

Tactile/Touch

- ☐ Sensitive to certain fabrics (clothes, bedding)
- ☐ Complains about having hair brushed and cut, taking showers, being gently kissed
- ☐ Avoids going barefoot, especially in grass or sand
- ☐ Becomes irritable with certain clothing textures, labels, seams in socks and pants; avoids wearing new clothes
- ☐ Reacts negatively to textures on hands, such as clay, finger paint, cookie crumbs, dirt
- ☐ Prefers strong hugs; is very ticklish

Visual

- ☐ Prefers low light to bright light
- ☐ Squints or gets headaches
- ☐ Likes to wear hats or caps to protect eyes from sun
- ☐ Avoids or seems threatened by eye contact
- ☐ Is bothered by or distracted by wall decoration or activity outside the window

Monica G. Osgood, et al. "*Profectum Parent Toolbox*. Individual Profile Form, Step 2, Webcast 12, Pgs. 4–7, Sensory Responsive Patterns." *Profectum Foundation*, 2015, www.profectum.org/. Used with permission of the Profectum Foundation.

Taste/Smell

☐ Gags on textured food

☐ Avoids certain tastes or smells that are typically a part of child's diet

☐ Does not like smells that others don't notice

Vestibular/Movement

☐ Becomes anxious or distressed when feet leave the ground

☐ Avoids climbing or jumping

☐ Is fearful of going up and down stairs

☐ Avoids or dislikes escalators

☐ May avoid having head tipped back when washing hair

☐ Avoids playground equipment that requires movement, swings, and slides

☐ May become anxious when moved by someone else

Monica G. Osgood, et al. "*Profectum Parent Toolbox*. Individual Profile Form, Step 2, Webcast 12, Pgs. 4–7, Sensory Responsive Patterns." *Profectum Foundation*, 2015, www.profectum.org/. Used with permission of the Profectum Foundation.

Sensory Under-Responsive Checklist

Place a check mark next to the symptoms that your child exhibits.

Auditory/Sound

- ☐ Has difficulty following directions, needs directions repeated
- ☐ May be nonresponsive when having name called
- ☐ May produce own sounds, hum, or talk to himself as he is completing tasks
- ☐ Enjoys loud sounds and music in the background

Tactile/Touch

- ☐ Is not bothered by injuries, cuts, or bruises
- ☐ May not notice when he is touched, bumped, or pushed, unless the impact is severe or forceful
- ☐ Is indifferent to the feel of various fabrics in clothes (cotton versus wool versus synthetic)

Visual

- ☐ Has difficulty following a moving object (or person) with his eyes
- ☐ May complain about having tired eyes
- ☐ Often loses place when reading and copying information down (off blackboard)
- ☐ May write on a significant slant
- ☐ May seem oblivious to details of objects and the surrounding environment

Taste/Smell

- ☐ May eat or drink something that is harmful without being aware of the smell or taste

Monica G. Osgood, et al. "*Profectum Parent Toolbox.* Individual Profile Form, Step 2, Webcast 12, Pgs. 4–7, Sensory Responsive Patterns." *Profectum Foundation*, 2015, www.profectum.org/. Used with permission of the Profectum Foundation.

- ☐ Usually does not notice odors and smells (which can be a safety concern as well)
- ☐ Often doesn't notice or care if food is spicy or bland

Vestibular/Movement

- ☐ Does not experience pleasure or even desire to explore his environment and move
- ☐ Displays a lack of participation in gym, sports, and playground activities
- ☐ Prefers sedentary activities, such as watching TV, using computer or video games, sitting around
- ☐ Often has poor muscle tone and slow motor responses
- ☐ Dislikes trying new physical activities and rarely initiates them
- ☐ Is not able to use his or her hands for a task without watching them

Monica G. Osgood, et al. "*Profectum Parent Toolbox*. Individual Profile Form, Step 2, Webcast 12, Pgs. 4–7, Sensory Responsive Patterns." *Profectum Foundation*, 2015, www.profectum.org/. Used with permission of the Profectum Foundation.

Sensory-Craving Checklist

Place a check mark next to the symptoms that your child exhibits.

Auditory/Sound

☐ Prefers the volume of the television and music at a level that is uncomfortably loud to others

☐ Uses a loud voice—possibly almost a shouting level—when speaking

☐ Unable to stop talking and has trouble taking turns in conversations

☐ Enjoys noisy environments, such as sports arenas or malls

Tactile/Touch

☐ Needs to constantly touch surfaces and textures, particularly soft and cuddly ones

☐ May cause others discomfort and a sense of violation of personal space with need to touch

☐ Frequently bumps into objects and people

☐ Wants to play with messy stimuli for long periods of time

☐ May mouth or bite objects beyond the appropriate developmental stages

☐ May rub or bite the skin

Visual

☐ Is attracted to watching flickering lights or nonmeaningful visual stimuli

☐ Tends to choose objects that are brightly colored

☐ Is captivated by and can spend hours in front of a television, computer, or video game

☐ Gazes at spinning objects for long periods of time

☐ Attends to one visual detail for a long time, such as a single page of a book, tire of a car

Taste/Smell/Oral-Motor

☐ Smells people, animals, and objects

☐ Licks objects, people, and foods (prior to tasting)

Monica G. Osgood, et al. "*Profectum Parent Toolbox.* Individual Profile Form, Step 2, Webcast 12, Pgs. 4–7, Sensory Responsive Patterns." *Profectum Foundation*, 2015, www.profectum.org/. Used with permission of the Profectum Foundation.

- ☐ Has a constant desire to chew gum
- ☐ Desires crunchy foods like chips, pretzels, and cookies
- ☐ Often particularly likes one type of food: sweet, sour, salty
- ☐ Bites on sleeves, pencil erasers, paper clips; always has something in his or her mouth

Vestibular/Movement

- ☐ Frequently falls on the floor and rolls intentionally
- ☐ Insists on intense movement input, such as flipping, turning, rotating, and being inverted; can spin for a long time without getting dizzy
- ☐ Is adamant about roughhousing, play fighting, and being tossed in the air
- ☐ Jumps on bed and couches aggressively
- ☐ Loves extreme fast-moving input, such as ice skating, skiing, sledding, bike-riding, rollerblading, skateboarding, riding roller coasters and other amusement park rides; may be an "extreme athlete"
- ☐ Is not calmed down by additional movement input; tends to get more aroused and disorganized as movement increases

Monica G. Osgood, et al. "*Profectum Parent Toolbox*. Individual Profile Form, Step 2, Webcast 12, Pgs. 4–7, Sensory Responsive Patterns." *Profectum Foundation*, 2015, www.profectum.org/. Used with permission of the Profectum Foundation.

If you marked multiple boxes within any of the checklists, it's worthwhile to seek additional information and/or guidance from an occupational therapist trained in sensory processing. (See Resources on page 268).

Most children process information through the senses without obvious difficulty. But when behavioral challenges start in infancy or toddlerhood and can't be explained by obvious factors such as relational stress or trauma—it's worth considering whether sensory-processing differences are a factor in the bigger picture of a child's emotions and behaviors.

Yvonne — Behavioral Challenges from Over-Reactivity in Processing Sounds

After Yvonne, an only child, was diagnosed at age three with speech and language challenges, her parents enrolled her in a specialized preschool for children with developmental differences. She adapted so well that the following year she moved into a mainstream kindergarten class.

A few weeks in, the teacher phoned Yvonne's parents to report a problem: Yvonne was humming and tapping on her desk to the point of disturbing her classmates. The instructor had repeatedly asked Yvonne to stop, even writing the girl's name on the board to call attention to the behavior. The teacher also tried positive strategies, offering Yvonne pretty stickers if she could refrain from the noises for five minutes. But none of these efforts curbed Yvonne's humming or tapping.

Yvonne's parents enlisted the help of an occupational therapist. After meeting several times with Yvonne and her parents and observing the girl in different settings, the OT offered an explanation for the behavior: Yvonne experienced such sensory over-reactivity in her auditory system that she had difficulty processing the classroom's background and foreground sounds. Her body's instinctive strategy to cope with that challenge was to make her *own* noises. Her noise making was a subconscious preemptive reaction to an auditory trigger. It made her feel better in the classroom.

Investigating Bottom-Up Causes

I have found over many years of working with infants and toddlers that early sensory processing differences can contribute to difficulties with the child's emotional and behavioral regulation and control. If your child or a child you are working with has had exaggerated behavioral responses to everyday activities or events from an early age, it's useful to reflect on the child's history of reactions to sensory experiences. As we learned in Chapter 2, these reactions are always dual-coded with emotions.

One reason that Yvonne reacted so defensively was that unlike at home, she didn't have a trusted adult nearby at school to help her manage her distress. Her behaviors weren't symptoms of a "disorder," per se, but a reflection of her subconscious "threat detection system" at work, assisting her in this new and challenging situation. Yvonne's seemingly inappropriate humming and tapping reflected her body's *adaptive defensive strategy*, her way of countering the sense of auditory threat she felt in a new classroom full of unfamiliar people, sights, and sounds.

The presence of a trusted and loving adult helps children to moderate their stress responses.

Yvonne's behaviors were, ironically, her way to calm her body in order to focus in the classroom. What some might have labeled "maladaptive" behaviors were actually an adaptation to her sensory over-reactivity, which was sending her onto the red pathway, causing *faulty* neuroception (experiencing threat in the environment when it's actually safe).

Understanding this apparent paradox enabled her parents and teacher to offer her additional support. The teacher arranged for Yvonne to sit closer to her, provided Yvonne with noise-canceling headphones, and during especially noisy times, made Yvonne feel special by creating enjoyable ways for her to be the "teacher's helper" in the classroom.

Those changes made all the difference. Within a month, Yvonne's "problem" behaviors decreased, much to the relief of her parents, teacher, and administrators. **When Yvonne's team came to understand the noises as adaptive strategies rather than inappropriate behavior or random attention seeking, they developed an appreciation for her behaviors and new ways to effectively solve the problem.** Yvonne's parents also felt a burden lift since previously they had secretly believed that they had somehow caused Yvonne's behaviors.

The team saw Yvonne in a new light, spontaneously engaging her with more compassion and warmth through their facial expressions, tone of voice, and emotional communication. The newfound understanding helped both Yvonne and the adults in her life find their way to a relationally co-regulated green pathway.

Assessing Each Child's Reactions to Physical Environments

Does the child have a history (beginning in toddlerhood) of repeatedly refusing or protesting certain experiences?
If so, list them:

_____

_____

_____

Are the experiences coinciding with specific sensory experiences or requirements? (e.g., touching certain substances, sounds, smells, movement, etc.) If so, list them:

_____

_____

_____

Does the child routinely resist trying new things or protest/avoid going to certain places? If so, list them:

_____

_____

_____

Can you identify any commonalities, from a sensory standpoint, that characterize the activities or places the child seeks to avoid?
If so, list them:

_____

_____

_____

Yvonne's Iceberg

Challenging behaviors: Humming

Tapping on desk

Classroom disruption

Non-compliance

Faulty neuroception

Need for adult emotional co-regulation

Auditory over-reactivity

Difficulty processing background and foreground sounds

Embarrassment

Mia — Under-reactive Threat Detection

While many children *overreact* to sensory aspects of the environment, sometimes children *underreact* to sensory information.

Mia, six, was adopted at birth and grew up with loving parents and a supportive community in a neighborhood filled with children. But her parents noticed early on how different she was from her peers. She would run around the playground, seemingly so unaware of her surroundings that she would bump into playground equipment— or collide with other children. She ran after other children, but didn't know how to play with them. Additionally, Mia fell often and skinned her knees, but that didn't seem to bother her. When her parents shared their concerns with Mia's pediatrician, he assured them that she was physically healthy, but referred the family to me to evaluate her social and emotional development.

After hearing her parents' concerns and observing Mia, I wondered whether she might be under-reactive in some of her sensory channels, so I suggested they have an occupational therapist colleague (someone I consult with on a regular basis) evaluate her. The OT later explained that our hunch was correct: Mia's *under-reactivity* to her sense of proprioception and touch caused a decrease in her awareness of her body. The feedback link from her body to her motor system, which should have informed her limbs how to move and react, was weak. Mia also seemed to have under-reactivity to pain—a fact that helped explain her nonchalant reactions to injuries.

Mia's behaviors were influenced by the way her body and brain registered sensory information, and had a profound impact on her play skills and relationships. Fortunately, we identified her differences early and devised an appropriate therapeutic approach. Over time, Mia developed increased body awareness, which led to fewer bumps and bruises and more successful peer interactions. Through play-based occupational therapy with her parents involved in each session—and with an emphasis on bottom-up strategies—Mia began to feel more connected to and aware of her own body. She became more confident and connected more naturally with her peers. As a result, she began to seek play experiences rather than avoid them, and her social-emotional development progressed and eventually flourished, with the support of a DIR®-based parent-child program.

Mia's Iceberg

Clumsiness

Difficulties interacting with peers

Seemingly high pain thresholds

Under-reactive to touch proprioception, pain

Weak sensory feedback loops to inform body how to move and react

Reduced awareness of her body in space

Jamal — Sensory Craving

Six-year-old Jamal had a natural urge to climb up on things. When he was two, the age at which toddlers explore the limits of what their bodies (and their parents) will allow them to do, he loved to climb on tables and chairs and jump off of them. On his second day of preschool, his teacher called his parents after he scaled her desk and leapt from the top. Jamal's parents had told him many times that he had to be careful, and they worried about him constantly. By the time he was three years old, he had visited the emergency room twice—once for a sprained ankle and once to get stitches in his forehead after a fall.

In his first semester as a kindergartener, an astute teacher recommended that the school's occupational therapist weigh in on his constant need to be in the air. She observed how much Jamal loved climbing and jumping off of structures on the playground and swinging. His parents reported that he could swing for hours on end if he was allowed to do so. The OT was trained in sensory processing and evaluated Jamal over several months. She noted that Jamal craved vestibular movement and proprioceptive input to his muscles and joints.

Jamal's sensory craving was so strong that it often overran Jamal's awareness of safety. Once Jamal's parents and teacher understood that he craved certain types of movement, they were better prepared to support him emotionally because they now saw his behaviors as adaptations to at least two of his sensory systems. With the guidance of the OT, they also now had practical suggestions to help him, including body-up strategies that helped calm him onto the green pathway at home and at school.

Jamal's Iceberg

Climbing and scaling furniture

Jumping off tables chairs, couches

Lack of safety awareness

Atypical sensory processing

Craving and seeking proprioceptive and vestibular input

Challenges in first four processes of social-emotional development

To review: the sensory systems react according to each individual's body and brain connections. These systems are influenced by genetics, constitutional factors such as the prenatal environment, the relational environment, and the physical environment. Sensory experiences are coded with an emotion and linked to memories. This explains why children are often triggered into defensive, fight-or-flight behaviors by a sensation, feeling, or thought related to earlier adverse experiences.

Now that we have discussed how the sensory systems influence emotions and behaviors, let's turn to see how feelings and thoughts can influence children's behaviors.

Behaviors Influenced by Feelings

Giana was eight years old when I met her and her concerned parents. They were looking for help for Giana's "big" emotions, which, in her parent's words, "dictated so much of each day" for the family. They reported that after Giana had started kindergarten, she suddenly began to worry about many things. Along with her anxiety came another behavior: each morning she asked questions whose answers she clearly already knew. Sometimes, she would ask her mother who was picking her up from school, even if she knew that her mom and dad picked her up on alternate days. On the weekends she asked if there was school that day, even though she certainly knew the answer.

Giana was often overwhelmed by her worries, and her parents wanted to give her tools to help her feel stronger and more resilient.

In our family sessions together, I observed Giana's play themes. Combined with her parents' descriptions, they revealed that she was experiencing generalized anxiety. Her fears, hypervigilance, and concerns were expanding into various parts of her life and affecting the whole family. In our sessions together, we explored childhood worries through a pathway that Giana loved, reading books. One book in particular that was (and is) a staple in my office, *What to Do When You Worry Too Much,* provided Giana explanations and solutions for her active limbic system and the resulting fears.[13]

One of the keys to helping Giana was to determine whether bibliotherapy (using books as a therapeutic tool, a top-down approach) was appropriate for this particular child's social and emotional development. As it turned out, it was. With the help of her attentive parents and some effective cognitive-behavioral strategies, Giana eventually found ways to manage her tendency toward worry and hypervigilance successfully.

Behaviors Influenced by Thoughts

Sergio was the third of six children. I met him at his after-school program, where, with his family's permission, he attended a social skills group that I led for a small group of behaviorally challenged children. (We called it that because "social skills group" sounded more positive than "behavior management group.") Sergio was gregarious and friendly. As we played games and talked about feelings, friends, and family, he often told jokes that made the other students in the group laugh. The school counselor had referred Sergio to the group to see if I could help him figure out how to stay calmer when things didn't go his way at school.

When Sergio couldn't quickly figure out an answer to a math problem, for example, he would become upset and sometimes cry. Writing a story or drawing a picture, he would immediately crumple up the paper and start over with a fresh sheet. His teacher would hear him mutter, "I'm not smart," or "I'm dumb at writing." When she tried explaining to Sergio that he wasn't expected to get things right the first time, he often became more upset. He also got agitated about simple spelling tests, explaining that he was worried about failing.

Sergio's biggest challenge was that he was a self-described "perfectionist." I guessed that his parents or other adults had used this word after witnessing how hard he was on himself when things didn't go his way.

Clearly, there were many potential contributing factors to Sergio's worries and thoughts. I contacted his concerned parents and suggested that a visit to a child therapist might help him (and them) unpack his strongly held ideas and thoughts, which seemed to be causing some of his dysregulation.

Months after the social skills group ended, I checked in on the parents, who told me Sergio had formed a strong relationship with his new therapist. The therapist approached children playfully, and Sergio enjoyed playing ping-pong with him at his office. His play therapy time included the whole family, giving Sergio an outlet to talk about his worries and thoughts. He was learning to sort out when thoughts were helpful or not. His parents appreciated how the therapist had helped Sergio learn to control what he called "hummingbird" thoughts, which flew around his mind. It appeared that the therapist's creatively delivered cognitive behavioral approach had helped Sergio approach the thoughts fueling his concerning behaviors in a new and effective way.

Behaviors Influenced by Thoughts and Feelings

Darius began the third grade at his new school a few months after his family relocated from their home in the Middle East. His father, a U.S. citizen, attended college and spent his adulthood in the Middle East, where he thought he would stay. Over time, the political situation prompted him and his wife to move to the U.S. to live with relatives. Their difficult decision meant Darius had to leave everyone and everything he knew: his friends, his house, and his school.

Shortly into the school year, his new teachers noticed that Darius often stood by the door of his classroom, refusing to go outside to recess.

His school counselor (who understood the importance of looking beneath behaviors) took a relational approach to helping children. Rather than meeting with students in her small office, she invited them to stroll with her on the school grounds and in this way got to know them. On such a walk, Darius told the counselor that when he looked at the soccer field on the playground, he thought about his friends back in his homeland. The counselor saw how his thoughts combined with feelings of overwhelming loss and sadness. She realized that discussing his life-changing losses was an avenue to understanding and solving his refusal to go outside. After a few months, Darius slowly began to feel better. One day, he ventured onto the soccer field, where his new peers discovered what a good player he was. Slowly, new positive memories began to replace his previously overwhelming, sad feelings and thoughts about his new life and home.

The Importance of a Team Approach

As we have seen in this chapter, when we are addressing challenging behaviors, it's essential to take into consideration a child's individual differences, whether those differences are in the realm of ***body processes, sensations, feelings, thoughts, or any combinations thereof.*** As the children's stories have shown, there are countless triggers and causes underlying challenging behaviors. Due to this complexity, we need to address all the various aspects of a child's behaviors comprehensively.

We start by understanding that no one person, or professional, or approach has all the answers to solving children's challenges. Most of us have been educated and trained with the assumption of the mind/body split; that's simply how our respective specialization programs are set up. Yet the brain/body connection is often best approached by a team of childhood professionals working together.

This is why it's useful to incorporate professionals from multiple disciplines on children's teams when standard approaches of a single discipline or profession don't yield the intended results. If you are a parent, it's important to include your child's pediatrician on the team as early as possible, to cover potential biomedical triggers or causes (and treatments, including evaluations for medication) when necessary. If you are a professional, working on teams, or having access to colleagues in different disciplines is a best-practice principle. Those in all childhood disciplines should work collaboratively to help solve children's behavioral challenges because they are everyone's responsibility, just as social and emotional development is every childhood provider's responsibility.[14]

Valuable information is gleaned from a child's team: those professionals who work together or consult with each other to help support families. Here's a partial list of pediatric professionals who can add valuable information when a child's behaviors are challenged.

- Pediatricians
- Mental Health and Counseling Professionals
- Occupational Therapists
- Developmental Pediatricians
- Educators and Special Educators
- Speech and Language Therapists
- Mindfulness Specialists
- Pediatric Neurologists
- Child Psychiatrists
- Nutritionists
- Physical Therapists
- Educational Therapists
- Music and Art Therapists
- Movement Specialists
- Developmental Optometrists

In previous chapters, we examined other common mistakes professionals and parents make in reacting to challenging behaviors: **(1) addressing behaviors before we understand their etiology; and (2) failing to use a developmental roadmap in addressing behaviors.** Now that we have discussed how individual differences are crucial to *understanding* behaviors, we're ready to turn to the real work: how we can *help* children who are struggling. In the next three chapters, Part Two of the book, we will turn to *personalized attunement*, the way to improve our current approaches by attuning to a child's individual needs and addressing the causes and triggers underlying behaviors.

Main Points —

- Individual differences are the characteristics and qualities that shape how we take in and respond to the world around us, including the way we experience processes in the body, sensations, feelings, thoughts, and combinations thereof.

- Children (and all human beings) understand and interpret the world through the sensory systems. It's necessary to have a basic understanding of sensory processing because it can help guide our interactive strategies for emotional regulation and co-regulation.

- When we appreciate a child's and caregiver's individual differences we can personalize our treatment, educational, and parenting approaches.

PART TWO

Solutions

4.
Safety Is the Starting Point

"Safety is treatment and treatment is safety."

Dr. Stephen Porges

It took only one day for me to see how Mateo's school team viewed him through a different lens than his parents and I did.*

His parents had noted his challenges early: he hadn't begun speaking yet at two-and-a-half. After two years of in-home services and an autism diagnosis, he entered a special-education program to address his challenges in communication, attention, peer relationships, and learning. Mateo's brain-wiring differences made it difficult for him to speak and to let others know what he was thinking. I was asked to work with him when he was eight and habitually wandered around his small special-education classroom, incessantly touching the walls—and often his classmates as well.

I watched Mateo in a group-learning session, trying to get the attention of his aide, seated beside him. When the aide didn't look his way, Mateo moved his arm until it glanced hers. Then she followed his Individualized Education Plan (IEP), which called for staff to ignore behaviors deemed as "nonpreferred." So instead of acknowledging him, she slid her chair sideways, out of Mateo's reach. He began to move his arms and torso more vigorously, leaning over and grabbing the arm of his aide, who then quietly asked him to pay attention to the teacher, and moved behind him, out of his view.

---

* The ideas contained in this chapter reflect the application of Porges's Polyvagal Theory and the concept of neuroception as a guiding principle in helping children with persistent behavioral challenges.

Seconds later, Mateo leaned back in his chair to see her—so far that he toppled over, landing loudly on his back. That prompted the teacher to instruct the aide to take Mateo to the "calm-down room," a plain closetlike space in the back of the classroom with a padded floor. Looking in through the one-way window, I watched Mateo, a flat and sad expression on his face, rhythmically kicking the wall while the aide sat to the side, avoiding any interaction.

In that one exchange, I saw evidence of all three of the concerns described in Chapter 1 about how our systems fall short in helping children with behavioral challenges: **(1) we fail to evaluate the underpinnings of behavioral challenges before we try to decrease them; (2) we don't put behaviors into the larger context of the child's social-emotional development; and (3) we use one-size-fits-all approaches.**

As I sat in the back of the room that day, I was reminded that we often target behaviors for elimination before we understand their adaptive purpose for a child.

Too often, we assume that a child is intentionally misbehaving when the child is actually responding to basic survival instincts, including the need to feel safe.[1] We need to consider whether or not children like Mateo are misbehaving on purpose or displaying that basic human response—and to design our approaches accordingly if that ability is still under construction. In Chapter 1, we learned that there are many reasons beneath the surface for children's behaviors. For Mateo, his ability to control his own motor actions was under construction, making "appropriate" communication impossible because of his brain wiring. *Adults mischaracterized his movement challenges as challenging behavior when, in fact, they were his attempts to feel safe.*

That moment between Mateo and his aide also illustrates the most profound concern I have about how many of our systems serving children view challenging behaviors: we see *the behaviors themselves* as the main problem or target, without recognizing that relationships and social engagement are key to helping children build behavioral and emotional control.[2] **Before we attempt to suppress behaviors, we need to ascertain whether the behaviors we are observing are a sign of a child's social engagement system in need of relational help.**

As I sat in the back of the class, watching Mateo descend into increasing levels of emotional distress, I heard Dr. Porges in the back of my mind: "To connect and to co-regulate with others is our biological imperative."[3] I was there to observe, but I had to stop myself from approaching the child and connecting with him myself. I looked around the room, expecting to see other adults concerned as I was about the child's emotional state. Instead I saw everyone trying to ignore the situation and continue teaching the other kids. It was a snapshot of valiant teachers and support staff following a mainstream approach to behavioral management, with the best of intentions. But as I mentioned in Chapter 1, that approach stands in contrast to what I have learned from translational neuroscience: the importance of relational safety in all aspects of child development. I returned to my office that day and wrote about the experience, adding it to similar entries in my journal, and pondering how to explain to his loving parents and his dedicated school team what I had witnessed.

When the aide misread Mateo's bids for help as noncompliance and moved her chair away, he moved from the green to the red pathway. Ironically, the plan to help the child *increased* his distress and further compromised his ability to co-regulate his emotions with others. The behavioral signs I observed—flat facial expression, kicking the wall, giving up on asking for help—were all signals that his social-engagement system had fatigued, yielding to the older brain circuitry linked to more basic survival instincts.

Personalized Attunement

This rest of this book focuses on how we can update the ways we help children by using approaches that respect the role of relationships in all areas of a child's development. I call this overarching approach personalized attunement: a way to tailor our interactions to meet each child's physical and emotional needs. We will learn how to use our knowledge of individual differences and how to leverage relationships and the environment in order to build the strongest foundation for development through the following steps:

1. Prioritizing the child's feelings of safety in relationships

2. Addressing the causes and triggers underlying the behaviors

3. Helping the child to develop new ways to cope

Practicing personalized attunement allows us to determine what each child needs in order to promote responsiveness, warmth, and engagement.

In this chapter, we'll focus on the first of the three steps: prioritizing relational safety for each child. We start here because I have observed that often, once a child's relational safety needs are properly met, many behavior challenges fade away naturally because the underlying reasons for the behaviors no longer exist.

Priming a Child for Success

Many of the techniques I learned decades ago in my psychology training conflict with what we now know about the workings of the autonomic nervous system. I was taught to view behaviors mainly at face value—as easily amenable to an array of cognitive and behavioral techniques aimed at changing them. This was well before the 1990s, known as the "Decade of the Brain," when neuroscientists' new understandings of the brain became widely known. The approaches I learned in school oversimplified ways to alter behaviors, mostly emphasizing the child's *thinking brain*, without considering the essential foundation that underlies all brain development: relational safety and emotional co-regulation.

As we learned in Chapter 2, the Polyvagal Theory sheds new light on the importance of adults' behaviors on the child's feelings of safety.[4] When a child feels truly safe with a trusted adult, social engagement behaviors emerge naturally. When a child experiences the neuroception of safety, defensive strategies are "turned off."[5] In other words, the child doesn't need to fight, run away or freeze up in order to feel safe on a subconscious level.

As in Mateo's case, when our actions diminish a child's sense of safety, we prime the child's system for defensive behaviors.[6] The behaviors that concerned his teacher—his wandering and constantly touching things in the classroom—were his way of coping with a neuroception of threat. He was a child with sensory over-reactivity to sounds and under-reactivity to proprioception, a child whose body needed to move in order to feel calmer and to find comfort in the physical environment and in others. **His attempts to touch his aide were not acting-out behaviors but rather reaching-out behaviors. They reflected a biologically-based strategy that human beings use to feel better when they are distressed. Yet we often label this strategy as misbehavior or "seeking negative attention."**

In short, I viewed Mateo's behaviors in class that day as his way of adapting to a suboptimal relational and physical environment that was ill suited to his individual needs. All children will benefit when we consider how to prime a child's nervous system for success by acknowledging and respecting the child's individual differences *and* need for relational connection.

Determining Neuroceptive State

When a child experiences a neuroception of safety, there's no need for protective, defensive behaviors, characteristic of the red pathway.[7] As the child relaxes onto the green pathway, cooperation, learning, play, and curiosity emerge naturally. Let's look at characteristics of the red and blue pathways that signify a child's adaptive responses to stress. Notice that I suggest that blue-pathway behaviors indicate very high levels of perceived threat. This is because the red pathway involves activation, or doing something active to feel better, which is more adaptive than disengaging, fading away, or dissociating. The blue pathway, in its final stages, indicates that the child's mind/body is essentially giving up and beginning to shut down in the face of a perceived life threat.

Is the Child Feeling Safe?

Characteristics of the **Red Pathway**

Look at the child's behavioral features, and mark any that you see.

☐ Face is angry, disgusted, clenched jaw, grimacing

☐ Face has raised eyebrows, furrowed brow, trembling lips or mouth, fake forced grin, startled expression, looks worried or scared

☐ Eyes may dart around, avoid or have intense eye contact, roll upward

☐ Child has fast or repetitive movements, trembling hands, clings, grabs, or flails around

☐ Child moans, groans in pain, quivering, whimpering sounds

☐ Voice is high pitched, loud, sarcastic, screaming, hostile, grumpy; uncontrolled laughter

☐ Body in motion, hitting, kicking, biting, spitting, pushing, shoving; threatening gestures

☐ Body motions are impulsive; child may bump into things or fall

How much time did the child spend in the red pathway?
_____minutes

What did adults do with the child when he/she was in the red pathway?

_____

_____

If you checked multiple boxes, consider that the child may be picking up threat in the physical or relational environment.

Adapted from *Infant/Child Mental Health, Early Intervention, and Relationship-Based Therapies: A Neurorelational Framework for Interdisciplinary Practice*, by Connie Lillas and Janiece Turnbull. Copyright © 2009 by Interdisciplinary Training Institute LLC and Janiece Turnbull. Used by permission of W.W. Norton & Company, Inc.

Is the Child Feeling Safe?

Characteristics of the **Blue Pathway**

Look at the child's behavioral features, and mark any that you see.

☐ Face looks flat, especially around eyes and forehead

☐ Voice sounds monotone, soft, and lacking in inflection or prosody

☐ Child is not talking or is making few sounds

☐ Child does not appear to be hearing what you are saying

☐ Body is slow moving; posture is slumped or frozen

☐ Child cowers or hides

☐ Child avoids interaction

How much time did the child spend in the blue pathway?
_____minutes

What did adults do with the child when he/she was in the blue pathway?

_____

_____

If you checked multiple boxes, consider that the child may be picking up **very** high levels of threat in the physical or relational environment.

Adapted from *Infant/Child Mental Health, Early Intervention, and Relationship-Based Therapies: A Neurorelational Framework for Interdisciplinary Practice*, by Connie Lillas and Janiece Turnbull. Copyright © 2009 by Interdisciplinary Training Institute LLC and Janiece Turnbull. Used by permission of W.W. Norton & Company, Inc.

Signs that a child is in the blue pathway often include a flat facial expression, a monotone voice, and a lack of interaction. In the red pathway, a child can physically have difficulty hearing, caused by the loss of neural tone that regulates the middle-ear muscles.[8] Before we decide on how to intervene, we should carefully observe these features of the child's face, voice, and postures.

Safety Is in the Eye of the Beholder

How can we know whether a child feels safe? What's important is the child's own *perception* of safety—not what adults think *ought to* constitute relational or environmental safety. In short, safety is in the "eye" (brain and body) of the beholder: the child. It is "defined by how the child feels, and not simply by the removal of threat."[9] I call this determining whether or not a child feels "Brain-Safe". We need to work toward providing what each child *interprets* as safety. What's critical isn't the general notion of an "optimal" environment, but each child's *response* to the environment. Many current treatment approaches and plans don't consider this important distinction. As much as possible, we need to tailor the physical, sensory, and relational environments to the needs of *each* individual child with persistent behavioral challenges and not make assumptions about what the child perceives as environmental or relational safety.

Providing relational support on the front end can be more cost effective in the long run because it saves us from spending time and money on plans that don't target the root causes of the behaviors. We can recruit new or existing personnel as emotional co-regulators to help support a child back to the green pathway as the first line of treatment. This concept is often overlooked when we fail to see relationships (with, for example, sensitive classroom aides) as essential elements of treatment plans. That obsolete view is not supported by current neuroscience principles about psychological resilience.[10]

> *We can recruit new or existing personnel as emotional co-regulators to help support a child back to the green pathway as the first line of treatment.*

A powerful modulator of a child's stress response is the safety of a relationship. That doesn't mean that the mere presence of a qualified adult is sufficient. We need to know *how* to help each child feel safe in mind and body. In my experiences as a child psychologist, I've found that with a modicum of training, adults can learn ways to *titrate their interactions* to provide the right cues of safety, according to each child's unique needs.

Max — Tailoring Relational Safety

Ten-year-old Max had multiple developmental delays and suffered from such severe anxiety that he routinely refused to leave his home to go to school. He was referred to my office for his long history of "school refusal." His parents had to "talk him out the door" each morning, and at school he often refused to speak, sometimes suffering meltdowns. He also had difficulty attending to his classroom work. The school assigned an aide to assist him academically, yet his difficulties continued.

During a subsequent school observation, I witnessed Max sucking on his fingers and biting his nails. His well-intentioned aide tried to help him follow the teacher's directions and keep up with his classwork by whispering to him to pay attention and helping him focus on each worksheet. What seemed to be missing, though, was an approach that considered Max's emotional state before focusing on academic tasks. He was clearly showing signs of distress throughout the school day, but his support plans didn't specifically address ways to support his emotional and regulatory state. When his parents asked the school to provide additional individualized, relationship-based training for the teacher and aide, the administrators refused, insisting that the aide was a longstanding employee with a good track record.

The problem was that Max's IEP plans were not effective in curbing his anxiety. His aide was in a losing battle to help him academically because his development was shaky at the foundations of regulation, attention, and social engagement. I suggested that the teacher and aide hone their emotional co-regulation skills with Max. (I explain how educators and other providers can do this in my book *Social and Emotional Development in Early Intervention*). **In short, Max was not progressing at school because his treatment plans failed to recognize the powerful importance of relational safety underlying his anxiety and affecting his ability to learn.**

Instead of using a generic lens to define emotional safety for all children, we should use the lens of each child's perceptions, based on the child's individual differences. Schools are wise to engage in discussions with parents and include them in the process of selecting the appropriate types of relational support for their child, because a child's emotional state has direct impact on the ability to learn. In my experience, classroom aides and paraprofessionals often are excluded from children's IEP team meetings. Instead, we need to honor the important role of paraprofessionals as essential emotional co-regulators with children and include them in those important gatherings.

Personalized Attunement: Safety Is in the Eye of the Child

Ask: Does the child perceive the adults in his or her life as supportive and providing cues of safety?

If so, what are the behavioral indications that the child perceives the adults in his or her life as providing safety cues?

_____

_____

If not, what are the behavioral indications that the child *does not* perceive the adults in his or her life as providing safety cues?

_____

_____

Determine how to increase safety cues to the child by communicating with the child's parents/caregivers and through careful observations of interactions.

What kinds of social interactions with caregivers help propel the child onto his or her green pathway of relational safety?

List: _____

_____

_____

_____

_____

What Is Stress?

In the 1930s, Hans Selye, a medical researcher, originally introduced the concept of stress as an emergency "general alarm reaction."[11] Our understanding of the impact of stress on the body has evolved since Selye's description. Bruce McKewen, a neuroscience researcher, describes two different kinds of stress responses. One is the body/brain's *adaptive* response to stress, called *allostasis*, when a challenge is successfully managed.[12] We sometimes think of this as "good stress," as in challenging experiences that can have benefits, lead to greater resiliency, and help us become more adaptive people.[13] "Bad stress," on the other hand, the kind that delivers a punch of wear and tear on the body, is known as "allostatic load." What we might call being "stressed out,"[14] an allostatic load can compromise stress resiliency and general health over time.[15]

We all go through difficult times, and not all stress is harmful. When children receive proper support, "manageable stress" helps them to build coping abilities and resilience.[16] That's beneficial, since we all face stressors every day. One problem with our current approaches to challenging behaviors is that we generally don't track stress (good or bad) in children's daily lives. Instead, we focus on compliance and managing surface behaviors, paying little heed to the child's internal stress. A more constructive approach would be to help children manage stressful situations and turn them into experiences that lead to growth.

> *One problem with our current approaches to challenging behaviors is that we generally don't track stress (good or bad) in children's daily lives.*

Too often, we prioritize compliance, teaching, or extinguishing behaviors without addressing the child's emotional state. We need to recognize instead that in addressing many behavioral challenges, *the starting point should be the child's sense of safety, not the behavior itself.* In this perspective, the adult's priority shifts to first *co-regulating* with a child if he isn't feeling safe in body and mind. That's what was missing from the treatment plans for Mateo, whom we discussed at the beginning of this chapter. If those working with him had recognized Mateo's behaviors as pleas for help, they might have approached him in an entirely different way.

"Good Stress" Helps Children Grow and Develop Resilience

Manageable stress helps children—and all of us—develop strengths and learn new things. It also helps children move outside of their comfort zones and develop new capacities and abilities. Each child tolerates stress differently. The key is to understand what is optimal—that is, what's enough good stress for a child to push past old fears or push the limits of a new motor action or other process to grow new strengths. Psychologist Lev Vygotsky describes this as the *zone of proximal development* (ZPD) or "the distance between the actual developmental level as determined by independent problem solving and the level of potential development as determined through problem solving under adult guidance or in collaboration with more capable peers."[17] In other words, children have a "zone" that helps push them forward and learn new things, as long as they have the proper support.

The key to helping children is to monitor their levels of stress and to make sure it's manageable.[18] According to Lillas and Turnbull, we should "make certain that the task or activity at hand is not too challenging. If so, go back to an earlier point of success to sustain alert processing. Once engaged, slowly increase the difficulty level and provide scaffolding and support as needed."[19] **In other words, we titrate our interactions and requirements of children in real time, making sure they are experiencing manageable stress and not the "bad" kind, which sends them into an allostatic load situation.[20]**

We can monitor children's levels of manageable stress by using our color pathways representing the different states of autonomic nervous system activation. When a child is at the edge of her green pathway, she's likely experiencing increased awareness and arousal that is supportive of learning and expanding experiences in the zone of proximal development (ZPD). I call this the "light green" path, when a child is edging towards the red pathway, but not quite there yet. *In other words, the child is activated and poised for learning something new and being challenged, but not overwhelmed by a task.* Such situations help children develop a greater *tolerance* for stressful situations.

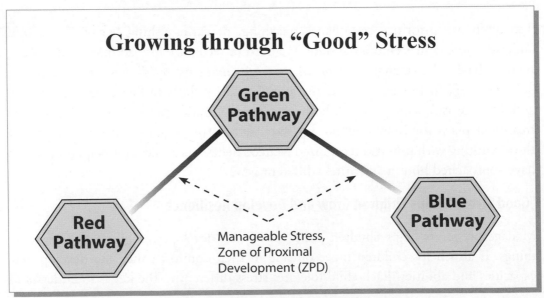

Vygotsky, 1978; Zones, Lillas & Turnbull, 2009

Helping Children Thrive and Learn through the Therapeutic Use of Self

We help children stay on the optimal pathway through our interactions with them. Let's now examine how all of us—parents, teachers, and professionals—can hone our skills for providing relational safety through supportive interactions. This practice—using our self to communicate emotional safety to a child—is known as the *"therapeutic use of self."* While many popular books and blogs discuss how to help children learn new helpful strategies to *calm themselves* (important and critical skills), we can do something even more powerful before *teaching* the ability to self-calm. We can prioritize the experience of being in a space of safety with another, and build a solid platform for children to grow and try new things that were previously difficult, thereby building their resilience.

Why Our Emotions Matter

Our emotional tone is the "raw material" that allows us to help children with behavior al challenges. As we learned in Chapter 2, this is transmitted through our body language. When we feel safe, we have soft eyes, a prosodic voice, and a relaxed posture.[21] Children pick up on these cues and are consciously and subconsciously influenced by them. *While this may seem like common sense, the reality is that it's difficult to maintain a flexible, engaged, green pathway of emotional regulation when our kids or the kids we work with struggle behaviorally.* The responsibility of doing our job well weighs heavily on us— parents, providers and teachers.

Parents often feel that they are on the front lines of a war to save their child. I have witnessed this firsthand with the families I have had the privilege to work with, and experienced it myself when I had to advocate for my child through the public education system. Parents are barraged with negative messages: "You're overreacting"; "You're being overprotective"; "You're asking too much." These messages can weigh heavily, taking a toll on physical and mental health. This criticism fuels second guessing, anger, and guilt. We'll now examine this dilemma, because we cannot take ourselves out of the equation when it comes to supporting children.

Supporting children isn't only about listening or even talking. Sometimes we support them merely by our physical presence through the therapeutic use of self. When we (the parent, teacher, or provider) offer a calming, warm presence, we make ourselves part of the equation of solving behavior problems by helping to calm a child's nervous system in a state of defense. **Many of our paradigms for helping children with persistent behavior challenges target the child's behaviors, but leave us—parents and providers—out of the equation.** In the developmental approach I describe here, our own emotional and physical presence with children is front and center.

So what does this look like? *It's beneficial for adults to take notice of our own reactions, starting by checking in with ourselves to determine whether we are experiencing calm attention in our own bodies and minds.* Our own awareness allows us to realize what kinds of emotional signals we are giving to children. Only then can we offer children what they need most when they are in distress: our calming presence to help them feel safe and calm again. This process of mutual support is known as emotional co-regulation.

To make the most of ourselves as therapeutic agents, we need to know how to determine which pathway *we* are on. Sometimes, when we witness a child in distress— whether the child is having a tantrum, hysterically laughing in an unnatural way, lashing out, or shutting down and ignoring us—our own sense of emotional safety can feel threatened. This is especially true for parents, since we carry such a heavy burden of responsibility to insure that our children thrive. When we witness our child struggling and feel the urge to "set them straight," our own stress responses can easily cause us to say or do things that we later regret.

How can we determine how ready we are to help children with behavioral challenges when they are struggling? Using a combination of the color pathways and house of social and emotional development described in Chapter 2, the first step involves reflecting and asking questions of ourselves to determine what pathway *we* are on.

We will revisit this worksheet later.

Survey for Adults: What Pathway Am I On?

Our first step in helping children with behavioral challenges is to assess ourselves before acting.

Create a moment of awareness by asking yourself: How am I feeling? What am I experiencing? Using the following checklist may help:

Green Pathway of Calm

_____ I'm breathing at a normal rate/rhythm

_____ I'm feeling calm in my body

_____ My voice is modulated, with nice variations (prosody)

_____ My facial muscles feel relaxed

_____ I can think

_____ I can plan

_____ I can come up with options

_____ I can ask for assistance from other adults or give myself a break if I'm too upset

Blue Pathway of Disconnection

_____ I feel slow to react

_____ I can't think fast enough

_____ I feel like I'm sinking or disappearing

_____ I don't feel up to managing the situation

_____ I feel helpless

_____ My voice is monotone

_____ My facial expressions feel frozen

_____ I feel sad

Red Pathway of Reactivity

_____ I'm upset

_____ I'm reacting quickly

_____ My breathing is shallow or heavy

_____ My body is tense

_____ I can't think

_____ I feel like I'm going to explode

_____ I'm talking loudly or yelling

_____ I can't stand or sit still

If you are on the green pathway, then you are ready to move to the next step in surveying your ability to serve as an emotional co-regulator ("Surveying Ourselves" on page 120). However, if you are on the red or blue pathway, or headed in that direction, this is where you **STOP**. Make sure your child or the child with whom you are working is physically safe, and find a moment to pause and reflect. The next few pages will focus on how we build up the green pathway for ourselves. Once we are solidly on the green pathway, we can determine how well we are framing our relationship with the child. We do this because if we are not calm and alert, we are not in a place to act thoughtfully and help the child. **In fact, we get into the most trouble when we react to a child's behavior challenge instinctively—sometimes with unfortunate results. This can happen when a child says or does something that feels disrespectful or is otherwise a personal "hot button" for us.**

Sometimes, when we say things we later regret, we feel badly about it, and our minds combat those bad feelings by creating a narrative that helps us believe the child needed or deserved our harsh reaction. That's a lonely place to be, and it's important to remember that you are not alone. This is a universally challenging predicament for all caregivers: maintaining emotional presence when the stakes—and the burden of responsibility—are so high.

Our own triggers—the many factors that cause us to act without thoughtful consideration—are just as powerful as the triggers we witness in our children or the children we work with. When our own neuroception is triggered into threat, and we can't shift, we are just as susceptible to emotional and behavioral challenges as our children. This isn't something to be ashamed of. As humans we *naturally cycle through a range of positive and negative emotions.* I have great compassion for parents who share with me the disappointment and natural longings for their child to be more "like those other kids at the park whose parents are relaxed and enjoying themselves." To be sure, raising a child with behavioral challenges can require constant hypervigilance. Many parents feel constantly "on edge," waiting for the child's next meltdown or tantrum, or the dreaded phone call from the school office.

The key is a compassionate awareness of all that we carry as parents and care-sharers. **Rather than berating ourselves or feeling guilty for ending up on the red or blue pathway (again), we can work on our own awareness and apply the self-care we need to get back to green.** If we can offer ourselves grace and acknowledge the full range of human feelings—negative and positive—then everyone benefits.

What feeds your green pathway and helps you feel more connected to yourself and to others? Whatever it is—connecting with a friend, walking, meditating, praying, yoga, exercising—it's helpful to create your own personalized self-regulation tools to guide you back to the green pathway and use them often.

Children benefit from our self-awareness as adults, because we can't hide our emotional state from a child. Emotions are transmitted from one person to the next, and through neuroception we pick up on them. Pretending to be just fine when you're really not can confuse a child and provide mixed messages about safety in relationships and how much a child can trust you to help her feel better.

At a time when you're away from the heat of such an exchange, you may find it useful to fill in this blank iceberg for yourself. If you feel that you are often overwhelmed by the burdens of your life or the burden of caring for children with behavioral challenges, consulting with a mental health professional can help to investigate your own emotional triggers and get you on a pathway to greater awareness, hope, and self-compassion.

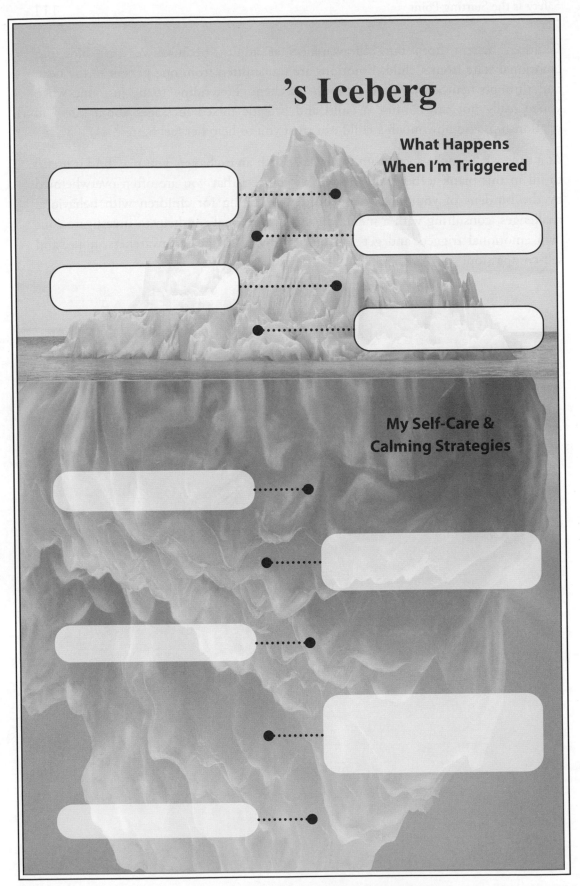

_____'s Iceberg

What Happens When I'm Triggered

My Self-Care & Calming Strategies

Self-Assessment and Self-Awareness: Staying Calm—Adults

Let's consider our own triggers.

Think about behaviors that you typically go to when your child or the children you work with experience behavioral challenges.

Reflect and write down those factors in your history or current situation that may challenge your ability to stay in the green pathway:

_____

_____

_____

_____

Consider and write down your own personal triggers that can lead you onto a red pathway when you are managing a child's behavior:

_____

_____

_____

These are some positive supports I can create for myself to counter such reactions: _____

_____

_____

_____

Fortunately, we can take action to counteract our own emotional triggers. We can find ways to support ourselves, benefiting our relationships as we experience (and model) awareness and compassion for ourselves. Think about your own self-regulatory tools. What are your strategies for calming and soothing yourself? It's helpful to make a list of them as a reminder to practice self-care, and actively build up your stores of resilience as you support your child or children who need you to be present through their emotional storms.

Mindful Awareness Aids the Therapeutic Use of Self

Caring human beings are the best therapeutic tool for children who are suffering, and we're most helpful when we can be emotionally present for them. *Mindful awareness* can help all of us—parents and professionals—and nurture relationships even when we are pulled by the sway of our child's (and our own) emotional upheavals.

Mindfulness is the capacity for moment-to-moment awareness without judgment.[22] Jon Kabat-Zinn brought its positive impact on health and well-being to the American public's attention in the 1980s, by developing a successful program for stress reduction at the University of Massachusetts Medical Center. Since then, studies have found mindfulness to improve psychological and medical outcomes, reduce stress, prevent burnout and "compassion fatigue," enhance satisfaction with the caregiving role, and increase well-being for parents of neurodiverse children.[23]

We can't truly help children with their behavioral challenges without *first helping ourselves* to be present, self-aware, and calm. This is the idea behind mindful self-compassion. Kristin Neff, the leading researcher on this form of mindfulness, describes mindful self-compassion as "when we suffer, caring for ourselves as we would care for someone we truly love." **She identifies self-compassion's three components: self-kindness, a sense of common humanity, and mindfulness.**[24] Dr. Neff's expansive research has demonstrated measurable benefits to caregivers of parents with children on the autism spectrum and a variety of other populations.[25]

Self-compassion may seem like a luxury, particularly in those moments when a child is on the red pathway and needs immediate assistance. But when we practice it over time, it can come as easily and naturally as . . . taking a breath.

Breathing in Moments of Relief for Caregivers

At the most basic level, we all have our breath available. Take a breath. Try to take one that is slow and deliberate. On the second or third breath, let your exhale be longer than your inhale. Continue for a few more breaths if you feel comfortable doing so. This is one way to slow the nervous system and begin to pump the brakes of the parasympathetic system—a most time-efficient way back to the green pathway.

Kristin Neff and psychologist Christopher Germer created a mindful self-compassion protocol that is helpful in supporting emotional regulation for parents and providers.[26] When facing a challenging moment with a child, it's helpful and calming to acknowledge quietly and say to yourself, "This is tough," or "This is a moment of suffering," and offer yourself grace. Just the momentary awareness that you are triggered is often enough to prevent you from saying or doing something impulsive that is not in the child's best interest.

If you're comfortable doing so, try the following exercise, which Drs. Neff and Germer designed to help stimulate calming in the body and engender positive feelings about yourself. Remember, as with all the exercises in this book, if you begin to feel distressed, simply stop—without self-judgment. Sometimes, stilling the body results in the activation of thoughts in the mind that can be uncomfortable for some people. (See page 267 for additional resources on mindfulness and mindful self-compassion.)

Affectionate Breathing

- Find a posture in which your body is comfortable and will feel supported for the length of the meditation. Then let your eyes gently close, partially or fully. Take a few slow, easy breaths, releasing any unnecessary tension in your body.

- If you like, try placing a hand over your heart or another soothing place as a reminder that we're bringing not only awareness, but affectionate awareness, to our breathing and to ourselves. You can leave your hand there or let it rest at any time.

- Begin to notice your breathing in your body, feeling your body breathe in and feeling your body breathe out.

- Notice how your body is nourished on the in-breath and relaxes with the out-breath.

- See if you can just let your body breathe. There is nothing you need to do.

- Now start to notice the *rhythm* of your breathing, flowing in and flowing out. Take some time to feel the natural rhythm of your breathing.

- Feel your whole body subtly moving with the breath, like the movement of the sea.

- Your mind will naturally wander like a curious child or a little puppy. When that happens, just gently returning to the rhythm of your breathing.

- Allow your whole body to be gently rocked and caressed—*internally caressed*—by your breathing.

- If it feels right, you can *give yourself over* to your breathing, letting your breathing be all there is. Just breathing. *Being* breathing.

- And now, gently release your attention on your breath, sitting quietly in your own experience, and allow yourself to feel whatever you're feeling and to be just as you are.

- Slowly and gently open your eyes.

From: *The Mindful Self-Compassion Workbook* (2018) by Kristin Neff, PhD, and Christopher Germer, PhD. Used by permission of Kristin Neff, PhD.

This concept of self-compassion is not popular in our culture, in which we often manage children first through our authority rather than through connection and engagement. Yet this valuable and powerful concept from mindfulness research supports the Polyvagal Theory's organizing principle: when human beings sense safety, their social-engagement behaviors (the opposite of challenging behaviors) unfold naturally, and the fight, flight, or freeze behaviors recede into the background since they are no longer necessary.[27]

We (adults, parents, caregivers, professionals) are the most important tools in the toolbox.

Our recognition that *how we are is as important as what we say*, compels us to take some time to reflect on the messages we provide children through our interactions with them.[28] In further considering how to help children connect to us, it's useful to take some time to reflect on the times in your life when you felt (or feel) truly safe with another person. This worksheet walks you through an exercise on experiencing memories of connection and safety.

Characteristics of Connection

Find a quiet place, sit still, and close your eyes. Think of a person in your life—from the past or present—who has made you feel safe, loved, and secure. Imagine the person's face and voice, and picture the soothing qualities this person embodies. If you can't think of someone who has offered this to you, then use your imagination to envision a loving and wise person with these qualities. Take some time to focus on that image and those qualities. Then open your eyes.

What feelings emerged as you did this exercise?

_____

_____

_____

What words or images come to mind as you thought about the interaction with this person?

_____

_____

_____

What kinds of things did the person say or do that made you feel safe, loved, and secure?

_____

_____

_____

The exercises and other self-care tools described earlier are intended to foster your ability to make yourself available to the children with whom you work or for whom you care. In other words, they are strategies that you can use to find the green pathway of calm. Just as it is important for children to build their house of social-emotional development, it is equally important for adults to track their own emotional reactions to ensure that they can serve as therapeutic agents for the child.

If your answers to the "What Pathway Am I On?" worksheet on page 111 indicate that you are indeed on the green pathway, then you are ready to move on to the next step, which involves surveying the quality of your engagement with the child. This worksheet, and the worksheets that follow, will take you through the remaining five steps that mirror the child's developmental processes.

Surveying Ourselves*

If we are on the green pathway, we then survey the quality of our engagement with the child.

Engagement and Relating for the Adult

___ Yes, I'm on the green pathway, and I'm feeling up to engaging with the child.

___ I can feel compassion or empathy for the child (even just a bit).

___ My facial expressions (especially the upper face, eyes, and forehead), body language, or other nonverbals are relaxed—signs that I am present on a mind/body level for the child.

___ I can use my words or my body language to reach out to the child in a way the child needs.

If you are generally able to do these things, then **continue to the next step.** If not, **STOP HERE** and back up to the *earliest* stage of challenge, starting with the exercises at the beginning of this chapter.

Adapted from Greenspan & Wieder, 2006

Nonverbal Interactions
for the Adult

The child knows I care and am present to help. I can now reach out.

_____ I can use words, gestures, or signals to see if we can communicate back and forth.

_____ I have the time and space to figure out what I can do to elicit positive signals of back-and-forth communication with the child.

_____ We are communicating in a relaxed back-and-forth exchange with gestures or words or a combination of both.

_____ We are engaging in a shared experience with a nice back-and-forth rhythm.

If you are able to do these things, then **continue to the next step.** If not, **STOP HERE** and go back to the earliest stage of challenge and work on that area first.

Adapted from Greenspan & Wieder, 2006

Shared Social Problem Solving for the Adult

___ I have the child's attention, and we are communicating in a back-and-forth way.

___ I can now piece together a few gestures or sentences to see if the child will add to what I am saying by gesturing to me with body language or with words.

___ We are engaging in a shared experience, with a nice back-and-forth rhythm that is leading us to a shared verbal or gestural "discussion."

___ I am beginning to understand what the child is communicating or needing from me.

If you are able to do these things, then **continue to the next step.** If not, **STOP HERE** and go back to the earliest stage of challenge and work on that area first.

Adapted from Greenspan & Wieder, 2006

Using Words, Ideas, and Play for the Adult

____ I am in a flow of communication with the child.

____ I can begin to deconstruct what may have just happened by guessing what the child is experiencing or by asking simple questions.

____ I can wonder with the child about what is happening and what the child thinks happened.

____ I can be reflective and open to the child's process of figuring out what he or she needs.

____ I am entering into a discussion with the child, through words, play, writing, or another creative means to deconstruct where the breakdown was and help the child find new ways to cope.

If you are able to do these things, then **continue to the next step.** If not, **STOP HERE** and go back to the earliest stage of challenge and work on that area first.

Adapted from Greenspan & Wieder, 2006

Building Bridges for the Adult

_____ I am beginning to understand how the child viewed his or her role and my role in what happened.

_____ We are putting the situation into context.

_____ We are forming plans for how to manage this in the future.

_____ I emphasize that people need each other during trying times and that I am open and available to the child.

Notes:

Adapted from Greenspan & Wieder, 2006

The processes described in the previous worksheets are dynamic, and will not necessarily happen in one sitting, but rather over time. With practice, surveying your emotional state and the child's state becomes easier. **This developmental model begins with emotional co-regulation between the child and us—the parent, teacher, professional, or caregiver. It puts relationships at the center, where they should be.**

Children Need Adults for Co-Regulation

As we have seen, a child who has a weak foundation of emotional regulation requires human assistance to find her way back to the green pathway. When we offer this kind of help, we're engaging in emotional co-regulation, attuning to and supporting another person through our presence. Stuart Shanker, an expert in emotional regulation, calls a child's ability to regulate emotions *Self-Reg*, for self-regulation.[29] Our interactions with children influence how they make sense of the world. Once a child feels safe in mind and body, the possibilities for learning and growth increase, expanding a child's tolerance for new experiences, sensations, feelings, and ideas.

Felix — The Power of Emotional Co-Regulation

Felix entered kindergarten with a reputation as an explosive child who was prone to pinching his classmates when they didn't do what he wanted. But his promising first grade teacher was known for helping students with behavioral challenges. From the beginning, she connected with Felix, each morning bending down on one knee, taking his hands into hers, and looking into his eyes with warmth, presence, and genuine connection as she searched his face for signals. If she sensed fear or hesitation, she would pause and spend a few more moments with him. Sometimes, if she saw signs of stress on his face or in his body, she designated a special task for him to assist with, ensuring that he stayed close to her. She knew that each day she needed to both evaluate and set the stage for Felix's relational security, and that he needed her cues of safety in order to stay calm and alert. The teacher intuitively valued and understood the benefits of emotional co-regulation to children.

Her approach proved effective. Felix pinched his classmates less frequently and increased his level of self-control, reaching out to his teacher when he was frustrated or needed help instead of pinching. The teacher communicated with Felix's parents on a regular basis, and they learned from each other about Felix's tolerance for various situations. On days that he woke up anxious or distressed, his teacher and father quickly (and privately, out of Felix's earshot) exchanged information— "It's a green morning!" or "It's been a red start to the day!"—so that the teacher could adjust her interactions and requirements for Felix. The information proved valuable to her understanding of how to titrate Felix's schedule and workload for the day.

A few months into the school year, the teacher had to miss a week of school on short notice. Sensing that Felix was still vulnerable, she left extensive notes, warning the substitute teacher that Felix would likely need emotional support from the substitute each morning and throughout the day. She genuinely cared for the child and understood that his behavioral control depended on the safety of adult emotional co-regulation.

The substitute dutifully followed the instructions, but unfortunately, Felix didn't feel the same connection with her. On the substitute's second morning, he pinched her. She had been trained to maintain neutrality when faced with negative behaviors so as not to reinforce them, so she tried to ignore the pinches, but they only increased in subsequent days.

So, what happened? The sudden departure of his beloved teacher caused Felix's threshold to drop, triggering his defensive behaviors. Far from an attempt to injure the teacher, his pinching was an instinctive impulse that he could not control because of his sudden shift onto a red pathway. And when she ignored his behavior, he felt even more unmoored.

Viewing emotional co-regulation as a frontline approach to persistent behavioral challenges is a shift from how we currently treat and manage our most behaviorally challenged children. One way of thinking about the necessity for this shift is to view children with the greatest behavioral challenges as those who are the most vulnerable.

When We Are Calm, We Can Provide Relational Cues of Safety

As we have seen, we can best support a child when we are calm ourselves. It's important to be aware that *how we say things is as important as what we say.* The first step when we attune to a child who is struggling is not telling, teaching, or instructing. It is *being present with* the child.

Providing Cues of Relational Safety for Children

According to the Polyvagal perspective, humans provide cues of safety or threat through tone of voice, facial expressions, posture, and other nonverbal forms of communication.[30]

Consider: Am I working off of an emotionally stable platform? Are the cues I am providing the child supportive of social engagement? Use the following questions to gauge your use of safety cues and check off those that apply to you.

Presence: Am I present with the child, attending to him or her singularly, and not distracted or multitasking? _____

Tone of voice: Is the volume of my voice appropriate to the child's needs? _____ Is there inflection or prosody in my voice? _____ Is there warmth and a caring tone to my voice? _____

Facial expression: Is my face expressive of safety and engagement?

_____

Pacing and timing: Am I approaching and pacing with the child in accordance to his or her immediate needs?

_____

Posture: Do I have a relaxed posture and inviting gestures? _____

Underlying Messages that Compromise Emotional Co-Regulation

Felix's experience with the two different teachers illustrates the importance of our interactions with children. They can feel the difference between fear or judgment and compassion and positive regard, but we can't expect ourselves to be able to deliver this message all the time. That's okay and to be expected.

Sending the most supportive message isn't always easy. Even when we're trying to be supportive sometimes we're not aware of *underlying messages* we're sending that compromise emotional co-regulation. This was the challenge for Natalie, who deeply wanted to help relieve her daughter Myra's anxiety, but in the process unknowingly exacerbated the problem.

Myra — The Importance of Parental "Hardiness"

Myra, a fifth grader, did well in school, but some of her behaviors deeply concerned her mother, Natalie. Myra constantly bit her nails and her lower lip—so much that she developed an open sore that wouldn't heal. Her pediatrician believed her behaviors were caused by stress and suggested family therapy. By all appearances, Myra had a comfortable life. Though her parents were divorced, both were deeply involved in her life. Natalie read the latest parenting books and tried to engage with Myra each day. The mother's heart would soar when Myra reported a good day, but she felt devastated on the days when Myra struggled. As much as she tried to hide her reactions, she constantly worried about her daughter.

When I met with Natalie alone to discuss a plan to help Myra, I asked how she was faring. She quickly grew emotional, pausing and tearing up. She told me that as a single mother, she felt a heavy, lonely burden in caring for her daughter.

First, a word about my personal reaction when I met Natalie. I resonated with her struggle as a sensitive mother myself. Her story naturally pulled me into a compassionate stance based on my own individual differences. And even though I didn't share personal information with her, I felt—and it seemed she did as well—an unspoken emotional connection over the immense responsibility of parenthood. In this natural moment of the therapeutic use of myself, I let my feelings guide how I interacted with her, knowing that allowing my own emotional presence to carry the moment, that is, what I chose not to do or say—was just as important as what I said.

That connection helped me to communicate an insight: over the next several weeks—in an atmosphere of joining rather than judgment—we both reflected on how children pick up on their parents' care and concern for them. I validated Natalie's reflections about how difficult it was to be a single parent and how impossible it was to always meet her daughter's behaviors with kindness and patience. I reassured her that that wasn't the goal—as humans we will naturally have our own reactions—and we discussed how important it was to be gentle with ourselves around this task. That interaction opened up a window of trust between us that allowed us to surmise that Myra was probably perceiving her mother's concern, and mother and daughter were unintentionally *increasing* each other's anxiety.

This is backed up by researchers, who have found that corumination (excessively talking with others about problems and dwelling on the negative feelings associated with them) can actually increase anxiety, especially in girls.[31] Natalie's way of showing her love for her daughter, coupled with her own stress, was likely making both of them feel less safe and connected through their interactions. Instead of helping each other to experience more calm, they were inadvertently making each other more anxious—decreasing, rather than increasing their sense of well-being. We discussed the concept of building resilience and how developing more "hardiness" in herself would also benefit her daughter.

Once Natalie realized the problem—that her own emotional tone, stress levels, and approach were hampering emotional co-regulation—she shifted her strategies. I recommended some free stress-reduction resources at a local university, and Natalie joined a mindfulness-based parenting support group. By examining herself, she learned that the best thing she could do for her daughter was to pay attention to her own social-emotional house first, building up her own resilience to be a parent who was more hardy and less vigilant and worried. Over time, her interactions with Myra shifted, and both mother and daughter began to relax more together. As Myra started talking openly to her mom about her concerns and fears, her lip and nail biting receded and eventually stopped.

Prioritizing Safety: Less Is More

While there's nothing inherently wrong with talking about difficulties, often we talk too soon. If a child isn't solidly in the upper processes of social-emotional development—able to internalize and make use of top-down advice—then discussing problems probably won't be very effective. In other words, using top-down solutions too soon has little benefit, because the child is functioning from the bottom up. Not only does talking not help, but it can make things worse. As in Natalie and Myra's case, rumination and dwelling on the stressor can *increase* the child's stress. Before we try to solve a problem with lecturing or consequences, we need to reflect on our own feelings and motivations, and consider whether what we are about to say will make the child feel better or worse.

Co-Regulation in Action: A Better Approach for Mateo

As we've seen in multiple ways, the key to helping children who are experiencing behavioral problems is providing a sense of safety first, setting a platform for ensuing growth and a greater tolerance for stress. That was what eventually helped Mateo, the student we met at the beginning of this chapter, who was sent to the "calm down" room and whose behaviors were stress responses due to a treatment plan that required decreasing cues of relational safety.

The first step was for the adults who worked with Mateo to begin *paying attention* to his behaviors instead of ignoring them. His aide learned that when Mateo began moving his body in certain ways, or glanced in her direction, he wasn't trying to be disruptive or merely seeking attention. *He was signaling the need for reassurance. With this new understanding, the aide began to pay attention, and instead of reacting by moving away, she leaned in.*

As it turned out, this approach was much better for the aide, a highly relational person who had never been comfortable with the IEP plan, which dictated that she ignore his behaviors. Over time, using her natural inclinations to soothe the child, she was able to help Mateo feel safer in his body and mind as she helped him tolerate manageable doses of stress, allowing him to become more engaged in the classroom.

As the other adults around him focused on *emotional co-regulation*, Mateo began to be more trusting. With this consistent emotional backing, he began to communicate more, first with gestures, then with signs, and eventually with a tablet computer. **Now the useful techniques offered by his behavioral team—breaking down tasks into smaller steps, predicting and developing routines, using visual schedules, and more—all gained synergy as he stepped into a whole new world of learning and engagement.**

When we understand how the human brain evolved over time, we come to understand that the foundation of treatment lies in acknowledging the loving and trusting core of humanity.[32] This essence may not be easy to test within the scientific boundaries of "evidence," but it is central to mental and physical health. When we acknowledge and integrate this truth into our systems of care, we will help many more children to thrive, connect, and flourish. **The concept of neuroception, currently not integrated into mental health, education, social work, or the criminal justice system has the power to change the way we view the treatment of challenging behaviors.**

Now we'll discover how we contextualize children's behaviors based on what we have learned so far and how this translates more specifically into *what we do* to help children. In Chapter 5, we'll learn ways to support children by focusing on bottom-up causes and triggers of behaviors before we launch in to top-down strategies, which will be the focus of Chapter 6.

Putting It All Together: Safety Is the Starting Point

When we approach a child, we can ask certain questions to help us better tailor our interactions in real time. In other words, we can titrate what we are asking of the child to his or her color pathway and developmental process.

1. **What pathway is the child on?** ___ Green ___ Red ___ Blue

2. **What is the quality of the pathway?**
   _____ Strong _____ Medium _____ Light

3. **What pathway is the adult on?** ___ Green ___ Red ___ Blue

4. **What is the quality of the pathway?**
   _____ Strong _____ Medium _____ Light

What developmental process(es) is the child working on? Check off all that apply.

☐ Calmness

☐ Connection and relatedness

☐ Communicating through back-and-forth rhythms

☐ Communicating through gestures (or technology if gestures aren't available)

☐ Connecting words/symbols to thoughts and ideas

☐ Crossing ideas and thoughts with others

Notes:

What helped? _____

What didn't help? _____

Main Points —

- The Polyvagal perspective of Dr. Porges posits that relational safety should be the starting point for all therapeutic interactions with children.

- It's important to assess whether or not a child feels "Brain-Safe".

- One of the first things we need to consider is whether challenging behaviors are a sign of a child's social engagement system in need of relational help.

- As parents and providers, we need to pay attention to our own green pathway and nurture our own nervous systems in order to co-regulate with a child emotionally.

- A child learns new things and develops increasing levels of stress tolerance and resilience when presented with manageable stress, individually titrated, in the presence of supportive adults.

- Parents and providers benefit from self-care and self-compassion because the "therapeutic use of self" is the most important tool we have.

5.

Addressing What Underlies Behavior: Working on Challenges from the Bottom Up

> *"The curriculum is so much necessary raw material, but warmth is the vital element for the growing plant and for the soul of the child."*
>
> **Carl Jung**

Morgan — Finding the Trigger

Morgan's parents described him as a "handful" from the day he was born. He had such severe colic as a baby that his nighttime crying bouts routinely stretched to three hours. Much to his parents' relief, when the bawling fits ended around five months, Morgan became a dynamic, affable, and joyful child.

That is, when he was happy. When he wasn't, he became moody, irritable, and controlling. He would protest and cry when his parents dropped him off at school. Though he managed first grade, his teachers expressed concern about his social skills. Though his environment seemed optimal—loving parents in a stable home where all of his basic needs were met—he still struggled. Why? There was good reason, but it took some digging to identify.

In this chapter we'll look more deeply at how to address individual differences as they relate to behavioral challenges. In short, we aim to identify anything that contributes to a child's challenges so that we can address it through supportive intervention. That means pinpointing anything that moves a child away from the green pathway and toward lashing out, running away, avoidance, hypervigilance, ignoring, or shutting down.

We'll examine how we work to connect body-up and top-down strategies, in order to help children learn new ways to cope. We'll examine how to use interactions to address developmental constrictions and increase a child's tolerance of new experiences. We will also examine how a variety of professionals from fields outside of mental health—including a child's pediatrician—can contribute to a comprehensive approach to addressing the underpinnings of behavioral challenges.

The process we followed to support Morgan provides a useful guide for looking beneath the surface of behaviors and determining what types of interactions and targeted therapeutic support each child needs. The four activities spell out IDEA, an acronym to remind us that we should use our thoughts and ideas to create a unique supportive approach for the behavioral challenges of each child.

> **I**nquire about the child's history and track behaviors to discover patterns
>
> **D**etermine what circumstances contribute to the child's distress
>
> **E**xamine what our investigation reveals about the triggers and underlying causes
>
> **A**ddress developmental challenges contributing to the behaviors through our interactions and targeted therapeutic support

Inquire About the Child's History and Track Behaviors To Discover Patterns

A Child's History

In the subspecialty field of infant mental health, it's standard practice to obtain a complete history of a child, including the mother's pregnancy, delivery, and circumstances around the child's first year. Experts in the field of neuroscience have confirmed how important the child's relationships are in establishing brain architecture in the first few years of life.[1] We can learn about the influences of the child's early relationships and environment by asking about them, and if you are a parent, thinking about the circumstances of your child's early experiences.

The following worksheets cover basic information about a child's history. I use these as part of a conversation with parents when I meet with them for an initial consultation (without the child present). If a child is fostered or adopted and some of the information isn't available, the caregivers can share whatever information was shared with them.

Pregnancy and Early Months

(To be completed by parent or caregiver)

1. **Please describe specific circumstances and details around the pregnancy:**

   _____

   _____

2. **Maternal/fetus physical health during pregnancy:**

   _____

   _____

3. **Were there any complications during the pregnancy?**
   _____No _____Yes

   Describe: _____

4. **Maternal stress levels during the pregnancy:** _____Low _____ Moderate _____High

   Describe: _____

5. **Was the pregnancy full term (37 weeks or more)?**
   _____No _____Yes

   Preterm? _____No _____Yes (_____weeks)

6. **Labor and delivery:** _____Unremarkable _____Complications or difficulties

   Describe: _____

7. **Did the baby have any health or developmental challenges in the first year?** _____No _____Yes

   Describe: _____

8. **What were the baby's sleep patterns/habits during the first 6 months?** _____

   Second 6 months? _____

   2–5 years old? _____

   Presently? _____

Early History

(To be completed by parent or caregiver)

1. How would you describe the child's first year? (check all that apply)

_____ What I expected _____ Enjoyable _____ Manageable

_____ Moderately stressful _____ Highly stressful

Explain: _____

2. Who was the child's primary caregiver(s) in the first two years?
(Include daycare, parents, babysitters, extended family, nanny, etc.)

_____

a. Primary Caregiver(s):_____ Child's age with
   this caregiver: _____

   How many hours per day _____ or week _____ did this
   caregiver spend with the child?

   Length of time spent with this caregiver: _____

b. Primary Caregiver(s)_____ Child's age with
   this caregiver _____

   How many hours per day _____ or week _____ did this
   caregiver spend with the child?

   Length of time spent with this caregiver: _____

3. Did the child enter into preschool prior to kindergarten?
   ___ No ___ Yes

   If yes, how old was the child? _____
   Years in preschool: _____

4. **Did any significant life stressors or adverse experiences happen in the family during:**

   a. The child's first year? _____ No _____ Yes

      Explain: _____

   b. Ages 2–5? _____ No _____ Yes

      Explain: _____

   c. Ages 6–9? _____ No _____ Yes

      Explain: _____

   d. Ages 10–13? _____ No _____ Yes

      Explain: _____

5. **Was there anything about your baby or toddler's behaviors that were confusing to you at any point?** _____ No _____ Yes

   If yes, describe the behaviors and explain: _____

   _____

   _____

6. **How old was your child when you first observed his or her behavioral or emotional challenges?** _____

   Describe nature of challenges: _____

   _____

   _____

Tracking Behaviors

Along with gathering information about a child's history, it's useful to track children's behaviors through a simple recording method that will provide clues as to patterns, causes, and triggers. By tracking behaviors, we can gain an appreciation for the *underlying needs* the behavior is potentially meeting for the child. We can also discover the *adaptive and protective* functions the behaviors serve for the child. Tracking the behaviors gives us the opportunity to learn more about each child's nervous system and how the child perceives the world. The following worksheet provides a template from which you can track these behaviors over the course of a couple of weeks.

Morgan's Parents' Journal

I asked Morgan's parents to keep a behavior journal for two weeks, ensuring that we tracked patterns with a degree of confidence and accuracy. When we first surveyed the journal, we found the information was rather confusing. We couldn't identify a clear pattern revealing the conditions or circumstances that contributed to Morgan's challenges. The triggers varied widely, from being asked to pick up his toys, to disliking dinner food, to battling his way through playdates. We couldn't readily identify patterns or situations that triggered him into various behaviors. As we will see, the lack of such patterns became useful information in and of itself.

Tracking Behaviors

Date: _____

Name of child: _____

Name of recorder: _____

Time of day: _____

Activity/Requirement/Trigger prior to the concerning behavior:

_____

Behavior observed: _____

Duration of behavior: _____

Recovery time (in minutes): _____

Date: _____

Name of child: _____

Name of recorder: _____

Time of day: _____

Activity/Requirement/Trigger prior to the concerning behavior:

_____

Behavior observed: _____

Duration of behavior: _____

Recovery time (in minutes): _____

Notes: _____

_____

_____

_____

_____

_____

_____

Determine What Circumstances Contribute to the Child's Distress

When patterns are not readily identifiable or observable, I ask parents and caregivers about an even *wider* range of basic health issues and processes for the child, starting with the most important: the child's sleep-wake cycle. When I had first met Morgan's parents, they had mentioned that as a toddler he'd had some difficulty sleeping. That wasn't a red flag at first, but at our second meeting, I delved more deeply into sleep issues. The parents recalled that back in Morgan's colic days, they would drive him around in the car to lull him to sleep, gently carrying him to his crib after an hour of driving.

As our discussion deepened, they admitted that they couldn't recall more than a couple of months when Morgan had slept soundly through the night. At age six, he was *still* waking multiple times each night, sometimes ending up in their bed or on the living-room couch. I soon discovered that nobody in the family had experienced consistent sleep for years. Getting Morgan to sleep was still a constant chore. His parents admitted that they had recently begun allowing Morgan to play video games on an iPad until he fell asleep. It was among the few strategies that had helped to settle him down at night.

After those revelations, we turned our attention to why Morgan's behavioral disruptions were so hard to predict and decipher and the role of his chronic lack of deep, restorative sleep in his emotional regulation. Now, our first priority was to further investigate the quality of the family's sleep patterns (or lack thereof).

Examine What Our Investigation Reveals About the Triggers and Underlying Causes

At my request, Morgan's parents arranged for a conference call with his pediatrician and me. On the call, we all agreed that we would focus first on improving the child's sleep. The pediatrician had suggestions for a supplement (a small dose of melatonin at bedtime), but first wanted the parents to work with me to see if improving the family's *sleep hygiene* would produce results. Perhaps once Morgan was sleeping better, we might see improvements in his emotional and behavioral regulation.

Morgan's Iceberg

Described as "moody, irritable, controlling"

Difficulties with separations

Inconsistent peer interactions

Frequent meltdowns

Immature social and emotional development

Chronic, unidentified deficits of deep-sleep cycling and restorative sleep patterns

Vulnerable stress recovery patterns

143

Address Developmental Challenges Through Our Interactions and Targeted Therapeutic Support

Morgan's iceberg revealed that his chronic sleep difficulties were likely contributing to his lower threshold for emotional regulation. This in turn influenced his ability to control his behaviors and impulses. His stress load fluctuated day by day, depending on his sleep the previous night and factors such as how many transitions he had to manage and how he was feeling *inside* his body (interoception). For example, through the tracking journal, his parents discovered a correlation between his occasional bouts of constipation and his emotional and behavioral outbursts. When he was constipated, the number of tantrums rose significantly.

One important step in managing developmental challenges contributing to behaviors is to track how much the child is dealing with to help titrate what is asked of the child at home, school, and in therapies. It's useful either to write down or keep in mind what a child is managing. While we need to take the history data only once and fill out behavior-tracking worksheets only as needed, I encourage parents, teachers, and providers to keep track of a child's stress load every day.

I often have parents write down or tell me how a child's day is going before we begin a therapy session. This helps us determine how much to ask of the child in the session. I also recommend that parents share such information with others who spend time with the child, so that each adult in the child's life can titrate the demands placed on the child depending on what the child is managing in his body and mind. Just as the parent of a child with Type 1 diabetes adjusts insulin levels according to blood sugar needs, we can use behavioral data points to tailor how much we ask of children.

Parents can fill out the following tracking sheet (or make one of their own) and share it with teachers or other providers before beginning a school day or session, so that he or she can modify interactions and requirements according to the child's allostatic load.

Tracking a Child's Stress Load in Real Time

Do you feel that your child is experiencing extra stress today?
_____ No _____ Yes

Explain: _____

How did the child sleep last night? _____ good night of sleep (at least 8–10 hours) _____ moderate sleep _____ (how many hours) poor sleep _____ (how many hours)

Is there anything unusual about the child's food intake today?
_____ No _____ Yes

Describe: _____

Is the child managing health issues today? _____ allergies _____ constipation _____ diarrhea _____ hunger _____ virus or other illness _____ other

Has the child experienced any additional stressors today?
_____ No _____ Yes

Describe: _____

Is there anything else you want me to know or that you observed today? _____

Our plan for Morgan started with focusing first on improving his sleep. In order to discover what calmed Morgan, his parents filled out checklists to identify his sensory soothing preferences—the sensations that their son enjoyed and that helped him feel calm. These included having a parent massage his hands, arms, and shoulders with firm pressure and listening to music through his headphones. Soothing a child through the sensations that bring comfort is a body-up strategy. We can use a child's sensory preferences to help prepare the child for restorative nighttime sleep.

We developed a plan for a new sleep-hygiene routine for the whole family. I recommended "setting the table" for sleep several hours before bedtime, starting when everyone got home around five p.m. I noted that the family's usual evening routine was generally chaotic and rushed, and probably had a negative impact on the sleep hygiene of both parents and child. I suggested that Morgan's parents rethink the schedule.

The parents agreed that their task-centered nighttime routine left little time for relaxation together—which emerged more naturally on weekends. They shared that they were rarely in green pathways *themselves* most weeknights and often felt stressed and fearful of Morgan's volatility. I explained the role of emotional co-regulation and the importance of being in the green pathway together as much as possible during the evening routine.

I met with Morgan's parents alone for a few meetings to fine-tune the details of a new family routine to improve mental and physical health, starting with encouraging each parent to manage stress better for themselves. To meet this goal, Morgan's mom downloaded a mindfulness app and she began doing a short meditation in her office after work, creating a space for herself and an intention to consciously calm her mind before she arrived home. His dad opted to shorten his workday by an hour for six months, picking up Morgan an hour earlier from his after-school program so he could arrive home less fatigued and with more time for dinner preparations.

Once they were home, the plan called for both parents to speak in softer tones since Morgan's sensory profile indicated that he was highly sensitive to adults' emotions and tone of voice. I suggested that they continue this warm and relaxed tone into dinner, when they could engage Morgan in playful, fun conversation—a shift from their habit of eating quickly with the news on television.

I also suggested that instead of everyone reverting to their screens, they begin a new ritual based on Morgan's interests—such as reading a book together after dinner. Other advice: dimming the lights throughout the house in the evening and playing some of Morgan's favorite soft, prosodic, vocal songs in the background, providing additional cues that it was time to slow down and relax.

Finally, I suggested curtailing screen time at least an hour before bedtime and offering Morgan a firm, comforting massage on his shoulders and back after his bath if he wanted one. His parents adopted the same sleep-hygiene strategy, switching off their own devices and the television so that the whole family could down-regulate together well before bedtime.

The approach to better sleep habits started with body-up suggestions for the whole family. To review:

- Parents considered their own personal stress levels and how this affected Morgan
- Mother began a short meditation practice after work and before coming home
- Father shortened his work day by one hour
- Both parents monitored their emotional regulation and spoke in softer tones
- Screen time for everyone stopped one hour prior to bedtime
- Parents shifted sensory ambience toward Morgan's preferences, with lights turned down and soft vocal music in the background
- Parents offered Morgan a shoulder massage after bath time
- The family began to read a book together as part of a bedtime routine

Fortunately, the change proved effective. Within two weeks, Morgan began waking just once per night—a major shift and surprise to his happy parents. After years of being awakened multiple times nightly with him, his parents felt rejuvenated, even with this small shift. It took a couple of months to tweak the routine, figuring out what to do about well-worn patterns, such as Morgan wandering into his parents' room during the night. (We'll discuss how we supported Morgan in breaking that pattern later in the chapter.) Still, within three months, the whole family was sleeping better than they could ever remember.

Research continues to demonstrate how important sleep is to our general health and well-being as well as our emotional regulation, the precursor to having control over our emotions and behavior.[2]

It is well worth the effort to inquire about the sleep quality and quantity of your child or the children you work with in order to evaluate whether poor sleep is contributing to a child's behavioral challenges.

Much to their relief, Morgan's parents reported that his irritability and moodiness decreased significantly once his sleep was uninterrupted and sound. *The next step was to address Morgan's social and emotional development, which was immature due to his history of regulatory challenges.* His teachers were concerned that he was usually either bossy with other children during recess or simply off playing by himself. But first, let's continue the discussion about how we use children's sensory preferences to help them find calmness in their bodies.

Using Sensory Preferences to Help Children Calm Their Physical Bodies

We can help children feel better when our interactions maximize and leverage the calming effects of sensory experiences. By recruiting a child's sensory preferences—and combining them with nonjudgmental, engaged interactions—we can better soothe a child when he or she experiences behavioral challenges. Just as sensations can send us into distress or unease, they can also help us feel comfortable and safe.

How do we learn about a particular child's preferences? Start with the following series of worksheets, which help identify a child's sensory preferences, beginning with auditory or sound preferences. The child's parent or caregiver should fill out these worksheets. Each of us has our own unique set of *sensory preferences* that can help us stay in the green pathway—or get back to it when we begin to feel stressed. For younger children, you can suggest or offer the sensory soothing activities that you have noted for each child. For older children and teenagers, it's useful to have a conversation about how various sensory experiences can help us feel calmer in our mind and body.

As you fill these out for a child, it's also useful to consider the types of sensory strategies that can benefit you, as a provider or caregiver. The scent of lavender, for example, may provide a calming effect to some people's nervous system.[3]

A note on tastes: these worksheets don't include a sensory-preference list for tastes because I don't generally recommend food as part of a sensory strategy to help individuals calm themselves. Using food as a soothing sensory strategy can lead to health consequences, including weight gain and avoidance of the threatening feelings underlying emotional-regulation challenges. For these reasons, it's best to use the other sensory systems to help children discover ways to calm their bodies and minds, and to use food more generally as a wonderful pathway to connect and socialize during family eating experiences.

Auditory Preferences

We can help children feel better by interacting with them in ways that maximize and leverage the calming effects of sensory experiences in the child's body.

1. **Sounds: What kinds of sounds in the environment does your child enjoy?** _____

2. **How does your child typically respond to:**

    Human voices _____

    Male voices _____

    Female voices _____

3. **What volume of voice does your child prefer?**

    _____ Softer volume _____ Higher volume

4. **What pitch/tone of voice does your child prefer?**

    _____

5. **What types of vocal music does your child prefer?**

    _____

6. **What types of popular music does your child prefer?**

    _____

7. **What types of instrumental music does your child prefer?**

    _____

8. **What types of nature sounds does your child prefer?**

    _____

Visual Preferences

Now let's turn to the visual system and look at how the child uses his or her visual system to navigate the world.

1. **What sorts of things does your child like to look at?**

   _____

2. **Does your child notice when things are out of place in the home?** _____ No _____ Yes

   If the child does notice, is his or her reaction typically:

   _____ Negative

   _____ Positive

   _____ Neutral

3. **Does your child take any action when her things are out of place?** _____ No _____ Yes

4. **Does your child find looking at faces comforting?** _____ No _____ Yes

5. **Does your child prefer to have:**

   _____ Direct eye contact

   _____ Peripheral eye contact (looking from the side of the eyes)

   _____ Other forms of indirect eye contact

   If so list: _____

6. **Have you observed if your child is calmer when lights are low and dim?** _____ No _____ Yes

7. **What kind of lighting seems to help settle your child?**

   _____

Touch Preferences

Touch is an important part of our lives. The following worksheet will help you identify the types of tactile sensations that your child finds calming.

1. **What types of touch does your child find soothing (hugs, massage, firm squeeze, light touch, etc.)?**

    _____

2. **Does your child prefer to be covered with a blanket when sleeping?** _____No _____Yes

3. **Does the weight of the blanket make a difference?**
    _____No _____Yes

    If yes, does your child:

    _____ Prefer a lightweight blanket or sheet

    _____ Prefer a heavy blanket that provides some pressure

4. **Where on the body does your child prefer to be touched (head, arm, hand, shoulder, back, feet, etc.)?**

    _____

5. **What kind of pressure does your child prefer?**
    _____ Deep pressure _____ Light pressure

Fragrance Preferences

The olfactory system (the sense of smell) links with memories in a powerful way. Adults and children often find certain kinds of smells comforting. The following worksheet will help you identify the types of smells that your child finds calming.

1. **What types of smells have you observed your child enjoying or having a positive reaction to?**

   _____

2. **Mark any of the following smells that your child enjoys:**

   _____ Food smells (what kind? _____)

   _____ Natural smells (what kind? _____)

   _____ Lavender

   _____ Rose

   _____ Pine

   _____ Citrus

   _____ Essential Oils (what kind? _____)

   _____ Other fragrances (what kind? _____)

3. **What kinds of smells/fragrances have you observed your child disliking or having a negative reaction to?**

   _____

4. **Under what circumstances did you observe the negative reaction to a certain smell or fragrance?**

   _____

Movement Preferences

Now let's turn to movement. Movement, in all its forms, is essential to helping children master their emotions and experiences.

1. What types of movement does your child enjoy?

_____ Crawling

_____ Walking

_____ Running

_____ Jumping

_____ Swinging

_____ Dancing

_____ Rocking or being rocked

_____ Skipping

_____ Sitting

_____ Lying down

_____ Clapping

_____ Tapping

_____ Flapping

_____ Other

2. When moving, what types of rate and rhythm does your child prefer?

Rate: _____ Fast _____ Moderate _____ Slow

_____ Fluctuating between fast and slow

Rhythm:

_____ Predictable pattern

_____ Steady, unchanging rhythm

_____ Unpredictable rhythm

A Note of Caution

Here's an important note of caution about working with sensory systems. We focused on determining sensory-calming strategies in Chapter 4 and in Chapter 3 saw how memories are sensory experiences that are coded with emotional tags.[4] So it's possible that a sensory experience—a smell, a touch, a sound, or sight—can trigger distress for a child, just as it can trigger safety and calmness. If at any point you find that a child has an aversive reaction to the sensory experiences you provide or suggest, simply stop the experience and provide an abundance of human connection in a way that comforts the child. Children who have experienced toxic stress or trauma are vulnerable in their nervous systems. Chapter 8 will explain some of those complexities. If you find that certain sensory experiences have a negative impact on a child (or yourself), it's helpful to work with a qualified provider to further investigate and find avenues for additional support.

Knowing the types of activities that a child seeks or enjoys gives us clues to the types of sensory experiences that we can use or suggest to help the child find calmness and relaxation in the physical body, leading in turn to better emotional regulation and green-pathway abilities. *It's important to apply these strategies in the context of warmly engaged interactions and not as an exercise for the child to do by himself.* Emotional co-regulation comes first, and this is how emotional self-regulation is developed. In doing so we recognize that the way to calm a child who is on the red pathway of sympathetic arousal or the blue pathway of disconnection is the same: human connection.

> ### *Emotional co-regulation comes first, and this is how emotional self-regulation is developed.*

Additionally, we should remember that sensory preferences are dynamic and constantly shifting. Just because a child likes a certain sensory experience at a given moment doesn't mean that he always will. It's useful to assess the child's *current* preferences (either by asking or by observing) before you suggest or offer a sensory experience, to make sure it's the appropriate choice for that moment. For this reason, I avoid suggesting "sensory diets" (e.g., providing the same sensory experiences to the child at a certain time of day or in response to a certain behavior). That approach overlooks the dynamic, ever-changing nature of our sensory and emotional experiences as humans. Instead, work with what helps the child in real time, as you apply or suggest different types of sensory input.

A New "Passive Pathway Intervention"

Recently, Dr. Porges introduced a "passive pathway" intervention, *the Safe and Sound Protocol*, which exercises neural pathways associated with regulating behavioral state and social engagement.[5] Early studies of the SSP with children and adolescents diagnosed on the autism spectrum have demonstrated improvement in autonomic regulation and auditory processing.[6] I have implemented the intervention with a small number of children and seen similar positive results, as have many of my occupational therapy colleagues. I look forward to following the continuing research on this new and promising *auditory intervention*—presented to children in a safe, relaxed environment.

> Our sensory tolerances and thresholds are always shifting. What we experience as soothing one moment may feel unpleasant the next hour or the next day. Always work with the child as a partner, and closely observe the child, eliciting feedback in order to understand which experiences feel calming and positive. Helping a child develop calming sensory strategies can provide lifelong benefits to physical and mental health.

Body-Up and De-Escalation Strategies: Discovering What Works for Each Child

As we learned in Chapter 2, when a child is on a red pathway, his hearing decreases as the body prepares to battle or run away. Before treatment, Morgan often spiraled into tantrums that came on so quickly (and often in public) that Morgan's parents didn't know what to do to help him. You can use the sensory preferences in this chapter as a starting point to discover and experiment with various strategies to help each child de-escalate. The general strategy, however, is to reduce the amount of input a child is coping with if he or she is in a red pathway.

Start Low and Slow

In general, if a child is in distress, it's a good idea to start low and slow. For example, if you are talking to the child and nothing is getting through, lower your volume and try a different tone, or stop talking all together. You can offer a hug or nonverbal, physical comfort with a gesture. If the child provides body language that signals a desire for physical touch, move in gently and slowly. If the child pushes you away, respect the child's preference. Each child and each situation will be different. After the escalated state is over (or even on another day) it's useful to ask the child what types of comforting support helps the most when he or she is struggling.

Connecting Kids on the Blue Pathway

If a child is on a blue pathway of disconnection, we also start low and slow, but our goal will be to bring the child back into engagement with us. In this case we are not helping to calm a child's revved-up nervous system but are wooing a child's system *back into* social engagement. Remember that children on the blue pathway are vulnerable and at high risk, so we must approach with love and connection, not demands or requirements.

De-Escalation Strategies for Children Behaviorally Activated on the Red Pathway

- Use respectful and empathic strategies to keep the child and those around him safe
- Provide cues of safety and stay regulated yourself, knowing this is a transient state
- Limit what you say to the child and remember that she may not hear you well
- Respect the child's communication and if the child pushes you away, provide comfort through your emotional presence and body language
- If the child wants physical space, move away slowly and respectfully
- Stay low and slow, moving to the child's level or sitting on the floor, and increasing your rate and rhythm of sounds and physical movement according to the child's body language
- At a later time, ask the child what helps him or her the most when struggling

Although Morgan's behavioral outbursts had declined significantly once he was sleeping better, he was still highly controlling of others and his environment, prone to disagree, and strongly attached to certain routines. That was to be expected, I assured his parents, because Morgan's emotional and physiological regulation—the body state that determines how we react and behave in the world—had such a rough start. This also explained why he had difficulty playing with his peers. It wasn't surprising that Morgan's developmental house was underdeveloped after years of challenges he faced at the foundational levels: solid sleep, emotional regulation, and social communication. Once he had more practice with his foundational levels, Morgan made rapid progress, probably because of his optimal early environment with his loving parents and his emerging top-down abilities.

Remember That Bottom-Up Strategies Lead to Top-Down Strategies

Before we had identified Morgan's fundamental challenges, he simply lacked the ability to cue in to his bodily sensations and figure out how to help himself. It is not unusual for children who have chronic difficulty settling their bodies (for a variety of reasons) to also have challenges in their behaviors and social-emotional abilities.

That explains why stabilizing Morgan's sleep patterns did not instantly free him from all of his behavioral challenges. His most explosive reactions decreased significantly after his sleep was better, but he still had other well-established patterns to contend with, including his habit of wandering into his parents' room when he woke up in the middle of the night.

Activities That Help Children Connect to Their Bodies and Minds

We have learned that children who have difficulty managing their emotions and behaviors likely have gaps or constrictions in some of the earlier developmental processes of their social-emotional house. Therapeutic activities, such as mindfulness meditation, yoga, group sports, and martial arts, can help children shore up these processes, especially if the child experiences the activity as pleasurable—and of course, safe. Such activities help increase "focused attention as well as sequencing and planning abilities," often challenged in children with early regulatory difficulties.[7]

One of my favorite therapeutic activities is to help children develop an appreciation of their amazing bodies and minds. When we help children become familiar with and appreciate their own nervous systems, it opens up a new world of self-care. Many of the children I work with have been given such consistent negative messages about their behaviors that they are pleasantly surprised to learn that our bodies (and behaviors) have their own wisdom, and we can learn from what our bodies are telling us if we pay close attention.

Moving to Top-Down Approaches

Once Morgan's sleep issues were addressed, the focus of our therapy sessions began to bolster his top-down thinking with increased self-awareness. *Our goal: to help him use his mind to calm his body; to use words to describe his feelings and ideas; and eventually to navigate his own solutions to challenges.* We knew we were ready to include more top-down "thinking" strategies when Morgan had the capacity to flex his social and emotional muscles with others through a more regulated (and not sleep-deprived) body and mind.

Mindfulness Exercises for Children

I have taught simple mindful awareness and breathing techniques to children with good results for many years. I'm not a mindfulness expert, but learned of its power years ago after experiencing the powerful benefits mindfulness brought when I was recovering from an unexpected medical issue. When my health challenge suddenly forced me to slow down, I discovered how comforting and life-changing my mindfulness practice became. I was amazed with the calming benefits of the breath, and with the power of *being* in the present moment without immediately trying to change anything.

I begin teaching children and parents about using the mind to calm the body through two strategies. First, we practice tuning in to the body and mind. This involves intentionally settling down, and allowing the child to pay attention to sensations emanating from the body. Second, we help children develop their own personalized strategies for meeting what their body needs.

I generally begin with explaining to children how important it is to exercise our "muscles" of awareness of the sensations and feelings in our minds and bodies. Here is a short practice that I sometimes do for small groups of children. It can be done with a single child as well. Try to memorize the gist of it and do it alongside the child or children, so that they can hear you coaching them but also experience your participation. Teaching these strategies is most effective when we adults send cues of engagement and safety to the child or children we are working with through our body language, prosody of voice, and positive emotional tone.

Tuning In to Our Minds and Bodies

Set-up: Create a quiet and uncluttered space for children to lie down on the floor. If possible, have blankets and pillows available for children to lie on, or cover up with, depending on their preferences.

Adult Narration:

We are going to practice listening to our bodies now. So, let's take a moment to settle down. We can sit on a pillow, or on the floor, lie down on our backs, or lean against a pillow. If we want to, we can close our eyes, but we don't have to. Do what feels most comfortable. Now, get comfortable, and make any adjustments you need to feel cozy.

Close your eyes and take a nice, deep breath, and blow out slowly. And one more nice, deep breath. Now, quietly and to yourself, simply pay attention to anything you are feeling right now. It might be an itch on your big toe, or the feel of the cool floor, or maybe it's even a thought or feeling running through your mind. Just try to pay attention and notice. There's nothing right or wrong about what we feel in our bodies or minds, so we don't need to change anything. For now, let's be very still and quiet so we can listen to our bodies. We'll take two minutes to do this and when I ring the bell or tell you it's time to sit up, we will sit up slowly and talk about what that was like.

Ring a bell or gently bring the children back after about two minutes.

Now wiggle your fingers and toes a bit, and sit up.

After the exercise ends, and once the children or child are sitting up, you can ask about what the experience was like. We want to support children noticing a range of experiences, including their sensations, feelings, or thoughts. The main point as you debrief is that there are no right or wrong answers. *Anything* a child reflects on (even if it's off-topic) is okay. For example, if a child says something silly, it might signal that he was uncomfortable stilling his body, so we can gently introduce the idea that sometimes our thoughts and bodies fight us calming down and we should expect that. An important part of this exercise is to model acceptance of the child's growing ability to notice sensations, thoughts, and feelings.

Developing an awareness of one's body/mind signals may sound simple. In reality, though, it's not easy for children (or adults) to slow down and to tune in to our own processes. Sometimes, this can even make us feel anxious or overwhelmed, so keep a close eye on the children and let them know that if they feel uncomfortable, they can open their eyes and sit up at any time.

More often than not, though, once a child gets the idea, tuning in begins to feel empowering because it helps children become proactive. After we help children develop an awareness of sensations, we can now move up to help children develop top-down strategies, based on their own thoughts and ideas. Of course, one strategy that we communicate is that we (the parent, teacher, therapist) are available to help the child or to simply be with the child when they need connection or reassurance.

Along with offering ourselves as support, we can also help children connect with ways to soothe and calm their own bodies with top-down strategies. We'll focus more on top-down strategies in the next chapter. Using these worksheets, we helped Morgan solve a remaining sleep issue: when he woke up in the middle of the night, he couldn't fall back asleep without getting up and wandering around until he found his parents. He explained that it was scary to walk down the hall at night, and he really wanted to stay in his own bed. So we helped Morgan to solve this problem by *asking him* about those things that help his body feel calm.

We can ask children about what feels calming for them by adapting the sensory calming worksheets from earlier in the chapter. When a child is on the green pathway and in a "top-down" thinking mood, we can help him discover ways to soothe himself.

Auditory Preferences

Ask the child and record his/her responses.

Sounds: What kinds of sounds do you enjoy? _____

If the child doesn't come up with specific sounds, you can prompt:
Music? _____ **What kind?** _____

Nature sounds? _____

Human voices?_____

What other sounds help you feel calm or happy? _____

Visual Preferences

Ask the child and record his/her responses.

What sorts of things do you like to look at?

_____

What are your favorite things to see in your bedroom?

_____

Our home?

_____

At school?

_____

In nature?

_____

Touch Preferences

Ask the child and record his/her responses.

What sort of touch is your favorite? Give examples: hugging, holding hands, massage, tapping, squeezing, etc.

List:

_____

Do you like to be covered with a heavy blanket when sleeping?
_____ yes _____no

Do you like to have a light sheet or no blanket at all?
_____ yes _____no

Do you like to hold onto anything to make you feel calm? If child doesn't answer give ideas.

_____

A favorite blanket or soft item?

_____

A favorite stuffed animal?

_____

A favorite toy?

_____

Other:

_____

Fragrance Preferences

Ask the child and record his/her responses.

What are your favorite things to smell?

_____

Food smells _____ what kind? _____

Nature smells _____ what kind? _____

Outdoor smells _____ what kind? _____

Other smells _____ what kind? _____

Movement Preferences

Ask the child and record his/her responses.

How does your body like to move?

_____ Walking

_____ Running

_____ Jumping

_____ Rocking or being rocked

_____ Swinging

_____ Dancing

_____ Skipping

_____ Sitting

_____ Lying down

_____ Clapping

_____ Tapping

_____ Flapping

_____ Other

Asking children about their sensory preferences has a twofold benefit. First, it offers an additional avenue to reinforce awareness of the body, and second, it provides children the opportunity to come up with their own self-generated solutions, which reinforces top-down thinking.

That was the case for Morgan. When we discussed what might help him fall back asleep instead of walking to his parents' room, Morgan thought of two things he could do: hug his teddy bear and look at a pretty shell-covered nightlight in his room. **As we engaged Morgan in connecting his body awareness to his thinking mind, he began to grow more confident and more empowered to try new things and create solutions using his top-down thinking.**

Morgan also benefited from guided imagery, a mind/body intervention that helps a child picture various scenarios that help produce calm in the body and mind. Two techniques he enjoyed the most were *mindful breathing* and *sending oneself and others friendly wishes*.

Mindful Breathing

As we learned in Chapter 4, just as we can use breathing to calm ourselves and co-regulate with a child, we can also teach children about breathing. Even preschoolers can learn to enjoy simple breathing exercises. I sometimes suggest that a child picture in her mind the act of breathing in by pretending to smell a beautiful flower, and then picture petals or a dandelion leaf and slowing blowing away the dandelion seeds with the outbreath. The Sesame Street in Communities website offers helpful aids, including a printable sheet with a flower breathing exercise, and a short video of the Count and Cookie Monster doing a "blowing out the candles on the cake" breathing exercise.[8]

Sending Friendly Wishes

Susan Kaiser Greenland's classic book *The Mindful Child*, offers context and overview to help children become more mindful.[9] It includes a practice that she developed with Gay McDonald, a master early-childhood educator, called "Sending Friendly Wishes." In this exercise, children learn to practice good will to others and to themselves. It begins with guided imagery that supports children from the body up (relaxed body and breathing) *and* the top down (thinking about the images).

"Ask your children to send friendly wishes to themselves, imaging that they are happy and having fun, that they're healthy, and that they're safe with their family and friends."[10] Next, children are asked to send friendly wishes to others in the room and in the world. The exercise closes with a "circle of friendly wishes"; the children say silently to themselves: "May I be happy, may I be healthy and strong, may I be cozy, safe, and living in peace with my family, my friends, my pets, and all those I love."[11]

Many mindfulness training programs for children have appeared in recent years, including the School Yoga Project, which has served thousands of children in the New York City area as well as trained teachers and school staff across the country.[12] For a list of mindfulness training programs and resources, please see page 267.

Conclusion: Successfully Combining Body-Up and Top-Down Approaches

By using a body-up approach and then layering in top-down strategies that Morgan chose for himself in dialogue with his parents, we helped him manage his behavioral challenges. Then came the day Morgan expressed pride about his first successful sleepover at his best friend's house. Over time, he gained confidence and enjoyed a positive and successful elementary school experience.

In this chapter we built a bridge between body-up strategies, starting with the sleep-wake cycle, and top-down strategies by engaging children in finding their own solutions. In the next chapter, we will look more closely at how play and top-down thinking can be used to help children find their own solutions to emotional and behavioral challenges.

Main Points —

- We start with body-up strategies when a child's developmental level (not chronological age) is primarily bottom up *or* if a child is currently in a stress response (red or blue pathway).

- Body-up strategies include working with children's individual differences, including their sensory preferences, to discover ways to soothe the stress response and the neuroception of threat.

- The most important tool in our toolbox is human connection.

- Mindfulness strategies bridge work from the body up and the top down.

6.

Working on Challenges from the Body Up to the Top Down

*"Creative thinking inspires ideas.
Ideas inspire change."*
Barbara Januszkiewicz

Darrell, age seven, found it difficult to manage his emotions in school—particularly at recess. Once, he was playing dodgeball when a ball hit him. When a classmate shouted, "You're out!" Darrell promptly punched him in the shoulder, then took hours to calm himself down again. Darrell came from a stable home and certainly knew that it was wrong to strike out at a peer. So he felt confused and embarrassed after his own explosive reactions.

How can we help children like Darrell, who display challenging behaviors even when they don't mean to? In this chapter, we turn our focus to building a bridge between *co-regulation* and the child's ability to *self-regulate* emotions and behaviors. Every child has a unique iceberg, so we need to patiently identify each child's situation from a fresh vantage point.

Four Steps to Identifying and Addressing Causes

I learned valuable lessons from working with Darrell, his parents, and his school to understand his behaviors. We followed the same four priorities described in the previous chapter to uncover the roadmap that helped Morgan. We used the acronym IDEA:

1. **Inquire** about the child's history and track behaviors to discover patterns

2. **Determine** what circumstances contribute to the child's distress

3. **Examine** what our investigation reveals about the triggers and underlying causes

4. **Address** developmental challenges contributing to the behaviors through our interactions and targeted therapeutic support

In the previous chapter, we discussed the importance of understanding a child's history. In this chapter we'll focus on the second, third, and fourth steps, learning in the process how to dive deeper into addressing the underlying causes of behavioral challenges and move up from there to support children's use of top-down strategies. We will learn how to help children strengthen their own emotional house and provide tools that they can use for *self-regulation.*

Inquire About the Child's History and Identify Surrounding Circumstances

In order to learn about their concerns, I always meet with parents first, without the child present. I conduct this session with caregivers because, too often, we talk about children in the third person in their presence, which increases the blame and shame they are likely already experiencing. I also routinely inquire about the child's attachment history in the first few years, with an eye on early relational safety and security.

Darrell's mother reported that the pregnancy was unremarkable, and Darrell's birth was "quick and easy" compared to the experiences of some of her friends. Early on, his parents were fortunate to have flexible schedules, with one of them working only part time from home, so that Darrell had one or both of them (or on occasion, their part-time baby sitter) caring for him until he started preschool at age three.

Track Behaviors with a Journal to Discover Patterns

After Darrell's parents and teacher filled out a behavior-tracking worksheet for two weeks, I met with them to analyze what they had recorded. We noticed a pattern: most of Darrell's challenging behaviors happened during unstructured times—on the playground, during outings at public places, or at family gatherings. These situations had a few common factors: a lack of an adult-imposed structure, the presence of other children, and reduced adult supervision.

His parents recalled that in Darrell's first year of preschool, an older student had bullied him. Adults discovered this only after several months, when Darrell suffered a deep scratch on his face, and he told a teacher that another child had hurt him. After investigating, the teachers learned that the peer had regularly targeted Darrell and others during free play in a treehouse structure, away from the watchful eyes of the supervising adults.

Eventually, the child who targeted peers left the school, and Darrell's parents and teachers assumed Darrell would move on without any lasting difficulties. What they didn't realize was how profoundly the incident had affected his threat detection system—how traumatized the interactions had left him on a subconscious level.

A child's history of interactions with others can influence how he perceives all future interactions and provides us with important information to help deconstruct the behaviors in question. With this new information, we now had a working hypothesis about Darrell's feelings of vulnerability on the playground and a possible trigger: his implicit (subconscious) memories of bullying at another school.

Though the bullying had happened many years before the more recent incidents, it probably still had an impact on Darrell's emotional and behavioral control. When we pieced together the events surrounding his troubling behaviors, the team—including his parents and teachers—now considered that his fight-or-flight behaviors were likely protective reactions, stemming from subconscious remnants of the preschool bullying incidents. This explained why he reacted so strongly and unpredictably to what seemed to be ordinary childhood experiences. Since it had happened so long ago and was never discussed with him, Darrell had not integrated these memories into his conscious awareness. Over time and under certain conditions, his nervous system became primed for defense, and he struck out at others. His faulty neuroception explained why he often picked up danger signals from peers who intended no harm.

Humans are complex; our triggers and reactions to stressful events are equally complex and have multiple causes. One child might experience something as stressful while another may not. Adverse experiences, especially if they are chronic, can affect the child's growing brain and how the child views the world.[1] Our individual differences coupled with our experiences predict how we react to situations, so we must pay close attention to each child's reactions.

When a child displays aggression, especially if the behaviors seem to happen without warning, we often mistakenly assume that the child intended to do harm, lacked discipline, or wanted attention. But Darrell, like many vulnerable children, simply didn't have top-down control of his behaviors when he was triggered. He sometimes made up reasons in order to explain his actions to others, but he actually had no idea what triggered his harmful interactions with peers.

Darrell's Iceberg

Emotional outbursts; Striking, hitting or kicking others

Unpredictable behaviors around peers

Faulty neuroception

Multiple early bullying experiences

Implicit memory fragments

Auditory, visual, and emotional triggers

Defensive, aggressive reactions

Reflexive, instinctive impulses to protect himself

Discover What the Investigation Reveals About Triggers and Causes

Equipped with a new understanding, Darrell's parents and teachers began to interpret his behaviors not as intentionally aggressive acts but as defensive reactions triggered by certain features of the relational and/or physical setting at school. Without his realizing it, certain sounds, sensations, and sights triggered a subconscious memory of the bullying he had experienced at preschool, resulting in *seemingly* unpredictable fight-or-flight reactions.

Darrell's early experiences led him to develop automatic defensive behaviors, including fighting and striking out at peers. *Over time, his threat detection system had shifted into overdrive, causing his intense reactions.* His early experiences set his thresholds for certain experiences at low levels, so he routinely overreacted to everyday events with peers such as the dodgeball incident.

This new insight surprised and relieved his parents, giving them a different way to understand his seemingly random physical acts. Equipped with a new working hypothesis, Darrell's teachers also felt more empathy for the child and better prepared to help him feel safe. The school administrators hired a classroom aide with a gentle, warm manner to keep a watchful eye on Darrell and his peers. Her calm presence helped to increase cues of relational safety for Darrell. She noted, for example, that he often reacted defensively if other children approached too quickly or without warning. Such observations helped to validate our working hypothesis.

It's important to discover as much information as possible about a child's past relational experiences. Often, subconscious memories can invisibly weaken a child's thresholds for tolerating certain experiences. Challenging behaviors can be precipitated by memories, thoughts, feelings, sights, smells, or sounds that trigger defensive reactions, unbeknownst to the child and to the adults around him.

Address Developmental Challenges Through Interactions and Therapeutic Support

In the meantime, I evaluated Darrell's social and emotional development. Not surprisingly, I discovered gaps in his social-emotional development that helped to further explain his sudden outbursts. When I told his parents about these issues, they were initially confused to hear that Darrell was so socially and emotionally immature; after all, their son was conversant and academically talented. Yet they agreed that it was difficult, if not impossible, for him to talk about his feelings, analyze his own behaviors, or reach out for help before he exploded with a behavior. When they discussed incidents with him, he often acted goofy, changed the topic, or concocted narratives ("He hit me first!") even when the adults knew otherwise.

The reason: The upper levels of Darrell's social-emotional house weren't solidly in place yet. This included process four (social problem solving), process five (symbolic development), and process six (building bridges)—those factors that allow a child to have perspective, label motivations and feelings, and build bridges between his ideas and others. To address these challenges, I met with his parents, teacher, and classroom aide to devise ways to bolster his social-emotional development through individualized, supportive interactions.

Building the Bridge from Co-Regulation to Successful Self-Regulation

We designed a program to support Darrell's top-down thinking by helping him learn how to recognize when he was triggered and find new ways to manage his reactions. **With relational safety leading the way, Darrell's team came together to help him to (1) recognize when he was triggered or began to feel upset; (2) do something to feel better including signaling for help from an adult if needed; and (3) learn to talk about his feelings and thoughts.** These three strategies were designed to decrease his automatic and aggressive (defensive) reactions.

We should always look for the *earliest* signs of challenge in the child's development and start working from that point. The most effective way to bolster top-down abilities is to shore up the child's sense of relational security because children learn to manage their emotions through attuned, consistent adult presence. That's why the school positioned a trusted adult to help the teacher in the classroom, and to *co-regulate* emotionally with Darrell in the hope of reducing his outbursts. The school's administrators needed to act quickly to reduce Darrell's time spent in the red pathway because the parents of other students in the class had voiced concerns for their own children's safety after Darrell pushed or shoved some of them.

Relational Strategies

When the classroom helper (or the teacher) observed Darrell veering off the green pathway, she physically moved closer to him, using engaging facial expressions and body posture; her naturally warm, prosodic voice; and her confident, relaxed emotional presence. Sometimes, when she saw Darrell's green pathway veering toward red, she took him outside and they played together for a while. Usually, this was enough to help Darrell move toward a stronger green pathway, so she faded into the background but remained quietly engaged with the classroom activities. **In a short period of time, the classroom and playground became imbued with cues of safety from these two dedicated adults who understood the healing and supportive power of relationships.**

Darrell's challenging behaviors decreased in frequency with each week that passed after the school hired the new, engaging aide. *The aide, who was mentored by a developmentally informed psychotherapist, understood the difference between monitoring a child's aggressive behaviors through intense surveillance and warnings and co-regulating with a child emotionally so that he felt safe.* I scheduled short weekly phone calls with her, the teacher, and Darrell's parents to check in and to discuss the strategies and principles of this approach.

Darrell's Adult Interaction Guide

1. Classroom aide and teacher monitor Darrell's green pathway and look for shifts

2. When Darrell exhibits behavior indicating that he is veering out of the green pathway and toward red, an attentive adult increases proximity

3. When in proximity, that adult provides Darrell with multiple cues of safety through engaging facial expression and body posture; warm, prosodic voice; confident, relaxed emotional presence

   *Note: As we have learned, the Polyvagal perspective suggests that certain sensory experiences such as voice prosody can be calming. Remember that children's individual sensory processing preferences will ultimately predict how they respond to our interactions.

Observing and Addressing Developmental Challenges

The classroom helper and teacher continued to observe Darrell's steady progress over the next few months. At this point, I scheduled an observation of free playtime and stayed after school for a team meeting with his parents, teacher, and helper to discuss Darrell's growth. We had all noticed that Darrell still showed immaturity in his social interactions with peers. Often, he had difficulty when a group of friends wanted to play a different game than he did. When it came to negotiating with peers in a free-play setting, he couldn't effectively solve problems, often giving up on his own agenda and wandering around to find other activities on his own. I explained that this was not unexpected because Darrell didn't have the necessary practice in social peer interactions in his early years due to the bullying incidents, which left him hypervigilant and highly reactive.

We decided that the next step was for family relationship-based play therapy to more deeply address and bolster Darrell's social-emotional development. **We took this step because the most direct and effective way we help children build social and emotional strength comes from the primary language of childhood: play.**

Play as a Neural Exercise: Healing Behavioral and Emotional Dysregulation

Dr. Porges describes play as a "neural exercise." It is a necessary tool in our toolbox for supporting children with behavioral challenges.[2] It's a neural exercise in that it flexes the "muscle" of emotional regulation through reciprocal interactions under conditions of safety with others. This definition of play requires that it is interactive, not solitary (such as playing a video game alone). Play allows for children to integrate and use bottom-up *and* top-down functioning in real time. It's one of the most therapeutic things we can do with children.

> ### *Children's play is practice to prepare for the complexity of the social world.*

A recent study examined an intervention that utilized one-on-one play with teachers of preschool-aged children. It sought to determine whether sensitive and responsive interactions with children would result in changes in their stress-response systems (activation of the sympathetic nervous system via the hypothalamic-pituitary-adrenal (HPA) axis).[3] It found that the children in the intervention (known as *Banking Time*) group showed significant declines in salivary cortisol levels (a physiological indicator of stress) compared to children in a control group. This pilot study is thought to be the first to document health benefits via a *biomarker* of a play-based intervention for preschoolers, highlighting the positive impact of engaged relationships in a school setting.

I learned about the benefits and intricacies of play from one of the world's leading authorities on symbolic play, Dr. Serena Wieder. Dr. Wieder's decades of practice and early research with Dr. Stanley Greenspan led them both to formulate the social-emotional development framework described in Chapter 2. Dr. Wieder emphasizes the richness of play and how it reveals much about a child's emotional life, including "positive feelings, longings, and wishes about being loved and cared for" as well as "negative feelings of jealousy, retaliation, fears and aggression."[4] Children's play is practice to prepare for the complexity of the social world.

Children are drawn to play, which allows them to connect with others as they tolerate a wide range of feelings and bodily states. From the Polyvagal perspective, play exercises the effective use of the social engagement system to down-regulate primitive fight-or-flight responses.[5] Through play, children "exercise" in the green pathway while inching close to the red pathway, as they safely experiment with a range of feelings and impulses. Play helps children manage their "big" emotions, fears, and concerns naturally.

Think about the simple game of peek-a-boo, and how alluring it is for babies to momentarily experience a loss of contact and then delight when the adult suddenly reappears. This early play exercise allows a child to experience a small dose of fear and then overcome it when the adult magically reappears.

Or consider the enjoyable and exciting game of hide-and-seek. The neural exercise begins as a child experiences a manageable amount of stress (sympathetic activation) as she quickly finds a place to hide. If she's in the green pathway, enabling "top-down" control, she can inhibit her giggles and wiggles so as not to be found. Children who are still developing the ability to inhibit their impulses often can't resist the urge to make a sound or otherwise signal for the other player to find them. That makes hide-and-seek a great litmus test for evaluating a child's developing capacity to inhibit impulses and have intentional control over behaviors.

Play allows children to experiment with negative and positive feeling states—they can alternatively be aggressive, competitive, or nurturing—in a safe and socially acceptable way, preparing them to manage the complexity of real life.[6] It also helps tame children's aggressive impulses by providing a symbolic pathway for them, a uniquely efficient way to exercise thinking and feeling in real time.[7]

In this age of academic, economic, social, and political pressure, all children (and adults) need more time to play.

Darrell had difficulty playing with other children on his own because his red pathway was activated so often during his critical preschool years. In response to his volatility, peers routinely avoided him or tried to manage his behaviors by telling him what to do if he wanted to play with them. This created a cycle in which he was regularly triggered into fight-or-flight responses instead of using more effective and appropriate behaviors. So it wasn't surprising that at age seven, Darrell's play skills were still weak. Stress harms children's natural curiosity and experimentation and affects their ability to have playful social connections. I encouraged his parents to engage Darrell in playful interactions on a daily basis to help grow these skills.

How Does Play Support Social and Emotional Development?

Let's consider why interactive play makes so much sense from a developmental perspective. It helps fill in the gaps of social and emotional development. Play is healing because it allows for resilience and emotional sturdiness to develop when manageable sympathetic arousal is paired with the safety of social engagement.[8] As we discussed in the previous two chapters, children with chronic behavioral challenges are generally more vulnerable, and one of our goals is to increase their tolerance for uncomfortable sensations, feelings, or thoughts.[9] That's what makes play the brilliant and natural language of childhood imbued with the capacity to strengthen children's stress tolerance. It's both alluring and fun, and helps kids develop a sense of mastery around the challenges they face every day, exploring themselves and their world at the same time.

Play helps children manage a range of positive and negative emotions through social engagement by flexing the muscles of emotional co-regulation and emergent symbolic development at the same time. Play is a helpful tool for all children growing up in a world that often feels threatening and unpredictable.

From a developmental perspective, play with parents and caregivers is one way to address developmental gaps so that children can bolster their abilities and eventually dispel the underlying reasons for challenging behaviors. Developmentally based play also prepares children to gain resources for controlling their behaviors, emotions, and impulses.

Characteristics of Therapeutic Developmental Play

Requires social interaction with an attentive, engaged adult care-sharer (is not solitary)

The child and adult are enjoying the play and feel safe, within a range of allostasis (good stress)

The child, not the adult, generally sets the agenda

The play is characterized by reciprocity and mutual engagement

Play Supports Top-Down Thinking

For children, play is a natural state that draws out subconscious concerns, fears, conflicts, aspirations, and joys. It is the most efficient way to discover what a child is thinking about and dealing with. Playing with a child gives you clues and answers that a child may not yet be able to discuss aloud. For example, before therapy, when Darrell's parents or teacher asked him repeatedly about his behaviors, he couldn't come up with a cohesive answer, instead changing the topic or fabricating a response. But when many adults in his life began to therapeutically play with Darrell, we engaged him—and found the answers in his play themes. **Children show us what their concerns are through play, often well before they can tell us about their concerns with their words.** Over time, play helps children develop the capacities to eventually talk about (or otherwise symbolize) their internal feelings and motivations more directly.

Follow the Bouncing Ball

Relationship-based, developmental play involves following the child's lead as the child shows us what he or she is dealing with through the actions, themes, emotions, and content of the play.[10] We lay the groundwork through our mere physical and relaxed emotional presence. When we allow ourselves to follow the child's lead and be a nonjudgmental, interactive partner in the play, we discover what's on a child's mind. The adult's role is not to lead, teach, or judge any aspect of the play. Rather, we follow where the child takes us with a nonjudgmental sense of curiosity, energy, and acceptance.

The types of physical movement, toys, themes, symbols, and ideas that the child naturally gravitates toward, lead us to increasingly higher levels of understanding the child's internal motivations, emotions, fears, and concerns.[11] This is how we came to help Darrell reconcile his early trauma with his current life stresses.

Over a couple of months, in weekly sessions, I supported the family as they learned how to play together. Encouraging his parents to go with the flow of the play, I used my "stage voice" (whispering reflections, suggestions, or encouragement) while they played with their son.

Darrell loved to play with his animal figurines. In our sessions, his parents played with Darrell as he pretended to be a ferocious lion or tiger actively grappling with problems such as getting lost in the forest, and wounding (or being wounded by) another animal. Working through emotional themes through symbols (being an animal or a super hero, for example) helps children to master their own feelings, impulses, fears, and desires, in a safe environment.[12] **As it does for many children, playing with his parents offered Darrell a perfect way to flex his emotional thinking and social problem solving, with benefits to his "real" life.**

Within a few months, Darrell's play evolved from focusing on wild animals to themes of "good guys and bad guys." He loved to set up dramas in which his mom or dad played the characters who did something wrong, and he delighted in being the police officer, king, or ruler who enacted swift punishment on them. He happily—and repeatedly—threw the "bad guys" in jail and delivered disciplinary actions for their offenses. Darrell's play themes were likely reenactments of his early traumatic experiences with the child who targeted him in preschool.

Allowing a Wide Range of Feelings in Play

Sometimes, the themes children choose in play—especially the more aggressive, negative themes—activate our parental instincts to teach appropriate behaviors. Early in Darrell's therapy, for example, when the imaginary bad guys broke the law and Darrell meted out severe punishments to offenders (like beating them), his parents cringed and tried to teach him to "be nice" in the session. I explained that his play was helping him reconcile very strong emotions. His play was robustly flexing his emotional range, a process that would actually make it *less* likely that he would engage in aggressive acts with peers. This helped his parents become more spontaneous in the play, freely letting his and their own characters express a range of emotions rather than stepping out of the flow to take advantage of a "teaching moment."

The Neural Exercises Continue

With a bit of coaching, Darrell's parents fell into their characters beautifully, connecting to their own inner children and enjoying the dramas that unfolded with their beloved son. They now understood that Darrell was working through his feelings of powerlessness that had once been deeply stressful for him. The play helped close the gaps in Darrell's social and emotional development, helping him learn how to talk about his thoughts, feelings and ideas, opening up the world of sharing experiences with others. *When a child can share experiences, he can begin to find his own solutions to problems. This leads to increasing abilities to self-regulate thanks to the development of top-down thinking, which modulates and inhibits the child's stress responses.*

In our debriefing sessions without Darrell present, his parents and I marveled at how the play gave voice to his early feelings of helplessness and vulnerability—feelings that were now finding their way out through the characters he created. I surmised that the play also helped Darrell reconcile and integrate the traumatic bullying incidents that happened so long ago, but that set his system on edge.

A Wide-Angle View of Play

Darrell benefited from what we might consider traditional "symbolic play," often using toys and themes of pretend. *But that's only one definition of play.* Some children don't enjoy playing with toys, preferring instead to throw a ball, take a walk in nature, or otherwise engage in a lively exchange of gestures and words. In this wide-angle view, play is whatever works as a pleasurable, organic, and back-and-forth flow of exchanges with others under conditions of interpersonal safety.

Play Basics

Play flexes the muscles of emotional regulation and builds symbolic channels to express oneself.

Tips for Developmental and Relationship-Based Play with Children:

- Unplug and let go of all distractions
- Have fun, relax, and stay curious
- Follow the child's lead and value her play needs/themes
- Let go of any agenda
- Be interactive and engaged
- Refrain from teaching or asking questions in play that you already know the answer to (such as, "What color is the snake?")
- Become the characters and connect to your spontaneous inner child
- Have fun!

Remember That Top-down Access is Dynamic and Shifts in Real Time

As we discuss the benefits of top-down control, it's worth remembering that regulation and attention shift in real time. All of us will cycle into and out of the green pathway at different times. Just because we have (or a child has) top-down abilities, doesn't mean we will be able to access our thinking brain at all times. When we veer onto the red pathway, we need to recognize it and recruit our bottom-up strategies, whatever they are (pausing, breathing, mindfulness activities, etc.), to find our way back to the green pathway, where we can once again access our thinking brain.

Seek Professional Support

It's important to seek support or consultation in order to use play therapeutically with your child or a child you work with, especially when you are unsure of the direction of the child's play or how play might benefit the child. Sometimes play can activate or temporarily increase difficult emotions or behaviors for children or even for ourselves as play partners. *Remember that if any activity you are doing with a child causes distress, you can compassionately end the activity and use it as data in personalizing attunement with the child.* Make sure you have support from a professional if the play activates painful or intrusive feelings or memories for the child or for you, knowing that child's play isn't always easy.

> ### *If you are a parent, it's important to seek out therapists who believe that the therapeutic "action" comes from the child's most trusted relationships—and not from the therapist to the child in the absence of caregivers.*

It's beyond the scope of this book to provide detailed instruction on the therapeutic nuances of play, and I highly recommend seeking the help of a trained professional if you are a parent, or seek training yourself if you are an allied childhood professional, as its benefits are so far-reaching and neurodevelopmentally supportive. Aspects of play can be integrated into virtually any childhood profession or role. This book's appendix includes a listing of helpful websites and resources on therapeutic, parent-mediated play. The appendix also includes names of agencies and therapists around the world who are trained in DIR® and other developmental approaches that are familiar with the therapeutic use of play and developmental/relationship–based therapies. These therapists often associate with developmental and relationship-based models, including DIR-Floortime®,[13] Child-Parent Psychotherapy (CPP),[14] Interpersonal Neurobiology,[15] and the Neurorelational Framework (NRF).[16]

Moving to Top-Down Processing: Engaging Children in the Process

Over time, Darrell learned how to engage with others and to overcome his default tendency to fight. The variety of classroom supports, combined with robust therapeutic play with his parents, strengthened his social-engagement system. In play, his truth, fears, and sense of powerlessness found a voice in the wild animals and action figures he "became," as he explored and "healed" the woes of his characters. This type of play strengthened his green pathway and symbolic capacities, reducing his outbursts. Now that his social-emotional house was stronger, he could access his top-down processing and reasoning by talking to trusted adults about his feelings and ideas.

Arriving home from school one day, he shared an experience with his father. "I felt sad," he said, "because my best friend sat with a new group at lunch today." In this one sentence, Darrell's remarkable progress shined through. He finally had access to the powerful top-down ability to *"Name it to tame it,"* as Drs. Siegel and Bryson put it.[17] Now, at last, what he had previously discharged as a push or a shove he turned into verbal communication. He was finally able to negotiate with peers rather than hitting them—and when he needed help, find an adult who would listen and provide support. With the help of loving and caring adults, Darrell developed from the bottom up (emotional regulation) to having top-down abilities—enabling him to talk about his feelings—including anger, jealousy and fears.

Celebrating the Power of the Thinking Brain

Acknowledge a child's expressions of her experience.

Validate the child's sharing his experience and provide positive, individualized solutions.

Celebrate the power of the thinking brain—it can help us turn bad experiences into manageable ones, as children become active participants in discovering their own solutions.

Context: We assure children that they now have the ability to find solutions to the specific problem and other future contexts, emphasizing the incredible power of awareness and human connection to help us feel better.

Helping a Child Develop Top-Down Strategies

I always wait to introduce these ideas until a child is developmentally ready. Why? As discussed in Chapter 1, too often we don't use a developmental roadmap to help children with challenges. Instead, we try to teach first, before the child (or teenager) is capable of doing what is being taught. Then we get frustrated when the child fails to do what was taught. But we shouldn't require that children mobilize their own self-regulation until we engage and nurture them first through emotional co-regulation. In other words, *being* with the child comes before disciplining or teaching the child.

The Exhilaration of Using the Brain to Calm the Body and Mind

Once a child has top-down abilities, she can use the incredible power of thinking to find effective ways to cope with challenges. This is what the field of mental health is built upon—the solid rock of interpersonal, healing exchanges that help individuals understand themselves better, reduce their own suffering, and find better ways to manage their difficult emotions.

Approaches that utilize top-down thinking are generally known as cognitive or cognitive-behavioral paradigms. Top-down control leads to endless opportunities for children to understand themselves better, connect with and soothe their own difficult emotions, and discover the power of their own minds. When a child or a teenager has the capacity for top-down thinking, a range of effective techniques and approaches will now be accessible. Such approaches, including Collaborative and Proactive Solutions (CPS)[18] and the blended approach of Dialectical Behavior Therapy (DBT), have been studied widely and proven helpful to individuals who struggle with intense emotions and disruptive behaviors.[19]

The following chart describes approaches for helping children in three categories, from body-up to hybrid approaches, which use both body-up and top-down strategies.

- **Top-Down Approaches:** Cognitive therapies; Cognitive—behavioral therapies; Collaborative and Proactive Solutions (CPS); Dialectical Behavior Therapy (DBT)

- **Hybrid Approaches:** DIR-Floortime®; Neuro Relational Framework (NRF); Theatre; Drama; Art therapy; Mindfulness practices

- **Bottom-Up Approaches:** Sensory-motor based occupational therapy; Adapted Physical Education (APE); Physical therapy; Yoga; Biofeedback; Movement therapies; Neurologic music therapy; Safe and Sound Protocol (SSP)

The rest of this chapter will describe some of the ways I use top-down exercises and teaching to help children use their minds to influence their thoughts, emotions, and behaviors.

Presentation Matters!

Let's start with the most important guiding principle of how we talk to children about their nervous systems. Remember that *how* we say something (our emotional tone) is as important as *what* we say (content). Children are more open to learning if they don't feel judged, talked down to, or under scrutiny. So check yourself at the door, make sure *you* are on the green pathway when you teach, and if you're not—have compassion for yourself, be flexible, and reschedule the teaching session!

As discussed in Chapter 2, I use colors because they are an effective way to help adults understand the child's autonomic pathway, which is our roadmap. But due to my own professional experiences and comments from parents, therapists, and teachers, I don't use colors to *teach* children about self-regulation. I have learned that using color charts can unintentionally send a message that certain autonomic states are "better" than others. For example, a teacher might ask a child to go to a chart and "change your color" if the child is misbehaving or having a difficult time settling down. When colors are used this way as part of a behavior management strategy, children receive the underlying message that red is "bad" and green is "good." Parents often tell me that their child, who witnessed classmates having to "change their colors," develops fears about having to do it herself.

There is no good or bad autonomic state. So while I have found the colors a useful way to guide *our* interactions with children as adults, I avoid using colors to *teach* children about self-regulation. I solve that problem in a developmental and individualized fashion by having children come up with their *own words to describe their own autonomic pathways.*

We start by helping children develop a healthy appreciation of the autonomic nervous system and how it protects us. We then teach them to recognize which of their pathways has been activated in response to what's going on inside their brain and body.

The following protocol is an example of what I use. I encourage you to tailor it to both the developmental level and the reactions of the children you are using it with. This particular activity is aimed at an elementary-school audience, but I have used it with older kids as well. It's easiest as a one-on-one experience, but can be tailored to a small group or classroom, with adult facilitators.

Teaching a Child to Recognize and Name His or Her Autonomic State

Narrative:

**Note to trainer: Present each pathway with a positive/neutral tone.

Our bodies are connected to our brain, which helps us think, solve problems, and figure out how we are feeling. Sometimes we feel things in our body, like a tummy ache or our heart beating fast, and sometimes we feel things in our minds, like an idea, thought, or a memory. All of us will feel calm and happy sometimes and scared, sad, or otherwise uncomfortable at other times. That's to be expected and simply a part of being alive. Our feelings are our body's way of protecting us and helping us stay healthy and safe. One way to help us figure out our feelings is to organize them using a special word. Today we will have fun choosing our own special words for our feelings in our minds and sensations in our bodies. We can use our special words to know what to do when we want to feel better.

Calm, Cozy, and Safe

Let's think about three different ways our bodies and minds can feel. Sometimes we feel calm, and we can also feel happy, cozy, and safe. When we feel this way we often want to play and do fun stuff with others. Can you (or "any of you" if it's a group) give an example of a time when you felt this way? What were you doing? Can you think of a word that describes your body and mind when you feel calm, cozy and safe?

Give plenty of time, and then ask each child to share his or her special word. Use the worksheet at the end of this exercise to have the child write the word and/or draw a picture of it.

Big Feelings and I Need to Move

Now let's talk about another way humans can feel. Sometimes we feel wiggly, scared, angry, or like we want to move—fast. When we feel this way we might do unexpected things we later feel bad about, like say or do something mean that surprises us. Can you (or "any of you") give an example of when you felt this way? Can you think of a word that describes your body and mind when you feel wiggly, angry, or like you want to get away from something or someone?

Give plenty of time, and then ask each child to share his or her special word. Use the worksheet at the end of this exercise to have the child write the word and/or draw a picture of it.

Sad, Lonely, and Slow

There's another way humans can feel. Sometimes we feel sad, lonely, or slowed down. This is when our body doesn't want to move very much, and we're not interested in doing things with our friends and family, not even fun things. Sometimes we can even feel "frozen," like our body can't move very fast. Can you (or "any of you" if it's a group) give an example of when you felt this way? Can you think of a word that describes your body and mind when you feel slow, low, or like you don't want to play or be around others?

Give plenty of time, and then ask each child to share his or her special word. Use the worksheet at the end of this exercise to have the child write the word and/or draw a picture of it.

_____'s Mind and Body

My special word for when I'm calm, cozy, and feel safe in my mind and body: _____. Here's my drawing of it.

My special word for when I have big feelings, am scared or angry, and I need to move: _____. Here's my drawing of it.

My special word for when I feel sad, lonely, or slow: _____. Here's my drawing of it.

The message we want to impart through this exercise is that all human beings regularly cycle through these various pathways as a part of being alive and living in a busy world. We want children to know that managing our range of emotions and bodily experiences is something natural and to be expected. The key is to help children recognize and become aware of their sensations and emotions so that they can self-calm and/or find help if they need assistance.

I have found that children find this exercise fun and liberating because, often, adults attempt to placate or extinguish negative behaviors and don't dig deeper or help the child associate them with adaptive emotions. This is why we need to remember to present all the autonomic pathways as neutrally as possible.

We want to provide a twofold message when teaching children about the pathways. First, we want to support their growing awareness of their physiological state and praise them for their growing awareness of their body/mind connection. "Wow, that's awesome that you paid attention to your body's signals!" is one suggestion, but of course we should tailor our language to each individual child. Secondly, we want to build on that information to help children recognize *what they need* when they find themselves outside of their calm pathway, which we will discuss next.

Helping Children Find Their Own Solutions

Once a child recognizes his or her autonomic state, the next step is to help the child to build his or her own personalized solutions to their life experiences. Remember that what matters most is a child's perception of the events—so we need to recruit the child's perceptions and experiences here. That's why, in keeping with the personalized attunement approach, we recruit children to develop their *own* understanding of reactions to life events. The following two templates help organize a child's framing of their stress responses and how they can proactively think about them. Remember that co-regulation sets the stage, so the atmosphere/tone of the conversation should be collaborative, positive, and hopeful.

We will use Darrell's worksheet as an example. Darrell first named and identified his different physiological states using the "Mind and Body" worksheet. Darrell filled it out with a parent, and these were his responses. He needed some help from his parents to come up with some of the answers.

Next, Darrell filled out the "Noticing My Reactions" worksheet. This is a template where the child identifies situations, people, places, things, etc., that cause him or her to feel each of these three ways in body and mind.

Finally, Darrell filled out the "Developing My Strategies" worksheet. This is a template where the child goes through each individual response in order to identify strategies or solutions that can help return him or her to the calm, cozy, and safe pathway.

Darrell's Mind and Body Experiences

My special word when I'm feeling calm, cozy, and safe in my mind and body is: Happy Camper
Here's my drawing of it.

My special word when I feel big feelings (scared, angry, and like I need to move) is: Explosion
Here's my drawing of it.

My special word when I when I feel sad, lonely, or slow is: Turtle
Here's my drawing of it.

Noticing My Reactions—Darrell

Things that make me feel like a Happy Camper:

Weekends

Carving pumpkins with Grandpa

Baking cookies with Grandma

Eating ice cream

Things that can send my body into the Explosion:

When too many kids are on the climber during recess at school

When Mommy and Daddy leave me with a babysitter

When I have a sore throat or tummy ache

Things that can send my body into a Turtle:

When my hamster died

When my friend Jamal broke his leg

When I throw up

When my friends call me names

When my teacher asks me to go outside and stand by myself

Developing My Strategies—Darrell

How I can help myself get back to a Happy Camper when I'm an Explosion:

Blow the petals off the flower (his favorite breathing exercise)

Wait until the climber has only two or three people on it

Talk to Mommy and Daddy about staying with Grandma instead of a babysitter

Tell an adult how I'm feeling

Lie down

Ask Mommy to read me a story

How I can help myself get back to a Happy Camper when I'm a Turtle:

Draw a picture of my hamster, Hamlet

Think about my hamster or my Mom and Dad

Go and see my friend Jamal and bring him a hamburger

Ask for Mommy to sit by me when I feel like throwing up

Find someone to talk to when my friends call me names

Ask Mommy to talk to my teacher about not sending me outside anymore

_____'s Noticing
My Reactions

Things that make me feel like a _____.

_____

_____

_____

Things that can send my body into _____ (child's word for big feelings from the "Mind and Body" worksheet):

_____

_____

_____

Things that can send my body into _____ (child's word for sad, lonely, or slow from the "Mind and Body" worksheet):

_____

_____

_____

Developing My Strategies

How I can help myself get back to my _____ (child's word for calm, cozy, and safe) **when I'm in the** _____ (child's word for big feelings):

_____

_____

_____

_____

_____

_____

How I can help myself get back to my _____ (child's word for calm, cozy, and safe) **when I'm in the** _____ (child's word for sad, lonely, or slow):

_____

_____

_____

_____

_____

_____

This is how we helped Darrell create his own self-regulation solutions, through conversations that helped him discover his own top-down strategies for calming down when he felt distressed. *Since these solutions were self-generated, and not created by adults, they connected to his body and brain in a way that made sense to him and increased their effectiveness.*

Finding Opportunities for Top-Down Thinking

Oftentimes, the most creative solutions and strategies come from children themselves. During a walk or a conversation in the car, we can ask the child about how he or she perceives our adult help. Prospective questions, such as "When you are upset, what can I do to support you or help you feel better?" help the child proactively solve problems and plan ahead.

Recalling and Forecasting

One activity that parents and therapists can do with children is to create a "What to do" chart together, in which a child imagines certain situations and then creates plans in case those situations arise. It's a variation of the "Developing My Strategies" worksheet, a simple top-down exercise in *recalling* difficult situations and *forecasting* different outcomes for those situations. It helps us to build additional strategies for self-regulation, as children become familiar with how to calm themselves. The chart can also help with planning and sequencing, important activities for building executive function.

Darrell enjoyed a particular activity and named it "The Situation Room with Darrell and Mom" after hearing on TV that the White House has a Situation Room. In this activity, Darrell and his mom wrote down the situations that concerned him in one column, his feelings about the situation in the next column, and in the third column, a reminder about what he could do to stay calm. Here is an example of Darrell's chart, followed by a blank template that you can personalize.

Situation Room with Darrell and Mom

What Happened	How I Felt	What I Can Do
Kids made fun of me in dodgeball game	Embarrassed	I stay calm by: Saying to myself, "It's ok to feel embarrassed," talk to a friend or my parents about it
When my neighbor won't share his iPad with me	Mad	Set a timer on Mom's iPhone for 5 minutes, so we can share the iPad

Situation Room or "What to Do" Chart

What Happened	How I Felt	What I Can Do

Encouraging Top-Down Processing Through Our Interactions and Conversations

We can encourage top-down thinking by creating an atmosphere of exploration and nonjudgment. If you are a parent, try to find time to be with your child without distractions and create a space for conversations away from devices, internet, television, and other disruptions.

We can model top-down thinking through our own self-reflections. For example, if you and a child experienced a difficult time together you can reflect on how it was for you, as the adult, then pause and see if the child picks up on your thoughts by sharing how she felt.

For example, one day in session, Darrell's mom said, "I'm sorry I yelled at you the other day. I was anxious when we couldn't find our dog and lost my temper as a result." This prompted Darrell to talk about how it felt for him when his mother lost her temper as well as how scared he was that their beloved dog may have been run over by a car. (Fortunately, by then, the dog was safe at home, found by a neighbor.)

Shifting Targets from Child to Relationships

What was the most significant ingredient in helping Darrell heal the wounds that were subconsciously affecting his emotional and behavioral regulation? His team shifted from thinking of the child's *behaviors* as the target of change to prioritizing *supportive relationships* and *individualized developmental support*. This proved to be just what Darrell needed: the healing power of relationships targeting the social and emotional constrictions that were causing the challenges in the first place. Once his autonomic regulation was more stable, he was also more open and eager to learn top-down strategies that helped him use his mind to calm his body. His bottom-up *and* top-down abilities were supported by the many adults in his life—his parents, teachers, therapists, extended family, and community—who loved and wanted to help him.

Reducing Stigma and Promoting Mental Health Hygiene

Unfortunately, there's still a stigma in our culture about mental health. I witness this from the professional side in interactions and meetings where a child's mental health issues are treated differently from their academic or medical needs. In reality, emotional needs are no different than other needs, but they aren't as well understood because they involve aspects of the mind, somehow seem more mysterious and less tangible.

We tend to talk about mental hygiene less often and with a different tone than we talk about physical health. Children benefit when we, as adults, talk more about our own emotions and concepts—such as vulnerability, fear, and shame—in a relaxed way that lets kids know that emotional (and behavioral) swings are a part of being human. I highly recommend the work of Brene' Brown, whose programs, books, and life's work focus on helping us embrace our vulnerability rather than hide it away.[20]

The Wonders of Top-Down Thinking

Over time, Darrell developed the ability to use his thinking brain to understand his body's often-unpredictable red-pathway responses. **Something quite amazing happened: He was experiencing neuroception and turning it into perception.**[21] In other words, he was developing self-awareness. One day, during a session after a difficult day at school, Darrell said: "Happy Camper and my Explosion were fighting with each other today." His father asked: "Who won?" Darrell simply gestured, a thumbs up. The smile on Darrell's face and his dad's reaction were a lovely example of the wonder—and efficiency—of using the brain to calm and organize how the body feels.[22]

Main Points —

The IDEA in helping children with behavioral challenges involves:

1. **Inquiring** about the child's history and tracking behaviors to discover patterns.

2. **Determining** what circumstances contribute to the child's distress.

3. **Examining** what our investigation revealed about the triggers and underlying causes.

4. **Addressing** developmental challenges contributing to the behaviors, first through our interactions and, if necessary, targeted therapeutic support.

   - Play helps narrow the gaps in children's social and emotional development, helping them learn how to talk about thoughts, feelings, and ideas, and opening up the world of sharing their experiences with others.

   - When a child is functioning in a top-down mode, we can successfully introduce strategies and conversations about the power and wonders of using the mind to self-regulate, plan ahead, and problem solve.

PART THREE

Neurodiversity, Trauma, and Looking to the Future

7.
Behaviors in Autism and Neurodiversity: Handle with Care

> *"Change the way you look at things, and the things you look at change."*
>
> **Dr. Wayne Dyer**

Norton, an eight-year-old, had received a diagnosis of "high functioning" autism when he was four. As soon as they could, his parents sought treatment for him, including speech therapy, occupational therapy, and a social-skills group, and he responded well to the interventions. When I called his pediatrician to introduce myself as his developmental psychologist, she described Norton as "quirky and brilliant." We both agreed that he was a joyful, inquisitive child who would likely do well academically.

Norton's parents enrolled him at a local private school, where he excelled, thanks to his excellent visual and auditory memory. But his school had little tolerance for his behavioral differences, including one particular habit: he often snapped his fingers. The snapping was loud enough to attract attention, though Norton was capable of snapping more quietly when he could watch his fingers. His parents weren't concerned about the snapping, but when he entered second grade, his teacher, concerned that the snapping was disruptive, asked for the school to provide a behavioral intervention plan.

Soon after the teacher's request, Norton's parents and I met to discuss various options for support. At the heart of the discussion was a dilemma: Should we automatically target this behavior for change or first reflect on its meaning and value to Norton?

That is an essential question any time we consider a neurodiverse child's atypical behaviors: Should we encourage a child to change his or her behavior before we understand its functionality for the child? Or do we instead change our beliefs and expectations about the role the behaviors serve for the child?

Over the years, I have become increasingly concerned about how behaviors are understood, interpreted, and managed for children diagnosed on the autism spectrum. I am most concerned for those children and teens with complex communication challenges. These children are often referred to as "nonverbal," a term I find both inaccurate and insensitive. *I refer to these children as "nonspeakers" or sometimes "individuals who type to communicate." These terms reflect acknowledgment that the child's challenge is not necessarily at the verbal/thinking level.* Adults often treat these children with rigorous "top-down" approaches that focus on changing surface behaviors. I devote an entire chapter in this book to exploring different approaches.

As mentioned in an earlier chapter, my post-doctoral experiences on multidisciplinary teams showed me the importance of respecting a child's *individual differences.*[1] Respecting individual differences in autism support is essential because there are endless variations for each person, and no two people are the same. As a member of a multidisciplinary team that included speech and language therapists, occupational therapists, vision therapists, physical therapists, pediatricians, pediatric neurologists, and others, I gained a perspective about how a child's brain/body processing affects development, behaviors, and mental health. With so much rich information from individuals whose professions essentially represented different brain areas, I developed an appreciation for the *adaptations* children make to adjust to their unique brain/body connections. This appreciation led me to be curious about behaviors rather than perceive them as necessarily "disordered."

Researchers have studied many critical areas that are helpful in understanding children's behaviors in autism, including sensory over-responsivity, gastrointestinal issues, sleep disturbances, and anxiety.[2] Many children on the autism spectrum experience challenges in one or more of these areas. Sensory over-responsivity (SOR) is an extreme reaction to sensory stimuli.[3] The incidence of SOR in autism was so compelling that it was added to the criteria for the diagnosis of autism (in addition to sensory under-responsivity or hypo-reactivity) in the latest version of the *DSM*, the *DSM-5*. Researchers estimate that at least 56 to 70 percent of children diagnosed with autism meet the criteria for sensory over-responsivity.[4]

It's essential to understand how a child's sensory responsivity and other individual differences influence observable behaviors and to use this understanding in determining how to support each child.

Even two decades ago, I didn't sound alarm bells for the parents of my patients; I didn't urgently warn them to change "aberrant" behaviors in autism. Rather I advocated for first respecting and understanding these behaviors. I sometimes doubted my own instincts. What if I was wrong? Early development was a huge window of opportunity, and every moment in a child's day was a critical opportunity to support the child's development.

Rather than guiding our treatment, recognizing the heavy stress loads many children carry is often left unaddressed.

Fortunately, during that same time (the 1990s), rich information was emerging about the application of neuroscience principles to clinical practices. In 2000, a groundbreaking report, "From Neurons to Neighborhoods," synthesized the rich research about children's brain and social development and provided the data I needed to counter my hesitations about the strength-based approach I was using.[5] One core concept stood out as most salient to my work with families and young children. **The committee stated: "The growth of self-regulation is a cornerstone of early childhood development that cuts across all domains of behavior."[6]** Many of the treatment plans I saw involved shifting behaviors without regard for the impact on the child's emotional regulation. But to me emotional regulation was *the* primary issue, and I encouraged parents to send this message to their child's teams.

Two decades later, experts agree that supporting emotional regulation through relationships should guide our clinical practices.[7] Nowhere is this needed more than in the area of autism support. Autism expert and author Teresa Hamlin believes that the effects of anxiety and stress are often overlooked in treatment approaches for autism.[8] Rather than guiding our treatment, recognizing the heavy stress loads many children carry is often left unaddressed. She writes, "Most treatments today are focused on increasing socialization, communication and school behavior. What is often overlooked is the idea that without addressing stress, these goals cannot be actualized."[9]

Additional validation for the developmental and relationship-based approach I used came from the delightful opportunity to meet again with many of my former clients, now young adults. Many of these individuals are happy to report what they liked and disliked about their various therapies. Hearing about their life stories has been inspirational and also resonates with the perspectives of many other young adults whom I have met at conferences, or whose books or blog posts I have read.

I routinely ask former patients and their parents what they remember about our work together. The young adults often tell me, "I always had fun here." The parents tell me, "You encouraged us to presume competence in our child." Let's look at some of the issues that surface as we think about behaviors in children diagnosed on the autism spectrum.

What happens when we attempt to alter surface behaviors without considering the behavior's adaptive benefit for the child or how the intervention can affect the child's developing sense of self and trust in others? In this chapter, we'll explore the answers to these questions and discuss the benefits of being supportive rather than judgmental of children's behaviors *until we discover what they represent in the child's experience of his own body and mind.*

Appreciating—Instead of Judging—Individual Differences

The truth is that we scrutinize children's behavior from the time they're born. "She's such a good baby!" we might say of a newborn who is easy to care for, doesn't cry too much, sleeps through the night, and whose moods are predictable and easy to read. Without realizing it, we're betraying our culture's (understandable) bias toward valuing behaviors that we can easily understand and that make our own lives easier as caregivers, teachers, or other providers. As children reach school age, we lavish praise and good grades on those who are good listeners, follow directions, and can sit still and perform well on tests.

We often reward these "good" behaviors with positive recognition, not realizing the messages we are sending to children whose natural tendencies fall outside of the "easy child" profile, particularly in the educational arena (e.g., those who can sit still are better than those who cannot; quiet is better than loud). While these messages may well serve the purposes of group education, they ignore the importance of understanding and appreciating—and not judging—the range of children's individual differences demonstrated through their behaviors.

Too often, professionals label a child's behavioral differences as a part of a checklist of the autism diagnosis rather than seeing them as adaptations to how information is processed through the child's body/brain information highways. Since all behaviors involve movement and sensation, autism researcher Anne Donnelan uses the term "sensory and movement differences" to describe individual variations in the behaviors of individuals diagnosed as autistic.[10]

Lots of children move their bodies in more ways than a particular setting might allow or tolerate, especially if the behaviors can disturb other children. While it's understandable that teachers need to manage behavior in their classrooms, what is often missing is an appreciation for the "constellation of adjustments and adaptations labeled people make to ease the circumstances of their lives."[11]

The Importance of Presuming Competence

When we insist that children do things their bodies aren't naturally inclined or ready to do, we can negatively influence their self-perception and create additional stress for them. Autistic author Ido Kedar, who types to communicate, wrote that, "My body is its own challenge, all by itself."[12] He goes on to say that the "experts" didn't understand how to help him. "Maybe they assumed I was too dumb, or they simply couldn't see what I had learned because I learned it in a different way than their methods."[13]

We should appreciate how children's bodies and brains use behaviors to help them manage their surroundings and their experience of being in the world.

That doesn't mean that we should adopt a laissez-faire attitude toward behaviors. To the contrary, we need to pay *closer* attention and take note of differences without presuming that a child's behaviors are pathological or disordered, or somehow reflect an intentional choice to be difficult. When we *presume competence* in children, we assume that their behaviors reflect necessary adaptations to their body's signals. We should appreciate how children's bodies and brains use behaviors to help them manage their surroundings and their experience of being in the world. Once we appreciate the adaptive functions of a behavior, we can then decide if and how to intervene in order to increase a child's sense of autonomy and independent decision-making.

Of course, if a child's behaviors are disruptive to family life or substantially interfere in a school setting, it's often necessary to make respectful modifications and accommodations. And parents should always work with a supportive multidisciplinary team when concerns arise around these issues. Further, as we'll examine in Chapter 8, we also need to pay attention to behaviors that signal that a child is *additionally* in a toxic stress pattern or has experienced trauma. In such cases, behaviors can indicate a child's immediate need for relational safety and intensive, positive relational support.

So why should we make an effort to *understand* behaviors before we attempt to *eliminate* them? The body carries its own wisdom, and we should help children to understand that. Too often we adults have hair-trigger responses to behaviors, and we instinctively try to teach children how to behave as our first response. Sometimes, that's simply part of being a good parent or teacher and maintaining order in a classroom. However, I believe it's a good idea to pause and rethink our quick reactions to behavioral differences in the neurodiverse child. *In doing so, we can begin to teach children to respect the signals from their own bodies and involve children in devising their own creative solutions that honor their individual differences.* This stands in contrast to the cajoling, reinforcing (and nonreinforcing) of behaviors that are often part of intensive services as soon as a child is diagnosed on the autism spectrum.

In the case of Norton, who couldn't resist snapping his fingers, various approaches over several years proved ineffective at reducing the snapping. At one point, his teacher tried introducing a behavior chart, with Norton earning stickers when he refrained from snapping. But his inability to earn enough stickers for a weekly prize caused Norton so much distress, monitoring, and hypervigilance that the teacher decided to halt that approach.

Meanwhile in our parent-mediated play therapy sessions at my office, Norton enjoyed role-playing various scenarios that caused him stress in daily life. Our sessions provided a natural and enjoyable outlet for him to communicate to his parents and me what was on his mind. During one session he asked me to play the part of his school behavior therapist, and he opted to play himself. Knowing how much his behavior therapist was working to reduce Norton's snapping, I took the opportunity to investigate. "Tell me," I asked in my role as the behavior therapist, "does it bother you when I tell you not to snap so much?"

"Yes!" Norton replied quickly. "I snap when I'm anxious."

Norton's parents and I paused to take in this powerful moment. In this safe space, interacting playfully with the people Norton trusted most, he was able to label a feeling with a word. The moment represented an important developmental milestone. Norton was offering us a window into his experience of the world, explaining how he truly felt about adults trying to alter a behavior that was actually helping him cope when he felt anxious.

I often wonder about the similar messages we give to children about their bodies' adaptations when we ask them to "quiet" their hands or bodies or otherwise conform behaviorally. What happens to their nervous system (positively or negatively) when we ask them to stop an action that their body is instructing them to do?

Luckily, I was videotaping the session that day (as I often do so that we can replay in parent debriefing sessions). Watching the tape, we were all struck again by Norton's succinct and profound explanation of his behavior. I often use that video clip (with Norton's parents' gracious permission) when I train fellow providers about social and emotional development and autism treatment/support.

Many of us are more comfortable with teaching an autistic child, as opposed to learning from him. Some professionals teach the language of emotions, for example. One common strategy, the well-intentioned effort of flipping through cards or books with different facial expressions, comes to mind. But as we learned in the last chapter, we can also achieve this goal more organically, while we playfully and patiently support the child discovering feelings, sensations, and thoughts in his own body. This is often referred to as the *embodiment* of experiences.[14] **It's a much different experience to feel what it's like to be sad or angry in one's body, than to identify pictures or drawings as a drill or exercise.**

After Norton's breakthrough session, we convened a team meeting that included his teachers and specialists to coordinate our various approaches to his behavior. Some people on the team wanted to encourage Norton to switch to another, less noticeable strategy. But I encouraged us to first consider the negative message they would potentially be sending Norton about his body's natural inclinations and his developing sense of self-identity now that he had explained the snapping helped alleviate his anxiety.

At the meeting, the team decided to reframe the finger snapping as a form of movement that felt familiar and soothing to Norton and to honor it as such. Instead of offering sticker charts to get rid of the behaviors, his teachers decided to ask him questions and offer comments that supported Norton's self-confidence and that demonstrated compassion and the presumption of his competence when he snapped his fingers. They would deliver them within a therapeutic use of self. That is, accessing their own green pathways to convey warmth and acceptance and asking the child: "Is your body telling you something about how you feel or what you need right now?" or "Is there anything I can do to help you right now?"

Of course, the team could have moved quickly to helping Norton discover other, less distracting ways to alleviate his anxiety. There's nothing inherently wrong with helping a child find a replacement behavior. However, there are benefits to becoming more intentional in the messages we give children about their behaviors. We can offer hopeful messages of tolerance and self-acceptance to the neurodiverse child—and every child in the classroom.

> ### *In this case, the message is that diversity of movement and behaviors shouldn't be automatically judged as negative.*

Instead of expressing frustration that Norton wasn't trying hard enough to stop snapping, the adults in his life began to show more compassion and tolerance. These messages helped create a stronger green pathway, and before the team suggested replacement behaviors (the topic of its meeting the following week), Norton's finger snapping decreased by about a third without any other intervention. *I surmised that his stress load decreased after he was encouraged to share more verbally about his anxiety.*

Norton benefitted from this new understanding of his behavior. His teacher was less bothered by it and allowed him to snap, while working to help him to figure out additional ways to calm his body. In the meantime, his occupational therapist, who participated in our team meetings, gently explored replacement behaviors by encouraging Norton to explore a wider range of various sensory strategies that felt soothing to him. This eventually led Norton to choose squeezing his hands together for input when he felt the need for it, and he reported that it felt calming. **This collaborative solution worked because Norton felt valued, understood, and safe.** And now he had an additional new and powerful avenue to use when he felt anxious: seeking out support from the concerned adults around him.

Norton's ability to use a word for a feeling represented years of developmental nurturing through playful, safe, and engaged relationships that sowed the seeds for this capacity.[15] Chapter 2 explained how social-emotional development begins with emotional co-regulation with trusted adults, which leads to back-and-forth communication, social problem-solving, and a synergistic integrative ability to pin words to feelings and eventually share that information with others. **For Norton, all of the thousands of interactions over many years resulted in a connected sense of autonomy, collaboration, and communication.**

Norton's Iceberg

Finger snapping

Sensory and movement differences

Fluctuating stress load

Anxiety and hypervigilance

Natural movement preferences

Adaptive movements and resultant behaviors

Presume Competence

In this new paradigm, rather than focusing on disorder and neurotypical standards, we come to appreciate the adaptive nature of what we often consider behavioral challenges. In this approach, we respect the wisdom of a child's brain/body connection. When we shift our lens to view the phylogenetic, adaptive nature of behaviors, we can appreciate their value rather than automatically disparaging them. **In the words of Dr. Porges: "Rather than investigating and understanding there is a neural substrate underlying the range of individual differences, we basically convey to these children that the behaviors are bad even if the behaviors are involuntary. Alternatively, the educational process could celebrate some of the unique sensitivities that people have."**[16]

This new perspective provides an opportunity for all of us to develop a deeper understanding and appreciation of the brain/body connection, an appreciation that is missing from mainstream autism treatment today.

Genelle — # When the Wrong Approach Makes Matters Worse

Genelle was diagnosed with an expressive and receptive communication delay when she was two and autism when she was three. She also had difficulty with social skills and mostly preferred to play by herself or with adults rather than peers. She often got into trouble for her behaviors, including her habits of singing parts of songs repetitively or touching her classmates on the head and arms during class time. This was a particular problem in her first-grade classroom because it disrupted other students.

A team at her school devised a behavior plan to help Genelle shift her behaviors to become more positive. Her teacher and classroom aide praised her and reinforced desired behaviors such as working quietly or not singing. This strategy yielded only mild measurable results, so a month later, they added an additional layer. The team then decided that when Genelle engaged in the targeted behaviors that the teacher should ask her to stop. If she didn't, after the third request, the classroom aide would accompany Genelle down the hall to a "calm-down room," a small former storage space set aside for kids who had difficulty in the classroom. The hope was that Genelle would learn that touching other children and singing songs would lead to a negative consequence.

The first time Genelle's teacher directed the aide to take her to the calm-down room, Genelle was confused. She didn't seem to understand the reason for being taken to the room, but she also picked up on the aide's cool emotional tone as the aide walked with her in silence to the room. Genelle was accustomed to adults speaking with her in friendly tones, so she found the silence, as well as the firm grasp her aide had on her hand, disquieting. The aide opened the door and instructed Genelle to go inside, following her, and then the door closed behind them with a loud, locking sound. The aide quietly told Genelle they would be there for three minutes then sat on a chair, not communicating with the child.

When Genelle returned to the classroom, she was quieter and didn't touch anyone. Her teacher thought that the technique had worked, but in reality, Genelle's nervous system had shifted from the green pathway to the blue pathway. The combination of sitting in a small empty room and an adult who was not providing cues of safety profoundly affected the child's autonomic nervous system, sending her into internal distress. Far from being a calming learning experience, it was stressful. Due to Genelle's developmental differences, she wasn't able to describe her feelings. And the extreme fear she felt degraded the relational platform of safety that her attentive and devoted parents had been helping her to build at school and at home.

The following week, when her mom was dropping her off at school, Genelle refused to leave the car. Her mother was surprised and concerned. The next day, when she and her mother went to a department store to shop, Genelle panicked when she saw a dressing room and heard a locking sound when it closed. Hyperventilating, she began to cry and her mother had no idea why. Concerned about this new behavior she had never before witnessed in her child, the mother phoned me the next day. We met without Genelle and deconstructed the situation with the help of Genelle's teacher and aide, who both kept a behavior log at school. I surmised that the incident at the calm-down room had created a traumatic memory for the child.

What happened? When adaptive individual differences are interpreted as malleable surface behaviors, and they are met by withdrawing social support from the child, *we can make matters worse*. We can create an *iatrogenic situation* where the *treatment causes additional problems*. This is what happened to Genelle.

Genelle's behaviors didn't signal an intent to disrupt or an attempt to seek attention. Her experience illustrates why when we work with autistic children, we need to discriminate between intentional misbehavior and responses to a child's unique brain wiring. Until we do, we may inadvertently add stress to vulnerable children by making false assumptions about behaviors, misbehaviors, and intentionality. Genelle's singing and touching peers were her body's instinctive, adaptive reactions to her sensory over-reactivity, her need for proprioceptive input, and her nervous system's responses inside a busy, sensory-rich classroom.

Emerging New Perspectives about Autism

Elizabeth Torres, a researcher in the field of computational neuroscience at Rutgers University, studies how behaviors in autism reflect the individual's attempts to cope with underlying physiological differences.[17] Her theoretical model of autism, known as the movement-sensing perspective, developed with fellow researcher Caroline Whyatt, implicates underlying differences in moving and sensing as a primary core feature of autism. This new model stands in stark contrast to the current *DSM* paradigm, which describes autism as a disorder of social cognition, interaction, and communication.[18] Their model, if correct, has profound implications in how we understand, treat, and support behavioral differences in autistic children.

When I first heard Elizabeth Torres present her research at an autism conference I co-chaired in 2013, I had to keep myself from cheering throughout her lecture. What she presented—a view of autism behaviors as representing complex differences within the nervous system's bidirectional information highway—made more sense to me than any of the current or past theories in circulation. Her work reminded me of what I had read through the years from Anne Donnelan, who, as mentioned earlier, believes that behaviors (movement) comprise the adjustments and adaptations people make naturally, according to their unique neurobiology. Her work also reminded me of the wisdom of Dr. Porges, who believes that behaviors are survival-based adaptations to an individual's neuroception of the environment (including the relational environment).

Behaviors and Autism

When we approach behavioral challenges in neurodiverse populations, we must expand beyond the notion that behaviors or traits are stable and "caused" by a disorder. At IEPs I often hear the statement, "This behavior is common for children with autism." While the intent might be to reassure parents, many tell me that such statements feel dismissive. *In fact, there are too many variations within autism and other developmental conditions to make such generalizations useful. They also undervalue a child's individuality.*

Another mistake is assuming that children's low scores on standardized cognitive testing accurately reflect intellectual functioning in neurodiverse populations. "Below-average cognitive function" is a particularly damaging label in autism and should be used with caution, because many traditional IQ tests underestimate intelligence in the special-needs population. They can underestimate skills because they were designed for neurotypical children with neurotypical motor functions. **A child might know the answer to a test question but be unable to show or tell the evaluator the answer due to a stress response or sensory and movement differences.**[19] This can have the unintended consequence of lowering expectations, IEP goals, and the educational curriculum for many students.

Again, let's consider Genelle, whose persistent singing of jingles and need to touch things and others caused concern at her school. Looking through the lens of a child's adaptation to her own physiology, we can understand why a punishment paradigm to decrease her "problematic" behaviors was unsuccessful. We decided to shift into an appreciation of the behaviors, but we had an additional problem: Genelle was now afraid of locked doors.

Looking at Bottom-Up Causes and Positive Supports

I encouraged the team to take a new approach. The first step was pausing and attempting to appreciate Genelle's behaviors, reflecting on how they were adaptive to her. The neuroscience rationale for taking the time to do this comes from Dr. Torres's work at Rutgers. Dr. Torres sheds light from the movement-sensing perspective, explaining that "many symptomatic behaviors, such as "stimming," averted gaze, and ritualistic routines *might be understood as coping mechanisms supporting stability and control of perception and action.*"[20] In other words, these behaviors we see in autism may be helping a child cope with taking in information from the world through their sensory systems and acting on that information.

I encouraged the team to reframe our thinking, understanding that Genelle's repetitive singing and ritualized touching of objects were actually adaptations and coping mechanisms. They occurred in the classroom because she had sensory over-reactivity (SOR) in her auditory system, and sensory under-reactivity in her proprioceptive system. As such, her behaviors were probably helping her tolerate—and feel more comfortable in—the classroom environment.

With this hypothesis in hand, we went to work to undo the stress and traumatic memory her visit to the calm-down room had caused. *First, we stopped all negative consequences to her behaviors and shifted to increasing relational security as the core strategy to help her feel safe in the classroom again.* Next, we agreed that we may have falsely assumed that her behaviors were attempts to gain attention or escape from a demand and shifted to considering that her behaviors were an adaptation to her physiology.

Our rationale for shifting our approach was that targeting the behaviors for elimination with top-down strategies ignored the fact that they were likely bottom-up processes. We had another choice: to view the behaviors as "personal accommodations" Genelle made on her own, much as you might adjust your posture without necessarily thinking about it when your body feels uncomfortable.[21]

With this major shift in our approach, I encouraged her parents to increase therapies that would *capitalize on the feedback to her body that Genelle was seeking naturally*—namely those involving music, touch, and rhythm. I recommended that we allow her to lean in to her natural tendencies rather than trying to extinguish them. In Dr. Torres's research lab, it's theorized that such experiences exercise sensory, somatic motor loops, which support other neurodevelopmental processes.[22]

Fortunately, Genelle's speech therapist connected her parents with a neurologic music therapist, whose techniques were a perfect fit for Genelle's natural inclinations.[23] In her sessions with Genelle, the therapist used various musical instruments, sounds, and rhythm to help Genelle feel more connected (and in control of) her body in motion. In the safety of the sessions, sounds were newly experienced as pleasurable as she explored them with a talented and highly relational therapist. Her mother recorded short video clips of the sessions and shared them with the rest of the team. We marveled at the innovative use of music and movement and the joyful look on Genelle's face as she danced and sang with her therapist and mom.

In addition, Genelle's occupational therapist met with the larger team to further discuss how we could collaborate to support pleasurable sensory and motor experiences, especially those that included sounds and various types of movement that increased Genelle's body awareness.

It's helpful to contextualize or put different therapeutic modalities and supports in their place from a neurodevelopmental perspective. In other words, we can ask if a certain therapy is more body up or top down. We can then ask if we are applying the most appropriate techniques based on where the child is functioning. Of course, no therapy is "purely" body up or top down, but we can categorize therapies in relation to these perspectives.

We can support a child's autonomy by offering activities that promote integration, improved communication, and self-advocacy, and most of all, relational joy and connectedness.

> *My hope is that understanding the difference between treating deficits and supporting development will help us to view behavioral differences with more respect and acceptance, no longer placing blame on autistic people or pressuring them to conform.*

A Shift in Perceptions

Our new conceptualization of Genelle's behaviors had a profound impact on the team. Now understanding her behaviors as personal accommodations to her own brain/body connections, her teacher and aide felt less pressure to change the behaviors. They decided to allow Genelle to engage in her naturally inclined behaviors unless they truly distracted other students in the class. To help her peers better understand Genelle, I co-led a classroom discussion with the teacher as we attempted to demystify and destigmatize Genelle's behaviors. The innocent and loving comments and questions from her classmates were an encouraging reminder to all of us about children's inherent tolerance, acceptance, and flexibility.

But Are We Reinforcing "Bad" Behaviors?

When we opt to appreciate behaviors rather than change them, do we run the risk of reinforcing *negative* behaviors? I think not. When we manage situations based on an integrated mind/body notion of child development, we can provide the most up-to-date therapeutic strategies and approaches, which will help children feel safe, take more risks, and realize their full potential. As discussed in previous chapters, that's far more beneficial to children than trying to eliminate behaviors before we truly understand them.

Don't Ignore Behaviors. Pay Attention to the Iceberg of Causality

Additionally, adopting this wider view of behaviors doesn't eliminate the need to enlist pediatricians and other professionals to help to identify the variety of triggers and causes beneath the tip of the iceberg—including the biomedical aspects of behaviors. Certain behaviors in children with impacted motor systems, particularly nonspeakers, can result from acute pain, physical sensations, or illness. As we have seen in the many children's stories in this book, the list of potential triggers is very long. *That's why it's important to have a team approach, allowing parents and specialists—including pediatricians, developmental pediatricians, and neurologists, among others—to weigh in on important treatment decisions and to make sure that the child isn't suffering from pain, infection, chronic conditions, or other medical issues that need attention.*[24]

Behaviors and Individual Differences in Autism and Other Forms of Neurodiversity

As noted earlier, the autism label can lead to "disorderism," the tendency of professionals to lower their expectations of a child, placing an invisible ceiling on the child's potential.[25] Labels can influence expectations because professionals are trained in the medical model of disability, which views patterns of developmental differences as deficiencies. But we can also change our culture's views of behavioral differences in autism, encouraging people to appreciate neurodiversity rather than seeking to change the child's behaviors to look more "normal."

I am not suggesting that we ignore atypical behaviors or that we do not support intensive, early intervention for children diagnosed with autism. But we should view behaviors through a new lens, not attempting to change them before we truly understand their functional purpose. Sometimes, behavior may have no purpose at all—*and that's okay too. Neurotypical observers may never understand why a child simply loves his own unique repetitive movements or topics of interest.* The adults in the child's life have a choice about the messages they give the child about his behaviors. What message do you want to send?

The most articulate teachers on this topic are autistic people themselves. In his blogging and books, Ido Kedar writes that people often judge his outward behaviors negatively and fail to presume his competence.[26]

Naoki Higashida, who types to communicate, is the author of *The Reason I Jump*, which echoes Ido Kedar's themes. "We don't even have proper control over our own bodies," he writes. "Both staying still and moving when we're told to are tricky—it's as if we're remote controlling a faulty robot. On top of this, we're always getting told off, and we can't even explain ourselves. I used to feel abandoned by the whole world."[27]

Ido Kedar's and Naoki Higashida's writings are a reminder that we should look for strengths rather than weaknesses, competence rather than incompetence, and we ought to emphasize each individual's potential with supports that are individualized and not one-size-fits-all.

Interpreting Behaviors in Neurodiverse Individuals

1. **Understand that a child's sensory and/or motor/movement profile may affect the child's ability to show you what the child is thinking and what the child can do.** Don't assume that children with movement differences (including those who can't speak) don't know the right answer, are purposefully misbehaving, or are purposely not cooperating. Instead, give each child the benefit of the doubt and assume that he understands but *needs the appropriate supports to be able to show you.*

2. **Confer with experts as soon as possible to help the child communicate.** Alternative and Augmentative Communication (AAC), including a subtype, Facilitated Communication (FC), are subspecialties in the field of speech and language therapy. Children with difficulties in spoken communication (nonspeakers) require support and assistance in finding alternative methods of communication. Some speech and language therapists have specialized training to help children with severe challenges in spoken language.

3. **All children need time to build relationships of trust in order to risk making mistakes.** Encouragement and reassuring adult presence helps children stay calm and alert. While it may not always be easy to communicate with neurodiverse children, all adults in a child's life should strive to discover a child's intentions and ideas. The first step is building a relationship of trust, enabling the child to feel safe, take chances, and persevere to show us all he or she knows.

Ignoring Behaviors When We Should Be Valuing Them

At a meeting I once attended, an autistic teenager recounted a frustrating episode from his childhood. At five years old, he was forty-five minutes into a session with his behavior therapist when he grew tired of the incessant drills and wanted to go home. Unable to use spoken language or even point or gesture, he simply ran to the window, pressed his nose against it, and stared intently out the window. It was his attempt to communicate to the therapist and his mother that he was ready to go.

But the therapist didn't get the message, instead dismissing his attempt to communicate as "stimming"—that is, a form of meaningless self-stimulation. They looked outside and saw a dog walker with a group of dogs he was walking. "He's fixating on the dogs," she told the boy's mother, assuming that the child's naturally strong interest in dogs was luring him to the window. "Let's ignore and try to get him back to the table." At seventeen, the boy recalled his great frustration trying to make himself understood.

The therapist wasn't being intentionally harsh. She was following a common treatment technique that reinforces desired behaviors and uses "planned" or "tactical" ignoring in an attempt to help children learn and acquire new behaviors. I have grown increasingly concerned about such approaches, because they operate outside of a complex understanding of autism. Perspectives that view behaviors only at "face value" presume that we need to change certain behaviors of autistic people rather than appreciating them as a form of communication, an expression of a child's stress load, of one's neurodiversity, or "merely part of the richness of human diversity."[28] The therapist's approach was based on a model that considers behavioral differences in autism to be deviant and in need of change.

> *Perhaps it's the systems and professionals who need to change their perceptions of autistic people's behavior, not the autistic children who need to be changed so they appear more neurotypical.*

Finally, from a developmental and relationship-based perspective, it is simply not appropriate to ignore children. We may think we are ignoring a specific behavior (not the child herself), but children don't necessarily make that distinction. When human beings feel ignored, it degrades the social engagement system that supports the green pathway. Doing so doesn't help the child, and can fuel confusion and decrease connection with others. Think about how you felt the last time somebody you cared about ignored you. **When we are ignored as human beings, it decreases our emotional links to other people, who should be our life rafts when we are suffering.**

- If a challenging behavior is a child's bid for communication (often the case for nonspeaking children on the spectrum), ignoring sends the wrong emotional message to the child. In short, the adult is saying, "I'm not interested in what you are trying to convey, and I'll pay attention only when you comply with my demands."

- Ignoring reflects an oversimplified understanding of the autistic child's behaviors without trying to discern the complexity of underlying thoughts and feelings.

- It is stressful for the child and stressful and unnatural for parents and caregivers to ignore children.

Instead of ignoring a challenging behavior, it's better to do the opposite—pay close attention to the child and ask: What is the child trying to tell us through the behaviors? And how can we help make it easier for the child to communicate? **When we presume competence, our priorities shift from achieving behavioral compliance to promoting growth, communication, and self-advocacy.** What makes the difference is the lens through which we view behaviors.

Expanding Our Understanding of Behaviors

When do we need to change the system rather than changing the child's behavior? In a world that doesn't always appreciate behavioral differences, we need to collaborate and expand our notions of and tolerance for behaviors that don't harm the child or others. Before we target behaviors because we find them disruptive, strange, or otherwise outside our comfort zone, we need to ask: is changing the behavior truly in the child's best interest?

The following worksheet will help you reflect on children's differences and natural inclinations in order to decide whether to intervene or to shift our own expectations and ideas about the child's behaviors.

Behaviors Have Meaning

Is it possible that the child's behavior is meeting a constitutional need? That is, does the child need to engage in the movement (behavior) in order to communicate something or to stay on his or her green pathway?

_____ Yes _____ No

If yes, note your observations of the child's needs:

_____

_____

_____

Is it possible that the child's behavior is signifying an underlying condition such as **physical pain** or **emotional distress**?

_____ Yes _____ No

If yes, note possible underlying conditions:

_____

_____

_____

Is there robust communication with the child's team, including the child's pediatrician, parents, and teachers about the underlying meanings of the behaviors?

_____ Yes _____ No

Explain:

_____

_____

_____

Classroom Application

The words we use to talk to children about their behaviors can impact every student in a classroom. It's useful to reflect on how we approach behaviors and other individual differences and the messages we give children about their preferences. The goal is twofold: (1) to help all of the children in the class appreciate signals from their bodies as valuable pieces of information rather than something to ignore or be ashamed of; and (2) to model acceptance of differences so that we begin to teach a new generation of children to respect human variations associated with the spectrum of autism and other forms of neurodiversity.

The following worksheets will help you to consider different needs that children may exhibit and how to approach these needs with a warm, engaging stance. Of course, these worksheets are only samples of situations and ways that you can respond. As discussed in Chapter 4, the therapeutic use of self should be our overarching guide for working with all children.

Talking to Children about Sensory Needs: Movement

Consider the differences between A and B in the following examples:

Child exhibiting movement differences in a classroom

A. Emotional tone is judgmental:

"You need to keep your body still; you are disrupting your neighbors."

B. Emotional tone is warm and engaging:

"I see your body is asking you to move around a bit. Would you like to stand up and stretch for a moment?"

Child lying on floor or desk instead of sitting up

A. Emotional tone is judgmental:

"Sit up straight. You can't lie down right now."

B. Emotional tone is warm and engaging:

"It seems a bit difficult for you to sit up straight right now. Perhaps you can prop yourself up right next to me with this nice pillow."

Create some phrases of your own to talk to each individual child about movement preferences and different needs.

Name of child: _____

Phrases: _____

_____

Talking to Children about Sensory Needs: Sound and Touch

Consider the differences between A and B in the following situations:

When you see a child reacting negatively to sounds

A. Emotional tone is neutral or judgmental:

"Please pay attention and sing along with us."

B. Emotional tone is warm and engaging:

"Would you like to sit by me? These sounds are new, and I'm here to support you."

"It seems that you feel it's a bit noisy in here. Feel free to grab your headphones if you need to."

When you see a child avoiding certain kinds of touch

A. Emotional tone is pressured:

"Better hurry! You haven't started finger painting. Time's running out."

B. Emotional tone is warm and engaging:

"I see you don't really like touching the paint. Does it feel funny on your skin, sweetheart?"

"Maybe I can try it with you."

Taking into account the impact of emotional tone, create some phrases of your own that you could use to talk to a child about sensory preferences and different needs.

Name of child: _____

Phrases: _____

_____

We need to shift our priorities and give children compassionate messages about the wisdom of their own bodies rather than singling them out for their natural inclinations and adaptive reactions. It's also so important to work with speech therapists and communication experts who have an expanded, neurodevelopmental lens, in order to help children communicate as early as possible. Communication aids the process of *emotional co-regulation*, the key platform for learning and memory and the healing balm for soothing children's distress.

Before we attempt to shift behaviors, we need to understand what the behaviors tell us about a child's needs and internal experiences. When we do, children will be more likely to appreciate their own body sensations and inclinations. This approach will help us move away from many current practices that reflect narrow definitions of what constitutes "appropriate" behaviors in the world of autism treatment and support.

Modeling Awareness and Self-Compassion

Many opportunities present themselves to demonstrate awareness and compassion for our bodies and minds, allowing us to model for children to do the same. The breathing and self-compassion exercises in Chapter 4, in addition to the mindfulness resources in the appendix, will help you connect to your body (if doing so doesn't come naturally for you). At a minimum, this requires *us* to slow down enough to pay attention to what our bodies are telling us. The following handout suggests phrases that draw compassionate attention to our bodies' signals, so we as adults can model for children how we attend to those signals.

When we adults demonstrate an appreciation of the signals our bodies give us, we help children develop an appreciation for their own body signals. We are demonstrating something that can be difficult for many children on the autism spectrum: planning, sequencing, and adjusting motor actions. These children's challenges often result from differences in how their bodies access sensory information and use it to generate responses.

Instead of demanding that children shift their behaviors, we need to shift *our* approach. If you see a child's facial expression, gestures, or posture shift away from the green pathway toward red or blue, try lovingly exploring the shift with the child. The worksheet offers examples of phrases we can use to help children better tolerate and communicate with us as they pay attention to feedback from their bodies. Remember that children labeled as autistic have higher rates of sensory processing differences, which can make "ordinary" environmental experiences uncomfortable.

Modeling Attention to the Body's Signals

Simple statements can help children see that adults make use of their own bodily experiences and follow through on what to do about it. When making such statements, don't call attention to the child in an attempt to make it an explicit teaching moment. Instead, find opportunities to make comments nonchalantly while on your calm, green pathway. The following are only examples, and you can use your own experiences as they arise.

"My body is telling me to sit down for a moment." (Then sit down.)

"Those police sirens make me pay close attention." (As you slow the car and pull to the side of the road.)

"My tummy is making noises, and I feel hungry" (Then eat.)

"My eyes are telling me it's too bright in here" (Turn lights down.)

Naming what we are feeling and honoring those feelings with an associated action provides a powerful message about listening to the wisdom of our bodies as well as an example for children to do the same.

Helping Children Notice and Appreciate Bodily Feelings

Consider ways you can help a child utilize the information coming from body sensations.

You can customize these statements for the child's developmental and communication level. They can be presented auditorily or visually (spoken or with written words or pictures):

"It looks like you felt something, sweetheart. What might that be?"

"Is your body telling you something right now?"

"Your eyes are big. Is your body telling you to pay attention to something?"

"Looks like your body wants to move." And always allow and suggest access to human comforting experiences; such as." What does your body feel like it needs right now?" or "Would you like to sit or walk (or _____) with me?"

Customize and record statements that work for your child or the child you are working with: _____

_____

Soothing children—and helping them soothe themselves—through our engaged relationships helps support social and emotional development across their lifespan, from reactive infants to children who can observe themselves and communicate about what is going on in their bodies and minds.

Ordering Our Priorities

When we make compliance our first priority, we sometimes send children an unintended message: ignore your body. That was the message the school communicated to Norton, the boy who snapped his fingers to cope with anxiety. After a difficult year at his first school, his parents decided to move him to a small private school (not a luxury all families have). At the new school, students had the option of sitting on large exercise balls rather than chairs—or even on the floor if they chose to. The school also allowed children—within reason—to seek the self-generated sensory experiences they needed in order to be calm and attentive. Norton thrived in this new setting, remained his unique self, and moved on to a small, progressive public high school. Excelling in academics thanks to his exquisite memory, he graduated as his high school's salutatorian.

His success is a reminder that when addressing a challenging behavior, it's essential to ask these questions: Can we take the time and effort to understand the adaptive nature of a child's behavior before we act on changing it? Is there an opportunity here to show tolerance and change our attitudes rather than simply changing the child's behavior? Can we use the child's behavioral differences as a roadmap to providing the most supportive and innovative approaches, solutions that respect each child's unique neurodevelopmental profile?

In the next chapter, we will turn to another population of children who benefit from this shift in our understanding of behavioral challenges: those experiencing toxic stress, trauma, and other adverse childhood experiences.

Main Points —

- Behaviors in neurodiverse populations include the "constellation of adjustments and adaptations labeled people make to ease the circumstances of their lives."[29]

- Children have their own unique ways of responding to the world based on their individual differences.

- We need to assess a behavior's meaning for the child before we intervene in order to support a child's sense of interpersonal safety, autonomy, and independent decision-making.

8.
Supporting Behavioral Challenges in Children Exposed to Toxic Stress and Trauma

> *"I believe that when we each find the courage to look this problem in the face, we will have the power to transform not only our health, but our world."*
>
> **Dr. Nadine Burke Harris**

When children have experienced trauma, unrelenting stress, or both, their nervous systems are likely highly vulnerable, so it is important to handle their behavior issues with sensitivity and compassion. As with any child, it can be difficult both to discern what provoked a particular behavior and to determine the best way to help the child. In this chapter, we'll consider the impact of toxic stress and the best ways to respond to behavioral challenges in children exposed to adverse experiences.

We will do that by examining the cases of four different children: Jessie, Matt, Loren, and Lena. As we'll see, their life experiences, the approaches of the adults trying to help them, and the children's outcomes vary greatly, but all of their stories can help us grasp the complexity of helping such children, the mistakes we might make along the way, and the potential to create a positive difference in these children's lives.

Before we examine the children's stories, it's important to understand the impact of stress on the developing brain.

The Impact of Early Adverse Experiences on Brain Development

Stressful or traumatic experiences are often precursors to problematic behaviors. Some children have risk factors that may predispose them to emotional and behavioral challenges, including a range of "adverse childhood experiences," known by the acronym ACEs.[1]

Kaiser conducted the original ACE Study in collaboration with the Centers for Disease Control (CDC) in California from 1995 to 1997. Over seventeen thousand patients completed surveys about their early childhood experiences and their current health and lifestyle. The researchers surveyed adults about their history of various childhood adverse experiences including:

- Physical abuse

- Sexual abuse

- Emotional abuse

- Physical neglect

- Emotional neglect

- Intimate partner violence

- Violent treatment of the patient's mother

- Substance misuse within the household

- Household mental illness

- Parental separation or divorce

- Incarcerated household members

The researchers found that the more cumulative adverse childhood experiences an adult had, the more likely the person was to have health, interpersonal, and behavioral problems throughout his or her lifespan. The study was among the first to bring attention to early-childhood risk factors and the impact of trauma. It showed that it's useful to learn about and consider each child's history.

Along with the recent focus on ACEs has come the recognition of Trauma-Informed Care, an approach to helping children that "recognizes the presence of trauma symptoms and acknowledges the role that trauma has played in their lives."[2] Dr. Nadine Burke Harris, a pediatrician and founder of the Center for Youth Wellness in

San Francisco, has studied the health impacts of childhood adversity on development for many years. Her book, *The Deepest Well: Healing the Long-Term Effects of Childhood Adversity*, eloquently describes the heavy toll that toxic stress has on children's developing brains and advocates for parents and providers to help children affected by ACEs.[3]

Dr. Burke Harris and her colleagues conducted a retrospective chart review of 701 children, investigating the connection between childhood ACEs and children's health. Their findings were sobering. Children with more than four ACEs in their history were *32.6 times more likely* to be diagnosed with learning and behavior problems than children with fewer or no ACEs.[4] Though her study was correlational and doesn't prove causality, the data highlights the need for continued research and increased awareness of how trauma and toxic stress affect development.

In an interview, Dr. Burke Harris reported that brain MRI studies on children exposed to high levels of adversity and toxic stress show "a shrinking of the hippocampus [a brain area important for memory and emotional regulation] and increased size of the amygdala, which is the brain's fear center. This can make you hypervigilant—overly sensitive to threats or challenges."[5] This biological finding explains why children with high ACE scores often have learning difficulties: the hippocampus is responsible for creating and maintaining memory.

In short, when the stress response is repeatedly activated, brain development can become compromised. Traumatized children's behaviors and learning difficulties reflect this harmful effect of stress on the developing brain.

With that background, let's see what we can learn from examining the cases of four different individuals, starting with Jessie.

Jessie — Threatening Feelings and Memories Influencing Behaviors

Jessie, a child born to Marla, a high school senior, came into the world with a loud cry. His mother and father, Joe, Marla's high school classmate, decided to raise the child together and live with Marla's parents until they graduated and could support themselves.

With his grandmother caring for him during the day while his parents were at school, Jessie thrived, meeting all of his milestones. The whole family took pride in Marla and Joe when they graduated from high school with their class, baby in tow. They moved into a studio apartment with their son shortly after graduation, securing jobs with staggered shifts at a local fast-food restaurant so that they could care for their son without putting him in daycare.

The move proved difficult for everyone, including Jessie. At three months he had slept through the night at his grandmother's, but in these new surroundings, at eleven months, he began waking multiple times each night. Exhausted, financially strapped, and stressed, Marla and Joe argued frequently and loudly in front of Jessie. Nobody considered the toll the tension was taking on the child until they placed him, at age two, in a daycare center where he started biting other children.

What caused this? The move from his grandmother's home and his parents' domestic conflicts proved to be ACEs—early adverse childhood experiences. Accustomed to being the center of his grandmother's day, he was suddenly thrust into new surroundings with his overwhelmed and exhausted parents. Jessie experienced the red pathway of threat when he heard his parents' incessant yelling. Because sensory experiences are also emotional experiences, the sound of his parents' raised voices likely created threatening memories associated with certain loud noises and voices. This became an important part of the puzzle when it came to helping Jessie.

When I met the family, we began putting all the pieces together. My main priority was to help Marla and Joe feel safe with me, and to not see me as another professional or parent figure blaming them for their child's misbehaviors. Once we established a relationship of trust, we looked at their sources of stress and, without judgment, began to appreciate what Jessie's behaviors were communicating about his emotions.

When we analyzed what had happened in Jessie's young life, we located several sources of stress. The move (which gave him less time with his grandmother), hearing his parents' loud and threatening voices, interrupted sleep cycles, and the dramatic shift in his daily routines all likely contributed to his rough start in daycare. In fact, we discovered that Jessie generally bit children at the busiest and noisiest times during the day: free playtime. We surmised that all of the changes in his life lowered his thresholds for self-regulation, since the behavioral concerns began after these changes. A mild speech delay further intensified his automatic behaviors, because he couldn't quickly and easily tell others what was on his mind. I guessed that certain situations quickly triggered Jessie onto the red pathway, and without an easy way to voice his concerns, that's when he bit whomever was in close proximity. He was managing the stress he felt in his body. His fight-or-flight response was an adaptation to perceived threat.

Jessie's exposure to early adverse experiences likely contributed to vulnerability in his nervous system. His parents did their very best, but the stress of moving away from his beloved grandmother, compromised cycling into deep sleep, and his parents' loud arguing, degraded Jessie's developing sense of security. Additionally, his daycare teachers imposed rules and consequences when he "misbehaved." His stress responses were misinterpreted as intentional behaviors, so the consequences the teachers issued with stern voices only served to increase his general stress load. In terms of his house of social-emotional development, he began to have problems in the foundation and the framing of relationships, leading to difficulties in emotional regulation, which gave rise to his behavioral challenges.

What eventually helped Jessie was a multipronged approach. First, everyone in his life—his parents, grandmother, and teachers—prioritized his feelings of safety and security. Second, I referred Jessie and his parents to a pediatric speech therapist to address his speech delay through a developmental and relationship-based approach. Around the same time, a rent increase forced Marla and Joe to move back in with Marla's mother, Jessie's beloved grandmother. Over the next few months, with increased relational warmth from adults, and the familiarity and security of his grandmother (who could now pick him up from preschool at noon, much earlier than his parents had retrieved him), Jessie's challenging behaviors decreased.

Jessie's Iceberg

Intermittent biting at preschool

Compromised sleep/wake cycles

Neuroception of threat

Speech delay

Changes in physical and relational environment

Moving away from security/comfort of grandmother

Parents' domestic conflicts

Memories of loud voices

Shifts in daily routines

School setting where memories/feelings were triggered

Matt — Recognizing Signs of Trauma

Julia and Samuel endured many years of unsuccessful infertility treatments before they decided to adopt. They were thrilled when a social worker phoned with news that a pair of brothers needed a loving home. After months of paperwork, they finally adopted Matt, age three, and his brother, Rett, who was a year younger.

Family life proved exciting and tumultuous. Rett adjusted easily, sleeping well and smoothly recovering from disappointments on most days. Matt, on the other hand, had difficulty from the start. He woke multiple times each night crying and had difficulty paying attention in preschool. In kindergarten, he rarely played with peers, instead sitting alone and reading books. At home, Matt wasn't connecting to his adoptive parents and often lashed out at them verbally when he was angry.

At age seven, Rett discovered that Matt had set a fire in the family's basement. Another time, during an argument, Matt grabbed the family hamster from its cage and flung it at a wall, killing it.

A psychologist diagnosed Matt with a reactive attachment disorder as well as a conduct disorder and expressed concern about his difficulties socializing with others. The school provided counseling for the child as well as a behavioral treatment plan to support him. His teachers and parents were instructed to provide structure and offer positive reinforcement when Matt acted appropriately and swift natural consequences (such as missing recess) when he misbehaved.

Unfortunately, the support plans proved ineffective. With few friends, Matt became known as a loner and spent much of his time playing videogames on his own. After he threw a large pot at his mother, threatening to kill her, his parents grew desperate and alerted the police.

When I met Matt's parents, they told me that they had known he had been abused and neglected as a toddler, but they had hoped that the security and love they offered would help him thrive just as his brother had.

Matt's behaviors—social disengagement, harming animals, setting fires, and threatening his parents—all revealed a brain and body constantly on defense. He had never established the capacity for emotional regulation—the ability to cycle into consistent green pathways with his primary caregivers. Subsequently, all of his other developmental milestones were challenged, including his ability to engage with others, think through problems and situations, express his feelings, and reach out for help. *His aggressive behaviors were an early signal that he was detecting danger or life threat in his environment even when he was safe.* Matt's early physical and emotional injuries caused trauma that deeply impaired his ability to manage his emotions and cognitive abilities. They also harmed his ability to link his own goals to a broader common good, and this deficit had serious impact on his sense of justice.[6]

His teachers, doctors, and previous therapists had treated him using models based on the assumption that he had "disorders" instead of recognizing that his behaviors were unintentional, survival-based adaptations to early trauma. He was prescribed medication to aid his emotional regulation, as well as an intervention plan that focused on rewarding surface behaviors and punishing "maladaptive" behaviors. None of this helped. **Unfortunately, the three systems working to help Matt—the education system, the medical system, and the mental health system—operated independently, not coordinating or communicating about the most important factor in his life: his early exposure to toxic stress.**

Professionals and teachers communicated to Matt that he needed to *change* his behaviors, but they lacked a unified approach on how to help him. In fact, there was a reason he acted the way he did: his actions were automatic responses dating from multiple traumatic experiences early in his life, when he sensed life threat from those upon whom he depended. In the absence of any conscious awareness of his severe abuse, and with adults punishing him for these subconscious survival-based behaviors, he began to think negatively of himself and others.

Matt's Iceberg

Attentional difficulties

Peer interaction challenges

Fighting

Conflicts with parents

Setting fires

Harming animals

Red and blue pathway behaviors

ACEs

Early abuse and neglect

Toxic stress history

Faulty neuroception

Hypervigilance

Struggles with emotional regulation

Disorganized thoughts

The problem with Matt's treatment was that it focused on shifting his behaviors, without considering the causality in light of his history and the impact this history had on his individual differences. Unfortunately, the treatment approaches only served to reinforce his dark, emerging thoughts and feelings about himself and the world. He developed a narrative that assumed others were his enemies, and he had to punish them. His actions were a preemptive strike coming from a traumatized brain. Unfortunately, the time-outs and other punishments meted out to him only deepened his sense of isolation and the narrative that others were "out to get him."

Matt and his family's journey eventually led to Matt's hospitalization as an inpatient when he suddenly became suicidal and threatened to run away. His lengthy stay at the hospital included the benefit of the family meeting a psychiatrist, who evaluated all of the medications that Matt had been prescribed over his young life. The psychiatrist had recently been trained in trauma-informed care and suggested a new plan with fewer medications and increased relational support. She joined Matt's team and attended meetings with his parents, as Matt transitioned back to his home. I appreciated the dedication of this provider, who viewed her role as much more than monitoring his medications. Matt's parents decided to home-school him for the first year of high school, and everyone on his team is hopeful that he will have a promising future.

Loren — Unrelenting Toxic Stress

By any measure, Loren had a difficult early life. He was only four when authorities seized him from his biological parents after police, who had arrested his father for dealing drugs, found Loren tied to a bed. His mother had abandoned the family months earlier, and Loren had suffered physical and emotional abuse and neglect from an early age.

Clearly, Loren was traumatized by unrelenting toxic stress—the unrelieved activation of the body's stress management system in the absence of protective adult support.[7]

From there, things didn't get much better. Trying to give him a more stable home, authorities placed Loren with distant relatives. But soon after arriving, Loren began attacking their toddler son, hitting the child or pulling his hair when the toddler came too close. Unable to manage Loren, the couple soon asked his social worker to find him a new home.

Next he was placed with a couple who had four other foster children and were known for running a "tight ship." Loren's social worker hoped the family's structure and rules would help the child, but instead, he seemed easily triggered, repeatedly experiencing explosive outbursts, knocking food and dishes off tables, and striking people. That placement lasted less than a year.

Diagnosed with Oppositional Defiant Disorder (ODD), Attention Deficit Hyperactivity Disorder (ADHD), and a serious learning disability, Loren spent most of the next six years in a therapeutic group home with its own school. He was twelve when a peer in the lunch line tapped him from behind and Loren, startled, punched the boy so hard he broke his nose.

Over time, Loren's brain had become wired not for safety but for *defense*. His early and prolonged adverse experiences led to his unpredictable red-pathway behaviors—instinctive, defensive reactions even to seemingly unthreatening circumstances, caused by faulty neuroception.[8] These incidents continued to accumulate until, eventually, Loren found himself in juvenile hall, another statistic in the "school-to-prison pipeline."[9] **Like Loren, most youths who experience similar fates have experienced stress-loading conditions, including exposure to poverty, food insecurity, racism, and implicit bias.[10]**

Why didn't Loren get the help he desperately needed? Unfortunately, most of the significant adults in Loren's life lacked training in trauma-informed care. They simply didn't understand how best to support a child whose brain and body were exposed to trauma and unrelenting toxic stress.

The Problem with Rewards and Punishments

The adults in Loren's life—undoubtedly well meaning—did their best to help him. His foster parents and teachers generally took the same approach: rewarding "positive" behavior and giving consequences for "negative" behavior.

This approach didn't help Loren. Why? What these adults didn't understand was that the rewards-and-consequences paradigm didn't account for the level of injury Loren carried in his brain and body. While the techniques they used might have temporarily increased or decreased the targeted behaviors, they didn't significantly help Loren do what he needed most to do: regulate his responses to stress.

This became apparent in IEP meetings, at which the professionals and educators who worked with Loren repeatedly described Loren's challenging behavior as intentional and purposeful, rather than perceiving it as a result of developmental trauma.

Consider one administrator's comments about Loren's behaviors and motivation to learn:

- *"Loren is capable of doing far more than what he actually does."*

- *"Loren makes the choice to work or not work in school."*

- *"Loren is basically lazy, and chooses not to do the work."*

- *"Loren understands far more of his math and reading than he wants you to know."*

- *"Loren sabotages progressing in his school work."*

- *"Loren has a very bad temper."*

For six years, from when Loren was six until he was twelve, his teams tried to alter his behaviors by offering significant incentives for positive behaviors and docking privileges (such as group field trips and outings) for negative behaviors. No matter how hard Loren tried, he mostly lost privileges. And his mental health fluctuated between the blue pathway (despairing and refusing to leave his room) and the red pathway (striking out at others). A psychiatrist tried to help with medications for his symptoms, but ultimately that did little good since many of them caused side effects, from weight gain to extreme lethargy and sleepiness.

Understanding the Impact of Trauma

When Loren's case came up at a workshop I conducted for one of the agencies serving him, we discussed Trauma Theory, which "presupposes a cause for one's difficulties, and that cause is not an individual character flaw, a moral weakness, or innate malevolence, but a result of injury."[11]

That led to a discussion of Loren's iceberg and how the attributions we make determine how we interact and plan treatment. The iceberg analogy provided a deeper understanding of the *context* of behaviors and a way to shift how we viewed Loren's behavioral challenges.

> *Understanding that Loren's traumatized brain and body were prone to instinctive, survival-based red-pathway behaviors helped us arrive at a different approach, one that looked at the causes of his behaviors rather than the behaviors themselves.*

We discussed how the Polyvagal Theory could help us see his behaviors as adaptations to the experience of life threat—in short, as survival instincts.[12] What would benefit Loren most was shifting the target from behaviors themselves to social engagement and relationships. We then created an iceberg for Loren and began to look at his behaviors from a more trauma-informed perspective.

Loren's Iceberg

The child's fault

Aggressive behaviors

"Hair trigger" responses

DSM diagnoses of ODD and ADHD

Defiant

Avoids tasks

Lazy

Bad temper

Tests limits

Adaptation to one's life experiences and individual differences

Childhood abuse and neglect

Trauma

Toxic stress

Faulty neuroception

Broken relational attachments

Learning and memory deficits

System on continual "high alert"

Survival instincts

Intermittent activation of blue and red pathways

Targeting Relationships, Not Behaviors

As we shifted the target from behaviors to relationships, the first step in helping Loren was to analyze his current sources of relational support.

"Does Loren have anyone in his life he trusts, someone who makes him feel safe?" I asked.

Loren's social worker told me there was: Mary, a retired teacher and volunteer at the group home, had known Loren since he was nine and had a caring relationship with him, helping him with homework, routinely taking him to dinner, and strolling the neighborhood with him.

Mary had also helped his school team create a program to address Loren's learning disabilities.

In all the years Mary had spent time with Loren, the child had experienced only two behavioral outbursts with her. Mary hadn't been trained in trauma care, but it seemed that she intuitively grasped that the way to help children is through relationships.

Mary's connection with Loren clearly showed how a relationship can support the neuroception of safety, eliminating the child's need for defensive, self-protective behaviors. We should expect that children with histories of toxic stress or trauma will exhibit challenging behaviors. (Indeed, the behaviors helped them to survive.) *By forging relationships with them, we can aid them in shifting those subconscious, self-protective reactions, realizing they are no longer necessary.*

Bruce Perry, MD, senior fellow of the Child Trauma Academy, has studied trauma's impact on children for many years. Acknowledging the harmful effects of childhood trauma, he points out that "strong relational health can help protect children from lasting damage connected to these experiences and is essential to their resilience."[13]

Instead of pathologizing the behaviors of children exposed to trauma, we ought to shift our lens and match our methodologies for support to this new perspective. We can create new narratives about children like Loren, who surely wanted to do well, but whose traumatized brain made it difficult for him to learn and behave, through no fault of his own. As his connection with Mary makes clear, the way to help shift children from a default of threat to safety is by rebuilding their sense of safety in relationships.

Helping Children Exposed to Toxic Stress or Trauma

As we have learned in previous chapters, once we make a shift to view behavioral challenges as serving *adaptive purposes* for children like Loren, our strategies to manage the behaviors shift as well. The basic pattern is the same for all behaviorally challenged children, but those exposed to trauma have additional emotional vulnerability. These children often exhibit extreme and unpredictable behavioral challenges, so we need to proceed with more caution and precision to avoid inadvertently making matters *more* stressful with solutions aimed at the wrong targets.

One important step is to obtain a comprehensive history of a child's relational and physical environment: At what age was she was exposed to adverse experiences? During the first year or two of life? Was the stress chronic or did the child have cycles of relational safety? Was there one consistent and stable adult in the child's life?

Providing Support and Acknowledging Injustices

Shifting how we conceptualize challenging behaviors in traumatized populations takes time, human resources, and training. What's essential is to collaborate with parents and caregivers to help children develop self-awareness and learn about emotional self-care in a culturally respectful way that suits their unique needs. It's important to provide children and families access to therapists trained in trauma-informed practices who will work with them while respecting each family's experiences, individual differences, culture, learning pathways and abilities, and social-emotional development. *This includes considering the impact of poverty, race, power, and privilege on an individual's perception of the world as safe or unsafe. In a world rife with injustices, we must acknowledge the additional burden of threat children of color experience.*

Providing Predictability and Preparing Children for Changes in Routines

Predictability is comforting to most children, especially those with exposure to adverse childhood experiences. Child trauma survivors often find it difficult to adapt to unexpected changes, think flexibly, or solve problems when things don't go as they anticipated. When changes happen too suddenly or without sufficient warning—even if adults perceive the changes as positive or benign—it can send a child down a red pathway.

Loren, for example, often experienced emotional disruptions when faced with unexpected changes, which came all too often in the foster-care system. Once, a benefactor offered Loren's social worker tickets for a baseball game just hours before the event. Knowing that Loren was a fan of the team, the social worker quickly arranged for him and some peers to attend the game. The problem: because of a communication error, nobody had told Loren about the plan until a driver arrived to pick up the group.

On the surface, Loren seemed to adjust to the unexpected outing, but inside, he was struggling to handle such a spontaneous shift in routine—even for an event he should have enjoyed. As soon as the group arrived at the stadium, Loren got into a fight with one of the other foster children, punching him in the stomach. In neurodevelopmental language, such an unpredictable outburst is called a *sensitized stress response*, a moment when a child's behavior appears to be unpredictable, and the child seems to be "walking on eggshells."[14]

Nobody on his team anticipated that the trip could be so powerful that it triggered him onto a bright red pathway. Disappointed in Loren's behavior and hoping to teach him that he needed to control himself better, a supervisor punished him for the outburst later, confiscating his iPad.

What might have prevented all of this? If the team had access to information about Loren's sensitivity to sudden changes or transitions, somebody could have taken the time to tell Loren what to expect from the experience, or, when things went awry, sensitively discussed with him how he felt about what happened. Trauma-informed practice helps caregivers learn how to understand and contextualize triggering life experiences for children in order to help them in their trauma recovery.

In Loren's case, circumstances continued to conspire against him. I learned a year after the workshop that Mary, who had forged such a strong connection with Loren, had moved away. Within months, Loren was back in juvenile detention—another statistic. **He had been propelled through the foster-care system, disconnected from practice guidelines that help trauma victims overcome the damage created by relational abuse and neglect.**

But there is hope for Loren and others like him. Programs such as Sandra Bloom's Sanctuary Model trainings aim directly at fixing this problem, through an informed approach about trauma and the brain, and could well become a standard of care for trauma victims.[15] Bruce Perry, a trauma expert, considers this model among the best, offering a range of trainings for individuals and agencies.[16]

Supporting Predictability and Managing Changes in Routine

We can help prevent emotional and behavioral disruptions through structured support to buffer the stress of unexpected changes in routines for children. While it's best to prepare children for changes (as described in the following worksheet), sometimes the unexpected happens. *When it does, our frontline tool is the therapeutic use of ourselves.* In such moments, it's important to increase emotional cues of safety to the child by sitting down or walking with the child as soon as possible. If possible, we should take a few moments to explain what the change is and when it will happen.

Children recovering from trauma and toxic stress benefit from predictability. We can increase predictability by communicating with children about their schedules in advance so that they know what to expect. In addition to talking about schedules, we can use visual signs, posters, or a whiteboard with pictures or words to help children prepare for each day and week. For children who have difficulty remembering or understanding sequences, seeing something in pictures or other symbols can make a big difference. And you can shift things on the board, adding or subtracting a picture or writing in the new plan when there's a change coming.

Supporting Predictability and Managing Changes in Routine

We can provide predictability by giving children a visual or auditory schedule or by combining the two.

Visual: If a child is a visual learner, then using a whiteboard, poster, or other visual device, write down the child's daily schedule, starting from the morning. If the child can better understand pictures, use photographs or pictures of the events and place them in sequence on the board. If a sudden change happens, alter the writing or the picture to reflect the change, so that the child sees it and can begin the mental process of shifting expectations and develop the ability to cope with the unexpected change in routine.

Auditory: If a child is an auditory learner, you can create a routine by talking to the child about the daily schedule starting in the morning. You can tailor the schedule to the child and make it fun and interactive by asking the child if she knows what comes first, second, third, etc., in her day, talking about or even singing about the sequence of the day, increasing the child's sense of predictability.

If a sudden change happens, talk about it as soon as possible, and engage the child using your own calming emotional green pathway to help her back to her own.

Allowing Flexibility, Control and Choices

To recap, while structure and predictability generally help children, it's even more important to attune to what each child's nervous system is requiring of them in real time. When we attune to what children need with an eye on whether or not they are feeling safe, we realize that we must also allow the child flexibility, control, and choices.

Children also benefit from having control and experiencing flexibility as they learn how to adapt to changes. This can be especially helpful when a child's pathway begins to veer away from the green and toward red. We need to remember that controlling one's environment (even if it is through an aggressive behavior) is an (unintentional) *adaptive* response for children who previously had *no control* over stressful or life-threatening circumstances.

We can help children gradually expand their flexibility by allowing choices over simple decisions such as the order in which they do things ("Would you like to do your spelling first or math?") or how they spend their free time or even small things such as who goes first in a board game. *We use the color pathways as a guide to titrate our interactions and help kids stretch to a "light green" pathway. I described this previously as Vygotsky's "zone of proximal development," in which children are poised to learn new things but not be overwhelmed by them.*

It's beneficial to build in the time and space for a child to decide flexibly (within reason) what the child wants to do based on what the child is managing at a given point in time. Doing so has the dual benefit of encouraging awareness in the present moment and flexing problem-solving muscles. We can also model flexibility in our own thinking as adults when the unexpected happens. (When the dinner casserole burns, for instance, we can joyfully opt to serve breakfast foods for dinner.)

> *Bruce Perry sums it up well: "We cannot emphasize enough how important it is for traumatized children to be given the most possible control, predictability, and ability to moderate the timing, duration, and intensity of their experiences."[17]*

Reducing Staff Turnover

It's also important to try avoiding staff turnover. Children in the foster-care system experience inordinately high turnover rates of their foster parents, therapists, counselors, and teachers. Consistency in relationships matters. The essential factor in helping children who suffer from the effects of toxic stress and trauma is to build (or rebuild) trust in human relationships. We use that which was absent and originally contributed to the trauma—caring adults to rescue the child—to begin the healing process while we create new memories of safety and protection to begin to build up the child's sense of trust. **As Dr. Porges teaches: "safety is treatment and treatment is safety."**[18]

Questions to Ask about Interventions for Children Exposed to Toxic Stress and Trauma

- Does my intervention increase or decrease the child's sense of safety?

- Am I encouraging consistent messages of safety through my interactions or techniques?

- Am I inadvertently sending messages to the child that something is inherently wrong with him or her?

- How is the child's behavior an adaptation or survival strategy that originally emerged to protect the child from the neuroception of threat?

What to Avoid in Working with Children Experiencing Trauma or Toxic Stress

When approaching behavioral challenges in vulnerable children or teens, we should avoid punitive measures—including paddling and other forms of corporal punishment, sequestering, isolating, ignoring, shaming, or blaming. Punishment can trigger a child into deeper levels of autonomic nervous system distress.

Point and Level Systems

We should also consider the potential adverse consequences of other popular behavior-management techniques, such as point and level systems (in which children lose or gain privileges or things according to their behaviors). If a child is not yet using his own top-down capacities to modulate bottom-up stress responses, such practices can have adverse consequences, moving the child away from the green pathway of relatedness. *Continually losing privileges can drive a child to hopelessness and despair, especially when the child continues to lose things because of behaviors the child cannot yet control.*

Disciplinary Techniques Not Recommended for Children

- Any type of physical or corporal punishment

- Seclusion, isolation, or solitary confinement

- Indiscriminate use of shackles on minors in court

- Isolating, sequestering, shaming, blaming, or ignoring

- Point and level systems for behavioral management

- Yelling, screaming at, shaming, or degrading children

Perhaps one day, experiences such as Loren's will enable researchers to pinpoint and discover better ways to address the impact of trauma and toxic stress on body and mind. Until then, we can use the wisdom of basic neuroscience to begin to shift how we view the underpinnings of behaviors in vulnerable populations. All of us who care for and work with vulnerable children can work toward an environment ensuring that safe, responsive relationships with caring adults become a frontline approach and standard of care to prevent or reverse the damaging effects of toxic stress and trauma in children.

Variations in the Experience of Trauma and Toxic Stress in Children

Children with a history of multiple adverse experiences run a higher risk of developmental, health, and mental health challenges, but how children interpret and respond to those experiences varies widely. As Lena's experience illustrates, even children without typical risk factors can experience intense stress reactions.

Lena — An Endless Series of Battles

When Ruth's husband moved abroad on short notice for a job opportunity, her eight-year-old daughter Lena took it in stride at first. But two months later, something shifted. Suddenly, Lena began turning every day into a series of battles—over everything from brushing her teeth to taking a shower to doing homework.

"Everyday life has become a challenge," the mother told me when she came to me for help, referred by Lena's pediatrician. Ruth felt defeated and exhausted by the constant fighting with her daughter, who would scream such harsh invective at Ruth that it brought the mother to tears.

I suggested that Ruth start a journal of her daughter's behaviors and reactions for a few weeks. Analyzing her entries in a session without Lena, the mother and I discovered a clear pattern: Lena mainly protested the activities that her father had supervised before his departure.

Before her husband had moved away, Ruth had worked night shifts as a nurse, sleeping by day. The father had been the one to pick up Lena from daycare, help with her homework, and supervise her bedtime routine. Instead of hiring a sitter after her husband relocated, Ruth switched to a day shift, thinking that her presence in the evening would help Lena tolerate her dad's absence and benefit their relationship.

After several sessions with the two, I privately suggested to Ruth that Lena's extreme and challenging reactions to previously unremarkable events were likely stress reactions to the departure of her father. With her beloved father away, Lena's emotional thresholds plummeted. Everyday activities that had been easy before became battlegrounds between mother and daughter.

Still, whenever mother asked daughter how she felt about her dad's departure, Lena insisted she was "fine." In truth, she wasn't. And Ruth's well-intentioned approach to parenting Lena—incentives, talking to her, and imploring her to behave better—only served to *increase* Lena's red-pathway behaviors. She had even purchased a book for Lena that taught children and teens how to deal with negative thoughts and feelings.

Lena, feeling defensive about most everything, wanted nothing to do with the book.

The problem: Ruth was using *top-down* approaches to try solving a *bottom-up* issue: Lena's feelings of loss and grief were stuck inside, without a way out through communication channels. Lena wasn't yet able to acknowledge, access, or even think about her feelings about her dad, so her mother's asking her to discuss them was premature. Lena's experience of suddenly losing the presence of her beloved father sent her into high levels of stress, which was channeled into her behaviors.

Ruth shifted in her perception of Lena, now grasping that her daughter wasn't *choosing* to be difficult—she was *suffering*. With more compassion and less judgment, Ruth changed her strategies to work from the bottom-up first: to engage first, talk less, and listen more. I urged Ruth to playfully engage her daughter on the green pathway as often as possible, as the first step in supporting her top-down abilities— that is, to *build up* Lena's ability to cope with her pain and suffering not by talking but by finding moments of joyful interaction together.

Ruth filled out sensory preference worksheets to match pleasurable experiences with joyful sensory interactions. Positive interactions became the template for Ruth to help her daughter fortify her social-emotional development and recover from the stress she experienced as a result of her father's sudden departure.

Lena's Iceberg

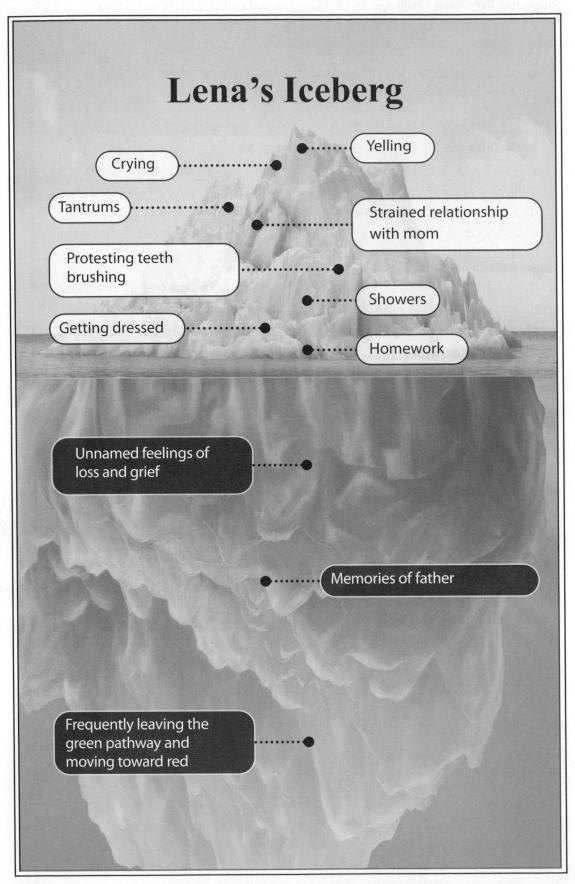

Yelling

Crying

Tantrums

Strained relationship with mom

Protesting teeth brushing

Showers

Getting dressed

Homework

Unnamed feelings of loss and grief

Memories of father

Frequently leaving the green pathway and moving toward red

I explained to Ruth that she needed to be on her own green pathway in order to create moments of joyful interaction with Lena—those connected moments that have the power to heal pain and sadness. She hadn't realized that her husband's abrupt departure had also stretched her own emotional resources. I began with a few sessions with Ruth by herself to focus on supporting her own emotional transition to being—temporarily—a single parent.

The focus of my therapeutic sessions with Lena and Ruth was to discover what brought them *both* into joyful interactions. Using the broad definition of play—*anything that supports and energizes a pleasurable, organic, and back-and-forth flow of exchanges*—I encouraged Ruth to follow Lena's lead and interests. As she began to study her daughter, she found that Lena loved hearing her mom sing songs from her childhood. We started at the foundation for both mother and child by helping Lena experience a warm, cozy green pathway through emotional co-regulation with her mom, who *also* needed emotional support.

At home, Ruth stayed closer physically to her daughter, offering to give her light "massages" when Lena took breaks from her homework. It wasn't long before their relationship warmed, as Lena enjoyed her mom's increased attention and empathy.

After a couple of months, we began to see progress in Lena's social-emotional house. More often on her green pathway, she began to give voice to her feelings and thoughts. The therapeutic work, promoting healing joyful interactions—the bottom-up foundation of emotional development—was now supporting the reemergence of her top-down abilities. In one of our final sessions together, Lena told her mother how much she missed her father and how lonely she felt without him. Finally, she had a way to express her feelings of loss and sadness through verbal communication within a trusting relationship with her mom, and her disruptive behaviors began to decrease.

Shifting the Lens and Understanding How Behaviors are Adaptive

When we view behaviors as *intentional*, we tend to use disciplinary strategies aimed at a surface target rather than the underlying cause of the behavior (a child's response to stress). When we view them instead as *adaptive coping mechanisms*, it leads to understanding and compassion. Ruth's experience with Lena shows that when a child is experiencing bottom-up reactions, our best response is to increase—not decrease—cues of relational engagement and safety.

When we appreciate children's behaviors for what they are telling us about the child's internal life, we experience a paradigm shift, moving from viewing behaviors negatively to seeing them as providing useful information about how to raise the child.

We move beyond the notion that children only use challenging behaviors to establish authority, test limits, or avoid tasks, to include the idea that challenging behaviors can be signals that the child is experiencing excessive stress.

Ross Greene, the founder of the Collaborative and Proactive Solutions (CPS) explains that when a child is challenging, it's a sign that something is getting in the way of the child meeting a demand.[19] In his groundbreaking and lens-shifting book *The Explosive Child*, Greene describes the factors that contribute to challenging behaviors as *unsolved problems* or *lagging skills* resulting in an inability to meet adult expectations.[20] The CPS approach brings the child and adults into a conversation in which each can share and collaborate in solving the behavior challenge. CPS is a revolutionary, excellent approach for children and teens once they are able to formulate and articulate their ideas and share them with concerned adults.

This was the happy point Ruth and Lena reached: relating, conversing, and exchanging information with each other as partners, not adversaries. Through a bottom-up approach, with relational interactions leading the way, Ruth no longer considered Lena a "problem child." Instead, she delighted in her daughter's newfound ability to talk about her struggles, a capacity that grew from her ability to co-regulate her emotions with her mom.

Aiming our Supports for Vulnerable Populations of Children

Clearly, Lena and Loren experienced starkly different outcomes. Loren, who suffered adversity in the first three years of his life, was more vulnerable. Bruce Perry's research at the Child Trauma Academy (and via a research network of clinical partners of over thirty thousand individuals) found significant increased vulnerability for children who were exposed to relational toxic stress in the first year of life.[21]

Professionals sometimes refer to "big-T" trauma and "little-t" trauma, to denote the differences in severity and accumulation of events in a person's life. Big-T trauma often involves helplessness and the perception of life threat, while little-t trauma involves life events that are distressing and exceed the person's ability to cope, but are not necessarily experienced as life-threatening.[22]

We can surmise that Loren experienced early, sustained, big-T trauma. Loren's and Lena's contrasting outcomes are likely related to the timing, duration, and severity of their exposure, as well as the fact that Loren didn't have a consistent, healthy adult presence once his friend Mary moved away.

It's worth noting that as a member of a minority group, Loren faced additional, lifelong risks in our culture with its implicit bias. As Dr. Perry points out, "True rehabilitation will not be possible without awareness of the multiple, complex effects of trauma, neglect, poverty, racism, and other developmental adversities."[23]

In contrast, Lena's privileged background didn't include the additional ACEs that Loren faced. Compared to Loren, she had more opportunities to develop psychological resilience, and a greater likelihood of stress tolerance. Her experience shows why this chapter's suggestions are so critical for children who don't or didn't have stability in their early relationships—including foster children and others whose early lives were disrupted and who lacked the buffering effect of adult support during those disruptions.

In almost thirty years of practice, I have witnessed children exposed to the wide range of trauma human beings can experience. I believe that when children's trauma is patiently addressed through loving, consistent relationships, as Dr. Porges writes, eventually the brain "can reorganize how our body feels."[24]

Main Points —

- Assume that a child exposed to toxic stress or trauma will exhibit behavioral challenges that are stress responses, remnants of protective, defensive responses to the originating events.

- Seek relational connection with the child as a first-line strategy, using bottom-up techniques before top-down approaches, and paying attention to the child's social-emotional development.

- Keep an eye on the child's color pathways (autonomic states) with the goal of attuning emotionally to help the child get back to the green pathway when activated onto the other two stress pathways.

- Work upward in the House of Social-Emotional Development to help a child symbolize feelings and thoughts to organize experiences, develop self-awareness, and contextualize stress responses.

9.

Hope for the Future and Plenty to Do Now

> *"When a flower doesn't bloom you fix the environment in which it grows, not the flower."*
> Alexander Den Heijer

Imagine this scenario: Lucia is a quiet and inquisitive three-year-old who struggles to control her behaviors. At a routine physical, her pediatrician observes how anxious Lucia is and warmly invites the family for a follow-up appointment. There, the mother fills out a simple questionnaire with details about Lucia's social and emotional development. The pediatrician reassures the mother that behavioral challenges in young children provide rich information about how best to tailor interactions and the environment for children. Her mother leaves feeling hopeful about helping her daughter and grateful for such a caring doctor.

A week later, Lucia's parents meet with the pediatrician to discuss a plan for precise support for their sweet daughter, who seems to spend too little time playing, laughing, and having fun—the "work" of toddlerhood. The pediatrician explains that one possible explanation for Lucia's challenges is that her autonomic nervous system tends to detect threat even in the comfort of her home and school environments.

"The earlier we discover a child's vulnerabilities," says the doctor, "the better we can support her physical and emotional development." A pediatric occupational therapist joins them, reviewing the information gathered by the pediatrician. In a reassuring tone, she asks the parents about Lucia. She's often "fine," they report, when the environment is predictable and she isn't facing unexpected events, but Lucia can struggle with simple and fun activities such as mall outings and dance classes. The parents schedule a "playdate" for Lucia in the OT's gym. Vulnerable children, the therapist explains, can learn to become "friends" with their nervous systems, and develop psychological resilience in the process.

Next, the pediatrician gives Lucia's parents a cute decorated wristband for Lucia to wear that will monitor the girl's stress load and sleep cycles. The device can detect when a child enters a physiological stress response as measured by electrodermal activity (EDA) through the skin. It will simultaneously deliver data to the parents' smartphones, and the pediatrician's confidential database, helping doctor and parents to discover what triggers Lucia's stress responses and, ultimately, how best to help her face life's challenges.

The parents leave the appointment filled with optimism and gratitude for these confident professionals who are helping their family and their beloved only child.

This is where I hope our understanding, research, and innovations are leading. I imagine a future in which parents enjoy the emotional support of a diverse team of childhood professionals who speak the same language of child development. I envision parents not being blamed and second-guessing themselves when their child has behavioral challenges. I envision a world in which we don't automatically label children with disorders, but rather appreciate their individual differences for the information they provide about how to best support the child.

The Future Is Now

This sort of world already exists at places like New York State's Center for Discovery, where autistic and neurodiverse individuals receive highly advanced, supportive, and holistic treatment informed by cutting-edge research. There, new "wearable" technology, like Lucia's wristband, measures EDA through biometric sensors, allowing experts to provide data on how stress contributes to challenging behaviors for individuals with vulnerable nervous systems.[1]

Instead of focusing on behavior management or teaching isolated skills, specialists at the center can measure how much cumulative stress a child experiences throughout the day. They partner with top universities including MIT and Harvard to conduct research that improves the quality of life for individuals and families by addressing underlying stress-inducing biomedical conditions, including sleep disorders, gastrointestinal problems, seizure disorders, obesity, immune and metabolic problems, and anxiety.[2]

To be sure, the Center for Discovery's approach is a new way to support individuals diagnosed with autism and complex medical and neurological profiles. This trend toward looking below the surface and valuing behaviors for what they tell us about an individual's needs, will enhance treatments, strategies, and approaches for all children, regardless of the diagnosis. I hope the Center for Discovery's research institute and its university affiliates will continue to study the complex feedback loops of the brain and body, providing a model with applications in many other settings. This new type of research, linking the physiological state with observable behaviors (through sense technology) has the potential to enlighten all of us about the impact of stress on multiple areas of functioning, helping us understand how to support individuals with persistent behavioral challenges.[3]

Already, national leaders in mental health research are encouraging us to move beyond our traditional understanding of "pathology" and labels. As we have discussed, the National Institutes of Mental Health (NIMH) now encourages research into *underlying processes* that cut across diagnoses and are relevant to a range of human behaviors and conditions rather than into simple *DSM* diagnoses.[4] This approach gives researchers "the freedom to address research questions beyond the constraints of *DSM* categories, in ways that integrate behavior and neuroscience."[5] The hope is that this will help provide useful, practical information that will reveal more effective ways of monitoring and decreasing children's stress loads. Technology and *new ways of thinking* will help us better understand how to support vulnerable children, teens, and adults, targeting the precursors of behaviors and not simply their end products—the behaviors themselves.

What We Can Do Now

We don't have to wait to help vulnerable children, however. Research on human stress has already given us a basic understanding of the value of moving away from reductionistic models in health care and mental health.[6]

As we have seen, we are social beings with social brains, and regardless of a child's challenges, the pathway to healing and support cannot circumvent attuned relationships. Psychologist Louis Cozolino reminds us that above all else, the brain is a "social organ of adaptation" that evolved over a long period to help human beings survive.[7] "And by a social organ," he says, "I mean that humans have evolved to be linked to and learn from other brains in the context of emotionally significant relationships."[8] To help our challenged children, there is no substitute for attuned relationships.

Over many years working with children, teenagers, and families, I have developed a profound appreciation for the brain's *adaptability*. Again and again I have witnessed that when a child's team values a behavior *for what it tells us about a child's needs* while diligently supporting the child's developmental processes through human engagement, behavioral challenges decrease.

Shifting Strongly Held Beliefs

Viewing the brain as a social organ of adaptation allows us to trust that children's behaviors hold valuable information. Rather than being a sign of a "disordered" or "willfully defiant" child, behavioral challenges are signals that the child's experience of the world compels adaptations.

> *When we use the lens of adaptation, as opposed to the lens of conscious misbehavior, we are better equipped to provide the necessary prerequisites to support children: compassion and understanding.*

Doing so requires dispelling some of the notions that fuel popular strategies based on top-down motivation (such as malicious intent), moving from viewing behaviors as necessarily negative (e.g., attention seeking) to viewing them as a roadmap for helping the child.

Combating the Negativity Bias

The reality is that many of us have our own reflexive, negative responses when children do things that confuse, anger, or frighten us. In fact, contemporary neuroscience can help us understand *why* children's negative behaviors are so triggering for adults: human beings experience a "negativity bias," a tendency to remember negative events more than positive or neutral ones.[9]

According to neuropsychologist Rick Hanson, PhD, this tendency emerged over the millions of years our brains developed, as remembering a predator or other threat was necessary and essential for survival.[10] That helps explain why we tend to overlook positive events in our lives and focus more on the negative. (It also explains why it's so compelling to watch or read the news—especially bad news.) In Dr. Hanson's words, "Your brain is like Velcro for negative experiences but Teflon for positive ones."[11] Children's behaviors can so easily activate the negativity bias because so much is at stake, and the burden of responsibility for the adults in charge is so high. (The next time your child or a child you work with triggers you into a less than optimal response, you can blame the negativity bias!)

Now let's step back for a moment and consider how the negativity bias influences our interactions with children. Since our brains are wired for paying attention to negative experiences over positive ones, when we witness a child doing something that we perceive will decrease their well-being, survival, or safety, it becomes our priority to shift the behavior (and protect the child) as quickly as possible. This is a natural tendency for well-meaning parents, caregivers, and providers. Understanding this helps those of us who parent and work with behaviorally challenged children perceive why we feel so compelled to act upon children's challenging behaviors as quickly as possible. The negativity bias simply makes it more likely for us to notice children's negative rather than positive behaviors.

This is likely a reason parents and caregivers of children with additional needs experience greater levels of anxiety and hypervigilance.[12] We carry an understandable burden of responsibility to protect and nurture our children. The burden gets supercharged under certain conditions because humans are hardwired to look out for negative or threatening events.[13]

But we can counteract the negativity bias through our awareness. When we demystify behaviors, we turn them into something we need not fear. When we fear less, we judge ourselves and our children's behaviors less harshly. And then we are that much closer to engaging together in ways that nourish the brain. This is good news, because most parents feel judged most of the time.[14] If we are calmer and less pressed into punitive action—which often compels us to "fix" a child as soon as possible—we nurture the very tool that holds the most promise for helping our children: ourselves.

Parents and caregivers of behaviorally challenged children face constant stress and vigilance. Few things are more threatening to a parent than learning that your child has a diagnosis or disability, that your child is aggressive and harming others, or that your child's mental health is compromised. Unfortunately, too many parents have told me that the unspoken, underlying message they receive all too often is that the child's negative behavior is somehow the result of their poor parenting.

The desire to make things better, mixed with the prevailing standards and approaches to behavioral challenges, often pits parents and providers against each other in IEPs or other educational meetings. It's useful for us to reflect on the large burden of responsibility we carry to protect the labeled child and those around him.

Hardwiring Happiness

How can we combat the negativity bias, live more freely on the green pathway, and help our kids realize their potential and grow up to be happy and resilient? It takes work, but we can actually "hardwire happiness," as Rick Hanson teaches.[15] When we have good experiences, they build up over time and begin to replace persistent negative thoughts or memories. Dr. Hanson describes the four steps with the acronym HEAL,[16] which stands for:

Have a positive experience

Enrich it

Absorb it

Link positive and negative material

I use the first three of these steps when I work with families and talk to parents and providers about supporting healthy brain/body connections for children.

Creating Positive, Enriching Experiences to Support the Child's (and Parent's) Green Pathways

We form memories through experience, and we can intentionally use positive experiences to build new neural connections in our brains, and the brains of our children or the children we work with.[17] Single moments, added together over time, create lasting memories. Simply stated, we can make a positive difference by increasing the number of positive experiences we and our children have. In doing so, we should let our hearts lead the way.

Too often, we are expected to have a reason, goal, or thought behind everything we do. In the flurry of prescribed activities, therapies, exercises, and data-tracking sheets, we sometimes lose sight of a vital element: experiencing playful, spontaneous joy, a potent elixir for children's development.

A Note for Parents

More and more, I prescribe not specific activities, but experiences. I encourage parents to trust their hearts more and engage their children in joyful experiences more often. Doing so often leads parents to feel spontaneous gratitude for the child as he is, rather than constantly working on pushing the child to where professionals, educators, or others want him to be. Sometimes it seems as if the message we give children is that they are "improvement projects." *To be sure, this doesn't mean we should reduce or dilute services for children or avoid professional help.* But we should prioritize children's developmental health first through attuned and connected relationships. Throughout the book, I have explained why this makes sense from a neurodevelopmental perspective.

When my daughter was in kindergarten, her teacher intuitively understood the power of human connection for a child's ability to learn. Every morning the teacher stood at the classroom door, greeting each student on a bent knee, shaking each student's hands or lightly touching each child on the arm or shoulder, offering greetings in a soothing, calm voice and with a beautiful smile. Her classroom was a happy place for my child, who thrived there.

Knowing that my daughter was in such good hands made me feel better as a mom, countering the hesitation and anxiety I felt because my daughter was among the youngest students in the class. Whether she realized it or not, the teacher was simultaneously teaching children and soothing parents through the therapeutic use of herself. It's simply reassuring to turn over your child over to an adult who you trust will value the child's emotional health as much as you do.

That point was also driven home by a viral video that captured Barry White Jr., a North Carolina teacher who welcomes every child in his elementary-school class with a different daily greeting.[18] Every single student and the teacher share a unique, choreographed handshake/dance move, which the teacher remembers and pulls off flawlessly. Like my daughter's kindergarten teacher, Mr. White helps each child feel safe, valued, and special. What better way to start a day than creatively infusing a child's environment with fun-filled personalized cues of interpersonal safety?

These educators both intuitively understand the power of interpersonal experiences in education. They intentionally create positive experiences when children need it the most—at the beginning of the school day, the most stressful moment for many children. And they don't stop there. They use techniques that set the best platform for learning. They take their time, enriching positive experiences, and in doing so, help children absorb the value of those experiences by making them last long enough to form memories, affecting the children's brains magnificently.[19]

Shifting the Experiences We Provide Children to HEAL

What can we learn from these teachers' examples? Our children's brains are transformed by experience, thanks to another neuroscientific phenomenon: neuroplasticity. In other words, our experiences constantly modify the neural connections in our brains.[20] In short, experiences matter! We need to make sure that the experiences we provide to children (and expose their parents to) are healthy and good for their developing brains. This book has presented examples of both types of experiences.

I hope those who oversee and work in the fields of education, behavioral support, mental health, juvenile justice, and social welfare (to name a few) will consider whether an intervention or approach is good for a child's brain before implementing that intervention or approach. Much has changed in a century and a half since many of our educational and training programs were established. We need to update those training programs based on what we now know about how to best support our children's growing and malleable minds and bodies.

It's Good to Increase Positive Experiences

It's worth asking: How many positive experiences are we providing and encouraging our children to have? Children, like adults, are also wired for the negativity bias, and we need to offer them positive experiences to counteract it.[21] When children are behaviorally challenged, adults routinely give them more negative than positive messages. One is that our positive attention is conditional and dependent upon their behaviors, a message that generates additional stress in children who don't yet have top-down control over their behaviors. *They find themselves in a no-win cycle: their uncontrolled behavioral responses meet up with negative interpersonal consequences, which increase their stress load, causing even more problematic behaviors—and on and on.*

Instead, we should provide positive relational experiences in order to fortify their social and emotional foundations. That's *not* to say that we should allow children to misbehave or make all the decisions or that we should downplay the logical consequences of behaviors. But we should make efforts to have more positive relational experiences with children.

Quantity Matters

Indeed, the quality and quantity of time we spend with children matters. Children need multiple positive experiences in order for the changes to register in their brain networks because *neurons that fire together wire together.*[22] In other words, the more you do something, the more it becomes ingrained into function and memory. By providing positive, enriching experiences for children we help them build their house of social and emotional development, one step at a time.

How do we start helping children in our overscheduled lives? One way is to rethink our priorities. It's important for children to have enriching academic experiences, but it's even more crucial to find time when they can connect with others through positive and joyful experiences. We can start by slowing down ourselves. Chapter 4 offered some suggestions for how we can do this as adults, allowing the benefits to extend to our children. If we are constantly *doing,* it sends children a message about how we value our time. Slowing down and modeling *being* more present with children, sends a different message. This notion is foundational to growing the green pathway, and decreasing the stress load our bodies are constantly managing. Many of us lead such busy lives that we don't slow down until the signals arrive too late, in the form of high blood pressure, physical illness, or chronic disrupted sleep. When we pay attention to our own pacing and biorhythms, we become more present and better able to signal cues of safety for our children and those we work with.

Here are some simple ideas to slow down and share positive, enriching experiences with children:

Intentionally look at the child with warmth and connection. Sit by the child and connect with your own state at the moment. If you are not on a solid green pathway, notice that without judgment, and try to recenter yourself so that you feel more present. Then, look momentarily at the child's eyes (or in the child's general direction if the child finds eye contact uncomfortable), with calmness, warmth, and presence. Try just to sit for a moment, focusing on the child and taking in the child's inherent goodness through your senses. Doing so can help us counterbalance our own (expected) hypervigilance and assessing, scrutinizing, teaching, or anticipating the next meltdown.

Ask the child what she would like to do with you. With all of the pressures and demands of raising and working with children, we often *tell* children what to do rather than *ask* what they would like to do with us. It's fine for children to occupy themselves, but the real magic happens when we are in connection and interaction with them. Connecting in this way also counteracts the disappearing human face-to-face engagement we experience due to our busy lives and the omnipresence of personal technology devices.

Take a mindful walk outside. Whether a walk is for minutes or hours, the key is to slow our pace to allow ourselves and children to take in experiences. By slowing and literally taking one small step at a time, we provide a powerful message to children about intentionality. We are more apt to feel a breeze or notice a leaf falling or ants scurrying on the ground. We are more apt to savor the feeling of a child's hand in ours and more prone to enjoy the myriad things that a child spontaneously notices and delights in that we may otherwise have missed altogether. A slow, mindful walk with a child yields so many benefits from a mind and body perspective.

Make mealtimes opportunities for social connection. Sometimes simply insuring that a child eats at the proper time is an accomplishment to be celebrated. But meals and snack times also offer rich opportunities to slow down and connect with children, rare moments in our busy lives. If possible, rather than simply feeding a child and doing something else (like watching TV or otherwise multitasking), try to eat together while enjoying a conversation (verbal or nonverbal). It's an undervalued and readily available opportunity to grow a child's emotional reserves.

Find time to play and have fun together. Play is one of the most beneficial activities for our health regardless of our age. The American Academy of Pediatrics recently promoted a major clinical report encouraging pediatricians and other pediatric professionals to emphasize the importance of play to parents in their developing children. The authors wrote: "*Research demonstrates that developmentally* *appropriate play with parents and peers is a singular opportunity to promote the social-emotional, cognitive, language, and self-regulation skills that build executive function and a prosocial brain.*"[23] What a powerful statement! Play shouldn't be an add-on for parents or professionals but rather an integral and valued part of every child's day. Enjoyable, playful activities with children decreases stress and anxiety and increases health and vitality.

Move the body. As children's free time decreases, so do their opportunities to move around at will. As we learned in Chapter 3, our bodies hold such wisdom and adapt our movements to address incoming signals from the brain/body connection. Allowing children to move their bodies at will—especially in joyful connection with others—is another sure boost to their social and emotional development and contributes to their ability to stay on the green pathway.

Listen to Music. Music can enrich, inspire, and encourage us to move. As we learned in Chapter 2, auditory information can increase a sense of safety, depending on how the child interprets the incoming sounds. It's well worth the effort to discover the types of music that bring joy to a child, and listen to, move, and dance with the music together.

I hope that this book has provided a new structure for you to contextualize and understand behavioral challenges. The various aspects of the book—the color pathways, the developmental iceberg, and the house of development—all point to the central message so eloquently captured in Den Heijer's statement, *"When a flower doesn't bloom you fix the environment in which it grows, not the flower."*[24] Our approaches fall short when we simply mist little flowers struggling to grow in parched soil. Instead, we need to tend the soil. In human beings, the "soil" is safety in relationships—safety as perceived by each child's nervous system, not as defined by adults for the child.

We are so accustomed to believing that children need to be taught or punished for "bad" behaviors that viewing behaviors from the lens of a stress response may seem unnatural or conflict with your discipline or profession—or how your own parents raised you. But over the years I have gained hope by watching schools, parents, and providers adopt a wider lens to view childhood difficulties. When we shift to more expansive brain/body notions of how to support vulnerable children, good things happen.

My hope is that many more families will come to share the experiences of those in this book, who have found answers for their children, in turn reducing suffering and increasing joyful connectedness. My wish is that this book's affirming messages help you to better understand and support children with behavioral challenges.

Resources

Blog, Information, and Speaking Requests

Mona Delahooke, PhD: www.monadelahooke.com

Brain and Social Development

The Child Mind Institute: https://childmind.org

The Center on the Developing Child: https://developingchild.harvard.edu

The NeuroRelational Framework (NRF) Institute: Research To Resilience: http://www.nrfr2r.com

Mindsight Institute: https://www.mindsightinstitute.com/team

Tina Bryson, PhD: https://www.tinabryson.com

Mindfulness and Mindful Self-Compassion

UCLA Mindful Awareness Research Center: https://www.uclahealth.org/marc/

Mindful: https://www.mindful.org/about-mindful/

Susan Kaiser Greenland: https://www.susankaisergreenland.com

Center for Mindful Self-Compassion: https://centerformsc.org

Rick Hanson, PhD: https://www.rickhanson.net

Parent-Mediated Interventions and Interdisciplinary Training

DIR® Floortime Model

The Profectum Foundation: https://profectum.org/about/dir/

The Play Project: https://www.playproject.org

The Interdisciplinary Council on Development and Learning: http://www.icdl.com

Collaborative and Proactive Solutions

Lives in the Balance: https://www.livesinthebalance.org/about-cps

Ross Greene, PhD: http://drrossgreene.com

Sensory Processing and Occupational Therapy

The Star Institute: https://www.spdstar.org

The American Occupational Therapy Association: https://www.aota.org

Polyvagal Theory and Applications

Stephen Porges, PhD: www.stephenporges.com

Deb Dana, LCSW: www.debdanalcsw.com

Rhythm of Regulation: https://www.rhythmofregulation.com

Trauma and Trauma-Informed Care

National Child Traumatic Stress Network: https://www.nctsn.org

Sanctuary Web: http://www.sanctuaryweb.com

Child Trauma: http://childtrauma.org

Trauma Center: http://www.traumacenter.org

Notes

Introduction

1. Stephen W. Porges and Deb Dana, eds., *Clinical Applications of the Polyvagal Theory: The Emergence of Polyvagal-Informed Therapies* (New York: W.W. Norton, 2018), 58.
2. Porges and Dana, *Clinical Applications of the Polyvagal Theory*, 61.
3. Stephen W. Porges, *The Pocket Guide to the Polyvagal Theory: The Transformative Power of Feeling Safe* (New York: W.W. Norton, 2017), 19.
4. Stanley Greenspan and Serena Wieder, *Engaging Autism: Using the Floortime Approach to Help Children Relate, Communicate, and Think* (Reading, MA: Perseus Press, 2006).
5. Stanley Greenspan and Serena Wieder, *The Child with Special Needs* (Reading, MA: Perseus Press, 1998), 14.
6. Lucy Jane Miller, *Sensational Kids: Hope and Help for Children with Sensory Processing Disorder* (New York: Penguin Books, 2007). See also "STAR Institute for Sensory Processing Disorder," The STAR Institute, accessed August 14, 2018, https://www.spdstar.org.
7. Mary Lea Johanning, "Premack Principle," in *Encyclopedia of School Psychology*, ed. Steven W. Lee (Thousand Oaks, CA: SAGE Publications, 2005), 395.
8. "National Parent Survey Overview and Key Insights," ZERO TO THREE, updated June 6, 2016, https://www.zerotothree.org/resources/1424-national-parent-survey-overview-and-key-insights.
9. Alexander Pope, "An Essay on Criticism: Part II," in *An Essay on Criticism* (London: W. Lewis, 1711), lines 215–216.

Chapter 1

1. Rasheed Malik, "New Data Reveal 250 Preschoolers Are Suspended or Expelled Every Day," Center for American Progress, November 6, 2017, https://www.americanprogress.org/issues/early-childhood/news/2017/11/06/442280/new-data-reveal-250-preschoolers-suspended-expelled-every-day/. See also "The National Survey of Children's Health," Data Resource for Child and Adolescent Health, accessed July 26, 2018, http://childhealthdata.org/learn/NSCH.
2. Greenspan and Wieder, *Child with Special Needs*, 11.
3. Connie Lillas and Janiece Turnbull, *Infant/Child Mental Health, Early Intervention, and Relationship-Based Therapies: A Neurorelational Framework for Interdisciplinary Practice* (New York: W.W. Norton, 2009), 32.
4. Greenspan and Wieder, *Child with Special Needs*, 11.
5. Greenspan and Wieder, *Child with Special Needs*.
6. "What is Precision Medicine?," Genetics Home Reference, U.S. National Library of Medicine, updated September 25, 2018, https://ghr.nlm.nih.gov/primer/precisionmedicine/definition.
7. "National Parent Survey Overview and Key Insights," ZERO TO THREE.
8. "National Parent Survey Overview and Key Insights," ZERO TO THREE.
9. "Toddlers and Self-Control: A Survival Guide for Parents," ZERO TO THREE, updated October 3, 2016, https://www.zerotothree.org/resources/1603-toddlers-and-self-control-a-survival-guide-for-parents. See also Amanda R. Tarullo et al., "Self-Control and the Developing Brain," *ZERO TO THREE* 29, no. 3 (2009): 31–37.
10. "Toddlers and Self-Control," ZERO TO THREE.
11. Greenspan and Wieder, *Child with Special Needs*, 70.

12. Lillas and Turnbull, *Infant/Child Mental Health*, 72. See also *The American Heritage Idioms Dictionary*, s.v. "Behavior," accessed July 26, 2018, http://www.dictionary.com/browse/behavior?s=t.

13. The iceberg is a common metaphor. Psychotherapist Virginia Satir, for example, used an iceberg as an analogy to help individuals understand their coping mechanisms and internal motivations in family therapy.

14. Sandra L. Bloom, "Creating Sanctuary in the School," *Journal for a Just and Caring Education* 1, no. 4 (October 1995): 403–433.

15. Mona Delahooke, *Social and Emotional Development in Early Intervention: A Skills Guide for Working with Children* (Eau Claire, WI: PESI Publishing & Media, 2017), 3.

16. Stephen W. Porges, *The Polyvagal Theory: Neurophysiological Foundations of Emotions, Attachment, Communication, and Self-Regulation* (New York: W.W. Norton, 2011). For further information, see Stephen W. Porges, "Articles and Interviews," accessed July 26, 2018, http://stephenporges.com/index.php/articles-and-interviews.

17. Stephen W. Porges, "The Polyvagal Theory: New Insights into Adaptive Reactions of the Autonomic Nervous System," *Cleveland Clinic Journal of Medicine* 76, no. 2 (April 2009): S86–S90.

18. Porges, *The Pocket Guide*, xv.

19. Porges, xv.

20. Stephen W. Porges, "Human Nature and Early Experience," *YouTube* Video, 46:38, October 24, 2014, https://www.youtube.com/watch?v=SRTkkYjQ_HU&t=1236s.

21. Porges, "Human Nature and Early Experience," 46:38.

22. Ross Greene describes a child's lagging skills as an underlying cause of behavioral problems in his best-selling book, *The Explosive Child* (New York: HarperCollins, 1998).

23. Stephen W. Porges, "Neuroception: A Subconscious System for Detecting Threats and Safety," *ZERO TO THREE* 24, no. 5 (2004):

24. Porges, "Neuroception", 19–24.

25. Porges, *Polyvagal Theory: Neurophysiological Foundations*, 24.

26. Porges, *The Pocket Guide*, 6.

27. Porges, "Neuroception," 19–24.

28. Bruce Perry and Maia Szalavitz, *The Boy Who Was Raised as a Dog: And Other Stories From a Child Psychiatrist's Notebook* (New York: Basic Books, 2006; New York: Basic Books, 2017). Citations refer to the 2017 edition, 347.

29. Daniel J. Siegel and Tina Payne Bryson, *The Whole Brain Child* (New York: Random House, 2011), 14.

30. *Diagnostic and Statistical Manual of Mental Disorders*, 3rd ed. (Washington, DC: American Psychiatric Association, 1980). The *DSM* is currently in its fifth edition (Arlington, VA: American Psychiatric Association, 2013). All subsequent citations refer to the 2013 edition.

31. "NIMH Funding to Shift Away from *DSM* Categories," American Psychological Association, last updated July/August 2013, http://www.apa.org/monitor/2013/07-08/nimh.aspx.

32. "Research Domain Criteria (RDoC)," National Institute of Mental Health, accessed July 26, 2018, https://www.nimh.nih.gov/research-priorities/rdoc/index.shtml. There are presently five RDoCs: negative valence systems, positive valence systems, cognitive systems, systems for social processes, and arousal/regulatory systems. Within each of these systems lies a complex matrix of domains that underlie aspects of human behavior and functioning. In keeping with this widespread shift, I have opted not to identify children described in this book with diagnostic labels unless those labels are critical to understanding the particular case.

Chapter 2

1.   Porges, "Neuroception," 19–24.

2.   Daniel Goleman and Richard J. Davidson, *Altered Traits: Science Reveals How Meditation Changes Your Mind, Brain, and Body* (New York: Random House, 2017), 140.

3.   Siegel and Bryson, *The Whole Brain Child*, 37.

4.   Bryan Kolb et al., "Experience and the Developing Prefrontal Cortex," Supplement, *Proceedings of the National Academy of Sciences of the United States of America* 109, no: S2 (2012): 17186–17193.

5.   "Parent Survey Reveals Expectation Gap for Parents of Young Children," ZERO TO THREE, updated October 13, 2016, https://www.zerotothree.org/resources/1612-parent-survey-reveals-expectation-gap-for-parents-of-young-children.

6.   "Executive Function & Self-Regulation," Center on the Developing Child, Harvard University, accessed August 13, 2018, https://developingchild.harvard.edu/science/key-concepts/executive-function/.

7.   Lillas and Turnbull, *Infant/Child Mental Health*, 42.

8.   Siegel and Bryson, *The Whole Brain Child*, 39.

9.   Goleman and Davidson, *Altered Traits,* 140–141.

10. Elizabeth B. Torres and Caroline Whyatt, eds., *Autism: The Movement-Sensing Perspective* (Boca Raton, FL: CRC Press, 2018), 178.

11. Porges and Dana, *Clinical Applications of the Polyvagal Theory*, 67.

12. Stanley Greenspan and Serena Wieder describe developmental milestones in the following books: Greenspan, *First Feelings: Milestones in the Emotional Development of Your Baby and Child* (New York: Viking Penguin, 1985); Greenspan, *Infancy and Early Childhood: The Practice of Clinical Assessment and Intervention with Emotional and Developmental Challenges* (Madison, CT: International Universities Press, 1992); and Greenspan and Wieder, *Infant and Early Childhood Mental Health: A Comprehensive Developmental Approach to Assessment and Intervention* (Washington, DC: American Psychiatric Publishing, 2006).

13. Robert R. Greene and Nancy P. Kropf, *Caregiving and Care Sharing: A Life Course Perspective* (Washington, DC: NASW Press, 2014).

14. Greenspan and Wieder, *Engaging Autism*, 386.

15. Dr. Serena Wieder in a discussion with the author at the World Association for Infant Mental Health Conference in Rome, Italy, May 2018.

16. Greenspan and Wieder, *Child with Special Needs*, 70.

17. For example, many educators use the following color system: Leah M. Kuypers, *The Zones of Regulation: A Curriculum Designed to Foster Self-Regulation and Emotional Control* (San Jose, CA: Think Social Publishing, 2011). Neuropsychologist Rick Hanson describes a "responsive" mode as a green zone and a "reactive" mode as a red zone in his book, *Hardwiring Happiness: The New Brain Science of Contentment, Calm and Confidence* (New York: Harmony Books, 2013), 38, 48.

18. Lillas and Turnbull, *Infant/Child Mental Health.*

19. Porges, *The Pocket Guide*, 5–6.

20. Porges, 5–6.

21. Porges, 5–6.

22. Deb Dana, *The Polyvagal Theory in Therapy: Engaging the Rhythm of Regulation* (New York: Norton & Company, 2018), 9.

23. Porges, *Polyvagal Theory: Neurophysiological Foundations,* 160–162.

24. Porges, 158.

25. Lillas and Turnbull, *Infant/Child Mental Health,* 46.

26. Nadine Burke Harris, *The Deepest Well: Healing the Long-Term Effects of Childhood Adversity* (New York: Houghton Mifflin Harcourt, 2018), 54.

27. Porges and Dana, *Clinical Applications of the Polyvagal Theory*, 67.

Chapter 3

1. Greenspan and Wieder, *Child with Special Needs*, 22.
2. Lillas and Turnbull, *Infant/Child Mental Health*, 42.
3. Siegel and Bryson, *The Whole Brain Child*, 27.
4. "PANDAS Questions and Answers," U.S. Department of Health and Human Services, National Institute of Mental Health, last modified September 2016, https://www.nimh.nih.gov/health/publications/pandas/index.shtml.
5. Jennifer Brout and Lucy Jane Miller, "*DSM-5* Application for Sensory Processing Disorder Appendix A (Part 1)," *ResearchGate*, December 2015, https://www.researchgate.net/publication/285591455_DSM-5_Application_for_Sensory_Processing_Disorder_Appendix_A_part_1.
6. Stanley Greenspan, *The Growth of the Mind: And the Endangered Origins of Intelligence* (Reading, MA: Perseus Books, 1997), 21.
7. Stanley Greenspan and Serena Wieder, eds., *Diagnostic Manual for Infancy and Early Childhood: Mental Health, Developmental, Regulatory-Sensory Processing, Language and Learning Disorders* (Bethesda, MD: Interdisciplinary Council on Developmental and Learning Disorders, 2005), 7.
8. Alice S. Carter, Ayelet Ben-Sasson, and Margaret J. Briggs-Gowan, "Sensory Over-Responsivity, Psychopathology, and Family Impairment in School-Aged Children," *Journal of the American Academy of Child and Adolescent Psychiatry* 50, no. 12 (2011): 1210–1219.
9. Miller, *Sensational Kids*, 4–5.
10. Doreit Bialer and Lucy Jane Miller, *No Longer a Secret: Unique Common Sense Strategies for Children with Sensory or Motor Challenges* (Arlington, TX: Future Horizons Press, 2011), 20.
11. Bialer and Miller, *No Longer a Secret*, 21.
12. The STAR Institute website offers an abundance of information on the topic of sensory processing disorder: https://www.spdstar.org.
13. Dawn Huebner and Bonnie Matthews, *What to Do When You Worry Too Much: A Kid's Guide to Overcoming Anxiety* (Washington, DC: Magination Press, 2006).
14. Delahooke, *Social and Emotional Development*, 3.

Chapter 4

1. Porges, "Neuroception."
2. Louis Cozolino, *The Social Neuroscience of Education: Optimizing Attachment and Learning in the Classroom* (New York: W.W. Norton, 2013), xxi.
3. Porges, *The Pocket Guide*, 51.
4. Porges, 45.
5. Porges, 45.
6. Porges, "Neuroception."
7. Porges, "Neuroception," 19-24.
8. Porges, *Polyvagal Theory: Neurophysiological Foundations*, 15.
9. Porges and Dana, *Clinical Applications of the Polyvagal Theory*, 61.
10. "Resilience," Center on the Developing Child, Harvard University, accessed August 15, 2018, https://developingchild.harvard.edu/science/key-concepts/resilience/.
11. Hans Selye, "A Syndrome Produced by Diverse Nocuous Agents," *Nature* 138, no. 3479 (1936): 32.
12. Bruce S. McEwen and Peter J. Gianaros, "Central Role of the Brain in Stress and Adaptation: Links to Socioeconomic Status, Health, and Disease," *Annals of the New York Academy of Sciences* 1186, no. 1 (2010): 2.

13. "Resilience," Center on the Developing Child.

14. Bruce S. McEwen, "Stressed or Stressed Out: What is the Difference?," *Journal of Psychiatry and Neuroscience* 30, no. 5 (2005): 315.

15. McEwen and Gianaros, "Central Role of the Brain."

16. "Resilience," Center on the Developing Child.

17. Lev S. Vygotsky, *Mind in Society: The Development of Higher Psychological Processes*, ed. Michael Cole, Vera John-Steiner, Sylvia Shribner, and Ellen Souberman (Cambridge, MA: Harvard University Press, 1978), 86.

18. Lillas and Turnbull, *Infant/Child Mental Health*, 178.

19. Lillas and Turnbull, 178.

20. McEwen, "Stressed or Stressed Out," 315.

21. Porges, *The Pocket Guide*, 44.

22. Jon Kabat-Zinn, *Full Catastrophe Living: Using the Wisdom of Your Body and Mind to Face Stress, Pain, and Illness* (New York: Random House, 1990), 2.

23. Suzannah J. Ferraioli and Sandra L. Harris, "Comparative Effects of Mindfulness and Skills-Based Parent Training Programs for Parents of Children with Autism: Feasibility and Preliminary Outcome Data," *Mindfulness* 4, no. 2 (2013): 89–101; Elissa Epel et al., "Can Meditation Slow Rate of Cellular Aging? Cognitive Stress, Mindfulness, and Telomeres," *Annals of the New York Academy of Sciences: Longevity, Regeneration, and Optimal Health* 1172, no. 1 (2009): 34–53; and Manika Petcharat and Patricia R. Liehr, "Mindfulness Training for Parents of Children with Special Needs: Guidance for Nurses in Mental Health Practice," *Journal of Child and Adolescent Psychiatric Nursing* 30, no. 1 (2017): 35–46.

24. Kristin Neff, *Self-Compassion: The Proven Power of Being Kind to Yourself* (New York: HarperCollins, 2011), 41.

25. Kristin D. Neff and Daniel J. Faso, "Self-Compassion and Well-Being in Parents of Children with Autism," *Mindfulness* 6, no. 4 (2015): 938–947. See also Kristin D. Neff, "The Self-Compassion Scale is a Valid and Theoretically Coherent Measure of Self-Compassion," *Mindfulness* 7, no. 1 (2016): 264–274.

26. Kristin Neff and Christopher Germer, *The Mindful Self-Compassion Workbook* (New York: Guilford Press, 2018).

27. Porges, *The Pocket Guide*, 45.

28. Jeree H. Paul and Maria St. John, *How You Are Is as Important as What You Do* (Washington, DC: ZERO TO THREE: National Center for Infants, Toddlers, and Families, 1998).

29. Stuart Shanker, *Self-Reg: How to Help Your Child (and You) Break the Stress Cycle and Successfully Engage with Life* (New York: Penguin Books, 2016).

30. Porges, *The Pocket Guide*, 44.

31. Erika M. Waller and Amanda J. Rose, "Brief Report: Adolescents' Co-Rumination with Mothers, Co-Rumination with Friends, and Internalizing Symptoms," *Journal of Adolescence* 36, no. 2 (2013): 429–433.

32. Porges, *The Pocket Guide*, 51.

Chapter 5

1. "Brain Architecture," Center on the Developing Child, Harvard University, accessed August 16, 2018, https://developingchild.harvard.edu/science/key-concepts/brain-architecture/. See also Bruce D. Perry, "Maltreatment and the Developing Child: How Early Childhood Experience Shapes Child and Culture" (inaugural lecture, The Margaret McCain Lecture Series, Centre for Children & Families in the Justice System, London, ON, September 23, 2004), https://childtrauma.org/wp-content/uploads/2013/11/McCainLecture_Perry.pdf.

2.   Els van der Helm and Matthew P. Walker, "Overnight Therapy? The Role of Sleep in Emotional Brain Processing," *Psychological Bulletin* 135, no. 5 (2009): 731–748. See also Christina O. Carlisi et al., "Sleep-Amount Differentially Affects Fear-Processing Neural Circuitry in Pediatric Anxiety: A Preliminary fMRI Investigation," *Cognitive, Affective, & Behavioral Neuroscience* 17, no. 6 (2017): 1098–1113.

3.   Peir H. Koulivand, Maryam Khaleghi Ghadiri, and Ali Gorji, "Lavender and the Nervous System," *Evidence-Based Complementary and Alternative Medicine*, no. 2013 (2013): 681304.

4.   Greenspan, *Growth of the Mind*, 21.

5.   Stephen W. Porges, *Associate Manual Safe and Sound Protocol* (Aurora, CO: Integrated Listening Systems, 2018).

6.   Stephen W. Porges et al., "Reducing Auditory Hypersensitivities in Autistic Spectrum Disorder: Preliminary Findings Evaluating the Listening Project Protocol," *Frontiers in Pediatrics* 2, no. 80 (2014): 1–10. See also Stephen W. Porges et al., "Respiratory Sinus Arrhythmia and Auditory Processing in Autism: Modifiable Deficits of an Integrated Social Engagement System?" *International Journal of Psychophysiology* 88, no. 3 (2013): 261–270.

7.   Lillas and Turnbull, *Infant/Child Mental Health*, 178.

8.   "Breathe," Sesame Street in Communities, accessed August 16, 2018, https://sesamestreetincommunities.org/activities/breathe-bundle/.

9.   Susan Kaiser Greenland, *The Mindful Child* (New York: Simon & Schuster, 2010).

10. Greenland, *Mindful Child*, 68.

11. Greenland, 69.

12. "The School Yoga Project," Little Flower Yoga, accessed August 16, 2018, http://littlefloweryoga.com/programs/the-school-yoga-project.

Chapter 6

1.   Bessel van der Kolk, *The Body Keeps the Score: Brain, Mind, and Body in the Healing of Trauma* (New York: Penguin Books, 2014), 159.

2.   Porges, *The Pocket Guide*, 22.

3.   Bridget E. Hatfield and Amanda P. Williford, "Cortisol Patterns for Young Children Displaying Disruptive Behavior: Links to a Teacher-Child, Relationship-Focused Intervention," *Prevention Science* 18, no. 1 (2017): 40–49.

4.   Serena Wieder, "PLAY: The Window into the Child's Emotional Experiences," Profectum Foundation, accessed August 16, 2018, https://profectum.org/wp-content/uploads/2015/03/PLAY-HANDOUT.pdf.

5.   Porges, *The Pocket Guide*, 22.

6.   Greenspan and Wieder, *Child with Special Needs*, 256–257.

7.   Wieder, "PLAY."

8.   Porges, *The Pocket Guide*, 22.

9.   Greenspan and Wieder, *Child with Special Needs*, 206–220.

10. Greenspan and Wieder, 256–257.

11. Greenspan and Wieder, 206–220.

12. Greenspan and Wieder. See also Wieder, "PLAY."

13. "What Is DIR and Why Is It Important?," Profectum Foundation, accessed August 16, 2018, https://profectum.org/about/dir/.

14. "Child-Parent Psychotherapy (CPP)," California Evidence-Based Clearinghouse for Child Welfare, last modified December 2015, http://www.cebc4cw.org/program/child-parent-psychotherapy/detailed.

15. "The Mindsight Approach to Well-Being: A Comprehensive Course in Interpersonal Neurobiology," Mindsight Institute, accessed August 16, 2018, https://www.mindsightinstitute.com/comprehensive-

course-in-ipnb.

16. "The NRF Manual," Neurorelational Framework Global Communities, accessed August 16, 2018, https://nrfr2r.com.

17. Siegel and Bryson, *The Whole Brain Child*, 27.

18. "About the CPS Model," Lives in the Balance, accessed August 16, 2018, https://www.livesinthebalance. org/about-cps.

19. "What is Dialectical Behavior Therapy (DBT)?," Behavioral Tech: A Linehan Institute Training Company, accessed September 27, 2018, https://behavioraltech.org/resources/faqs/dialectical-behavior-therapy-dbt/.

20. Brené Brown, *Daring Greatly* (New York: Random House, 2012).

21. Dana, *Polyvagal Theory in Therapy*, 101.

22. Porges, *The Pocket Guide*, 204.

Chapter 7

1. Greenspan and Wieder, *Child with Special Needs,* 11.

2. Virginia Chaidez, Robin L. Hansen, and Irva Hertz-Picciotto, "Gastrointestinal Problems in Children with Autism, Developmental Delays or Typical Development," *Journal of Autism and Developmental Disorders* 44, no. 5 (2014): 1117–1127; Preeti A. Devnani and Anaita U. Hegde, "Autism and Sleep Disorders," *Journal of Pediatric Neurosciences* 10, no. 4 (2015): 304–307; and Francisca J. A. van Steensel and Emma J. Heeman, "Anxiety Levels in Children with Autism Spectrum Disorder: A Meta-Analysis," *Journal of Child and Family Studies* 26, no. 7 (2017): 1753–1767.

3. Shulamite A. Green et al., "Neurobiology of Sensory Overresponsivity in Youth with Autism Spectrum Disorders," *JAMA Psychiatry* 72, no. 8 (2015): 778–786. See also Ayelet Ben-Sasson et al., "Extreme Sensory Modulation Behaviors in Toddlers with Autism Spectrum Disorders," *The American Journal of Occupational Therapy* 61, no. 5 (2007): 584–592.

4. *Diagnostic and Statistical Manual*, 50. See also Green et al., "Sensory Overresponsivity."

5. Jack P. Shonkoff and Deborah A. Phillips, eds., *From Neurons to Neighborhoods: The Science of Early Childhood Development* (Washington, DC: National Academy Press, 2000).

6. Ibid., 3.

7. "Resilience," Center on the Developing Child.

8. Theresa Hamlin, *Autism and the Stress Effect: A 4-Step Lifestyle Approach to Transform Your Child's Health, Happiness and Vitality* (London: Jessica Kingsley Publishers, 2016), 32.

9. Hamlin, *Autism and the Stress Effect*, 32.

10. Martha R. Leary and Anne M. Donnellan, *Autism: Sensory-Movement Differences and Diversity* (Cambridge, WI: Cambridge Book Review Press, 2012), 9.

11. Leary and Donnellan, *Autism*, 9.

12. Ido Kedar, *Ido in Autismland* (self-pub., 2012), 46.

13. Kedar, 47.

14. Samuel McNerney, "A Brief Guide to Embodied Cognition: Why You Are Not Your Brain," *Scientific American*, November 4, 2011, https://blogs.scientificamerican.com/guest-blog/a-brief-guide-to-embodied-cognition-why-you-are-not-your-brain/.

15. Greenspan and Wieder, *Engaging Autism*, 91.

16. Porges, *The Pocket Guide*, 219.

17. Torres and Whyatt, *Autism*, 3.

18. Torres and Whyatt, 3.

19. Anne M. Donnellan, David A. Hill, and Martha R. Leary, "Rethinking Autism: Implications of Sensory and Movement Differences for Understanding and Support," *Frontiers in Integrative Neuroscience* 6, no. 124 (2013): 124.

20. Torres and Whyatt, *Autism*, 18.

21. Torres and Whyatt, 18.

22. Torres and Whyatt, 27.

23. "Neurologic Music Therapy (NMT)," The Academy of Neurologic Music Therapy, accessed August 17, 2018, https://nmtacademy.co/home/clinic/. See also Michael H. Thaut, "A Music Therapy Treatment Model for Autistic Children," *Music Therapy Perspectives* 1, no. 4 (1984): 7–13.

24. Lonnie K. Zeltzer and Christina Blackett Schlank, *Conquering Your Child's Chronic Pain* (New York: HarperCollins, 2005).

25. Mona Delahooke, "Disorderism: How to Make Sure People See Your Child and Not a Diagnosis," *Mona's Blog*, June 21, 2015, https://www.monadelahooke.com/disorderism-how-to-make-sure-people-see-your-child-and-not-a-diagnosis/.

26. Kedar, *Ido in Autismland*.

27. Naoki Higashida, *The Reason I Jump*, trans. Keiko A. Yoshida and David Mitchell (New York: Random House, 2013), 21.

28. Leary and Donnellan, *Sensory-Movement Differences,* 9.

29. Leary and Donnellan, 9.

Chapter 8

1. "Adverse Childhood Experiences," Center for the Application of Prevention Technologies, Substance Abuse and Mental Health Services Administration, updated July 9, 2018, https://www.recoverymonth.gov/organizations-programs/national-center-trauma-informed-care-alternatives-seclusion-restraint-nctic .

2. "National Center for Trauma-Informed Care and Alternatives to Seclusion and Restraint (NCTIC)," Substance Abuse and Mental Health Services Administration, updated October 26, 2015, https://www.samhsa.gov/nctic/about.

3. Nadine Burke Harris, *The Deepest Well: Healing the Long-Term Effects of Childhood Adversity* (New York: Houghton Mifflin Harcourt, 2018).

4. Harris, *The Deepest Well*, 59.

5. David Bornstein, "Treating the Lifelong Harm of Childhood Trauma," *New York Times*, January 30, 3018, https://www.nytimes.com/2018/01/30/opinion/treating-the-lifelong-harm-of-childhood-trauma.html.

6. Sandra L. Bloom and Brian Farragher, *Restoring Sanctuary: A New Operating System for Trauma-Informed Systems of Care* (New York: Oxford University Press, 2013), 46.

7. "In Brief: The Impact of Early Adversity on Children's Development," Center on the Developing Child, Harvard University, accessed September 15, 2018, https://developingchild.harvard.edu/resources/inbrief-the-impact-of-early-adversity-on-childrens-development/.

8. Porges, *The Pocket Guide*, 20.

9. Libby Nelson and Dara Lind, "The School to Prison Pipeline, Explained," *Justice Policy Institute*, February 24, 2015, http://www.justicepolicy.org/news/8775.

10. Nelson and Lind, "The School to Prison Pipeline." See also Bloom and Farragher, *Restoring Sanctuary*.

11. Bloom and Farragher, *Restoring Sanctuary*, 5.

12. Porges, *The Pocket Guide*, 20.

13. Perry and Szalavitz, *Boy Raised as a Dog*, 328.

14. Perry and Szalavitz, 311.

15. Bloom and Farragher, *Restoring Sanctuary*. See also "The Sanctuary Model'" (website), SanctuaryWeb. com, Sandra L. Bloom, accessed September 15, 2018, http://www.sanctuaryweb.com/Home.aspx.

16. Perry and Szalavitz, *Boy Raised as a Dog*, 316.

17. Perry and Szalavitz, 313.

18. Porges and Dana, *Clinical Applications of the Polyvagal Theory*, 73.

19. Ross Greene, *The Explosive Child* (New York: HarperCollins, 1998).

20. Ross Greene, *The Explosive Child*, 19.

21. Perry and Szalavitz, 329.

22. Elyssa Barbash, "Different Types of Trauma: Small 't' Versus Large 'T'," *Psychology Today*, March 13, 2017, https://www.psychologytoday.com/us/blog/trauma-and-hope/201703/different-types-trauma-small-t-versus-large-t.

23. Perry and Szalavitz, *Boy Raised as a Dog*, 325.

24. Porges, *The Pocket Guide*, 204.

Chapter 9

1. Hamlin, *Autism and Stress Effect*, 64.

2. "Research Partners," The Center for Discovery, accessed September 4, 2018, https://thecenterfordiscovery. org/research-partners/.

3. "The Research Institute for Brain and Body Health," The Center for Discovery, accessed September 4, 2018, https://thecenterfordiscovery.org/brain-health-research-institute/.

4. "NIMH Funding to Shift Away from *DSM* Categories," American Psychological Association.

5. Ibid.

6. Sonia J. Lupien et al., "The *DSM-5*/RDoC Debate on the Future of Mental Health Research: Implication for Studies on Human Stress and Presentation of the Signature Bank," *Stress* 20, no. 1 (2017): 96.

7. Cozolino, *Social Neuroscience of Education*, xxi.

8. Cozolino, xxi.

9. Hanson, *Hardwiring Happiness*, 20. See also Paul Rozin and Edward B. Royzman, "Negativity Bias, Negativity Dominance, and Contagion," *Personality and Social Psychology Review* 5, no. 4 (2001): 296–320.

10. Hanson, *Hardwiring Happiness*, 20.

11. Hanson, 27.

12. Anna Dabrowska-Zimakowska and Ewa Pisula, "Parenting Stress and Coping Styles on Mothers and Fathers of Pre-School Children with Autism and Down Syndrome," *Journal of Intellectual Disability Research* 54, no. 3 (2010): 266–280. See also Elisabeth M. Dykens et al., "Reducing Distress in Mothers of Children with Autism and Other Disabilities: A Randomized Trial," *Pediatrics* 134, no. 2 (2014): e454-e463.

13. Hanson, *Hardwiring Happiness*, 15.

14. "National Parent Survey Overview and Key Insights," ZERO TO THREE.

15. Hanson, *Hardwiring Happiness*, 4.

16. Hanson, 60.

17. Hanson, 52.

18. 4th Ark, "Cool Teachers Greet Students with Personalized Handshakes," *YouTube* Video, 2:37, February 10, 2017, https://www.youtube.com/watch?v=V3dhHfhdTOE.

19. Hanson, *Hardwiring Happiness*, 61.

20. Dean V. Buonomano and Michael Merzenich, "Cortical Plasticity: From Synapses to Maps," *Annual Review of Neuroscience* 21, no. 1 (1998): 149–186.

21. Hanson, *Hardwiring Happiness*, 160.

22. Christian Keysers and Valeria Gazzola, "Hebbian Learning and Predictive Mirror Neurons for Actions, Sensations and Emotions," *Philosophical Transactions of the Royal Society B: Biological Sciences* 369, no. 1644 (2014): 20130175.

23. Michael Yogman et al., "The Power of Play: A Pediatric Role in Enhancing Development in Young Children," *Pediatrics* 142, no. 3 (2018): e20182058.

24. Alexander den Heijer (@purposologist), "When a flower doesn't bloom, you fix the environment in which it grows, not the flower," Twitter, May 26, 2015, 2:45 a.m., https://twitter.com/purposologist/status/603134967841988608.

Bibliography

4th Ark. "Cool Teachers Greet Students with Personalized Handshakes." *YouTube* video, 2:37. February 10, 2017. https://www.youtube.com/watch?v=V3dhHfhdTOE.

American Psychiatric Association. *Diagnostic and Statistical Manual of Mental Disorders*. 3rd ed. Washington, DC: American Psychiatric Association, 1980.

American Psychiatric Association. *Diagnostic and Statistical Manual of Mental Disorders*. 5th ed. Arlington, VA: American Psychiatric Association, 2013.

American Psychological Association. "NIMH Funding to Shift Away from *DSM* Categories." Updated July/August 2013. http://www.apa.org/monitor/2013/07-08/nimh.aspx.

Ayres, A. Jean. *Sensory Integration and the Child: Understanding Hidden Sensory Challenges*. Los Angeles: Western Psychological Services, 2005.

Baer, Ruth A., Emily L. B. Lykins, and Jessica R. Peters. "Mindfulness and Self-Compassion as Predictors of Psychological Wellbeing in Long-Term Meditators and Demographically Matched Nonmeditators." *Journal of Positive Psychology* 7, no. 3 (2012): 230–238.

Barbash, Elyssa. "Different Types of Trauma: Small 't' versus Large 'T'." *Psychology Today*, March 13, 2017. https://www.psychologytoday.com/us/blog/trauma-and-hope/201703/different-types-trauma-small-t-versus-large-t.

Bazarko, Dawn, Rebecca A. Cate, Francisca Azocar, and Mary Jo Kreitzer. "The Impact of an Innovative Mindfulness-Based Stress Reduction Program on the Health and Wellbeing of Nurses in a Corporate Setting." *Journal of Workplace Behavioural Health* 28, no. 2 (2013): 107–133.

Behavioral Tech. "What is Dialectical Behavior Therapy (DBT)?" Accessed September 27, 2018. https://behavioraltech.org/resources/faqs/dialectical-behavior-therapy-dbt/.

Ben-Sasson, Ayelet, Alice S. Carter, and Margaret J. Briggs-Gowan. "Sensory Over-Responsivity in Elementary School: Prevalence and Social-Emotional Correlates." *Journal of Abnormal Child Psychology* 37, no. 5 (2009): 705–716. doi:10.1007/s10802-008-9295-8.

Ben-Sasson, Ayelet, Alice S. Carter, and Margaret J. Briggs-Gowan. "The Development of Sensory Over-Responsivity from Infancy to Elementary School." *Journal of Abnormal Child Psychology* 38, no. 8 (2010): 1193–1202. doi:10.1007/s10802-010-9435-9.

Ben-Sasson, Ayelet, Sharon A. Cermak, Gael I. Orsmond, Helen Tager-Flusberg, Alice S. Carter, Mary Beth Kadlec, and Winnie Dunn. "Extreme Sensory Modulation Behaviors in Toddlers with Autism Spectrum Disorders." *The American Journal of Occupational Therapy* 61, no. 5 (2007): 584–592.

Benson, Paul R. "The Impact of Child Symptom Severity on Depressed Mood Among Parents of Children with ASD: The Mediating Role of Stress Proliferation." *Journal of Autism and Developmental Disorders* 36, no. 5 (2006): 685–695.

Benson, Paul R., and Kristie L. Karlof. "Anger, Stress Proliferation, and Depressed Mood Among Parents of Children with ASD: A Longitudinal Replication." *Journal of Autism and Developmental Disorders* 39, no. 2 (2009): 350–362. doi:10.1007/s10803-008-0632-0.

Bialer, Doreit, and Lucy Jane Miller. *No Longer a SECRET: Unique Common Sense Strategies for Children with Sensory or Motor Challenges*. Arlington, TX: Future Horizons Press, 2011.

Bloom, Sandra L. "The Sanctuary Model." SanctuaryWeb.com. Accessed September 15, 2018. http://www.sanctuaryweb.com/Home.aspx.

Bloom, Sandra L., and Brian Farragher. *Restoring Sanctuary: A New Operating System for Trauma-Informed Systems of Care*. New York: Oxford University Press, 2013.

Bluth, Karen, Patricia N. E. Roberson, Rhett M. Billen, and Juli M. Sams. "A Stress Model for Couples Parenting Children with Autism Spectrum Disorders and the Introduction of a Mindfulness Intervention." *Journal of Family Theory and Review* 5, no. 3 (2013): 194–213. doi:10.1111/jftr.12015.

Bornstein, David. "Treating the Lifelong Harm of Childhood Trauma." *New York Times*, January 30, 2018. https://www.nytimes.com/2018/01/30/opinion/treating-the-lifelong-harm-of-childhood-trauma.html.

Bradford, Kay. "Brief Education about Autism Spectrum Disorders for Family Therapists." *Journal of Family Psychotherapy* 21, no. 3 (2010): 161–179.

Brazelton, T. Berry. *Touchpoints: Your Child's Emotional and Behavioral Development.* New York: Addison-Wesley, 1992.

Brobst, Jennifer B., James R. Clopton, and Susan S. Hendrick. "Parenting Children with Autism Spectrum Disorders: The Couple's Relationship." *Focus on Autism and Other Developmental Disabilities* 24, no. 1 (2009): 38–49. doi:10.1177/1088357608323699.

Brout, Jennifer, and Lucy Jane Miller. "*DSM*-5 Application for Sensory Processing Disorder Appendix A (Part 1)." *ResearchGate*, December 2015. https://www.researchgate.net/publication/285591455_DSM-5_Application_for_Sensory_Processing_Disorder_Appendix_A_part_1.

Brown, Brené. *Daring Greatly.* New York: Random House, 2012.

Buonomano, Dean V., and Michael Merzenich. "Cortical Plasticity: From Synapses to Maps." *Annual Review of Neuroscience* 21, no. 1 (1998): 149–186.

Burke, Nadine J., Julia L. Hellman, Brandon G. Scott, Carl F. Weems, and Victor G. Carrion. "The Impact of Adverse Childhood Experiences on an Urban Pediatric Population." *Child Abuse & Neglect* 35, no. 6 (2011): 408–413. http://doi.org/10.1016/j.chiabu.2011.02.006.

Buron, Kari Dunn, and Mitzi Curtis. *The Incredible 5-Point Scale: The Significantly Improved and Expanded Second Edition.* Shawnee Mission, KS: AAPC Publishing, 2012.

California Evidence-Based Clearinghouse for Child Welfare. "Child-Parent Psychotherapy (CPP)." Last modified December 2015. http://www.cebc4cw.org/program/child-parent-psychotherapy/detailed.

Carlisi, Christina O., Kevin Hilbert, Amanda E. Guyer, and Monique Ernst. "Sleep-Amount Differentially Affects Fear-Processing Neural Circuitry in Pediatric Anxiety: A Preliminary fMRI Investigation." *Cognitive, Affective, & Behavioral Neuroscience* 17, no. 6 (2017): 1098–1113. doi:10.3758/s13415-017-0535-7.

Carter, Alice S., Ayelet Ben-Sasson, and Margaret J. Briggs-Gowan. "Sensory Over-Responsivity, Psychopathology, and Family Impairment in School-Aged Children." *Journal of the American Academy of Child and Adolescent Psychiatry* 50, no. 12 (2011): 1210–1219. doi:10.1016/j.jaac.2011.09.010.

Center for Discovery. "Research Partners." Accessed September 4, 2018. https://thecenterfordiscovery.org/research-partners/.

Center for Discovery. "The Research Institute for Brain and Body Health." Accessed September 4, 2018. https://thecenterfordiscovery.org/brain-health-research-institute/.

Center for the Application of Prevention Technologies, Substance Abuse and Mental Health Services Administration. "Adverse Childhood Experiences." Updated July 9, 2018. https://www.samhsa.gov/child-trauma/recognizing-and-treating-child-traumatic-stress.

Chaidez, Virginia, Robin L. Hansen, and Irva Hertz-Picciotto. "Gastrointestinal Problems in Children with Autism, Developmental Delays or Typical Development." *Journal of Autism and Developmental Disorders* 44, no. 5 (2014): 1117–1127. http://doi.org/10.1007/s10803-013-1973-x.

Cozolino, Louis. *The Social Neuroscience of Education: Optimizing Attachment and Learning in the Classroom.* New York: W.W. Norton, 2013.

Cozolino, Louis. *The Neuroscience of Relationships: Attachment and the Developing Social Brain.* New York: W.W. Norton, 2014.

Dabrowska-Zimakowska, Anna, and Ewa Pisula. "Parenting Stress and Coping Styles on Mothers and Fathers of Pre-School Children with Autism and Down Syndrome." *Journal of Intellectual Disability Research* 54, no. 3 (2010): 266–280. doi:10.1111/j.1365-2788.2010.01258.x.

Damasio, Antonio. *The Feeling of What Happens: Body and Emotion in the Making of Consciousness.* New York: Harcourt Brace, 1999.

Dana, Deb. *The Polyvagal Theory in Therapy: Engaging the Rhythm of Regulation.* New York: W.W. Norton, 2018.

Data Resource for Child and Adolescent Health. "The National Survey of Children's Health." Accessed July 26, 2018. http://childhealthdata.org/learn/NSCH.

Delahooke, Mona. "Disorderism: How to Make Sure People See Your Child and Not a Diagnosis." *Mona's Blog,* June 21, 2015. https://www.monadelahooke.com/disorderism-how-to-make-sure-people-see-your-child-and-not-a-diagnosis/.

Delahooke, Mona. *Social and Emotional Development in Early Intervention: A Skills Guide for Working with Children.* Eau Claire, WI: PESI Publishing and Media, 2017.

den Heijer, Alexander (@purposologist). "When a flower doesn't bloom, you fix the environment in which it grows, not the flower." Twitter, May 26, 2015. https://twitter.com/purposologist/status/603134967841988608.

Devnani, Preeti A., and Anaita U. Hegde. "Autism and Sleep Disorders." *Journal of Pediatric Neurosciences* 10, no. 4 (2015): 304–307. http://doi.org/10.4103/1817-1745.174438.

Donnellan, Anne M., David A. Hill, and Martha R. Leary. "Rethinking Autism: Implications of Sensory and Movement Differences for Understanding and Support." *Frontiers in Integrative Neuroscience*, no. 6 (2013): 124. doi:10.3389/fnint.2012.00124.

Duckworth, Angela, and Laurence Steinberg. "Unpacking Self-Control." *Child Development Perspectives* 9, no. 1 (2015): 32–37. http://doi.org/10.1111/cdep.12107.

Dunst, Carl, Carol M. Trivette, and Deborah W. Hamby. "Meta-Analysis of Studies Incorporating the Interests of Young Children with Autism Spectrum Disorders into Early Intervention Practice." *Autism Research and Treatment*, no. 2012 (2012): 462531.

Dykens, Elisabeth M., Marisa H. Fisher, Julie Lounds Taylor, Warren Lambert, and Nancy Miodrag. "Reducing Distress in Mothers of Children with Autism and Other Disabilities: A Randomized Trial." *Pediatrics* 134, no. 2 (2014): e454-e463. doi:10.1542/peds.2013-3164.

Eisenberg, Nancy, Claire Hofer, and Julie Vaughan. "Effortful Control and its Socioemotional Consequences." In *Handbook of Emotion Regulation*, edited by James J. Gross, 287–306. New York: Guilford Press, 2007.

Epel, Elissa, Jennifer Daubenmier, Judith T. Moskowitz, Susan Folkman, and Elizabeth Blackburn. "Can Meditation Slow Rate of Cellular Aging? Cognitive Stress, Mindfulness, and Telomeres." *Annals of the New York Academy of Sciences: Longevity, Regeneration, and Optimal Health* 1172, no. 1 (2009): 34–53. doi:10.1111/j.1749-6632.2009.04414.x.

Ferraioli, Suzannah J., and Sandra L. Harris. "Comparative Effects of Mindfulness and Skills-Based Parent Training Programs for Parents of Children with Autism: Feasibility and Preliminary Outcome Data." *Mindfulness* 4, no. 2 (2013): 89–101.

Fields-Meyer, Tom. *Following Ezra.* New York: Penguin Group, 2011.

Foley, Gilbert, and Jane Hochman. *Mental Health in Early Intervention: Achieving Unity in Principles and Practice.* Baltimore: Paul Brookes Publishing Company, 2006.

Fox, Sharon E., Pat Levitt, and Charles A. Nelson. "How the Timing and Quality of Early Experience Influence the Development of Brain Architecture." *Child Development* 81, no. 1 (2010): 28–40.

Freshwater, Dawn. *Counseling Skills for Nurses, Midwives, and Health Visitors.* Philadelphia: Open University Press, 2003.

Geary, Cara, and Susan L. Rosenthal. "Sustained Impact of MBSR on Stress, Well-Being, and Daily Spiritual Experiences for 1 Year in Academic Health Care Employees." *Journal of Alternative and Complementary Medicine* 17, no. 10 (2011): 939–944.

Goleman, David, and Richard J. Davidson. *Altered Traits: Science Reveals How Meditation Changes Your Mind, Brain, and Body*. New York: Random House, 2017.

Green, Jonathan, Andrew Pickles, Greg Pasco, Rachael Bedford, Ming Wai, Mayada Elsabbagh, Vicky Slonims et al. "Randomised Trial of a Parent-Mediated Intervention for Infants at High Risk for Autism: Longitudinal Outcomes to Age 3 Years." *Journal of Child Psychology and Psychiatry* 58, no. 12 (2017): 1330–1340. http://doi.org/10.1111/jcpp.12728.

Green, Shulamite A., Leanna Hernandez, Nim Tottenham, Kate Krasileva, Susan Y. Bookheimer, and Mirella Dapretto. "Neurobiology of Sensory Overresponsivity in Youth with Autism Spectrum Disorders." *JAMA Psychiatry* 72, no. 8 (2015): 778–786. doi: 10.1001/jamapsychiatry.2015.0737.

Greene, Ross. *The Explosive Child*. New York: HarperCollins, 1998.

Greene, Robert R., and Nancy P. Kropf. *Caregiving and Care Sharing: A Life Course Perspective*. Washington, DC: NASW Press, 2014.

Greenland, Susan Kaier. *The Mindful Child*. New York: Simon & Schuster, 2010.

Greenspan, Stanley. *First Feelings: Milestones in the Emotional Development of Your Baby and Child*. New York: Viking Penguin, 1985.

Greenspan, Stanley. *Infancy and Early Childhood: The Practice of Clinical Assessment and Intervention with Emotional and Developmental Challenges*. Madison, CT: International Universities Press, 1992.

Greenspan, Stanley. *The Growth of the Mind: And the Endangered Origins of Intelligence*. Reading, MA: Perseus Books, 1997.

Greenspan, Stanley. *Building Healthy Minds: The Six Experiences that Create Intelligence and Emotional Growth in Babies and Young Children*. Cambridge, MA: Perseus Books, 1999.

Greenspan, Stanley, and Stuart Shanker. *The First Idea: How Symbols, Language, and Intelligence Evolved from Our Primate Ancestors to Modern Humans*. Cambridge, MA: DeCapo Press, 2004.

Greenspan, Stanley, and Serena Wieder. *The Child with Special Needs*. Reading, MA: Perseus Press, 1998.

Greenspan, Stanley, and Serena Wieder, eds. *Diagnostic Manual for Infancy and Early Childhood: Mental Health, Developmental, Regulatory-Sensory Processing, Language and Learning Disorders*. Bethesda, MD: Interdisciplinary Council on Developmental and Learning Disorders, 2005.

Greenspan, Stanley, and Serena Wieder. *Engaging Autism: Using the Floortime Approach to Help Children Relate, Communicate, and Think*. Reading, MA: Perseus Press, 2006.

Greenspan, Stanley, and Serena Wieder. *Infant and Early Childhood Mental Health: A Comprehensive Developmental Approach to Assessment and Intervention*. Washington, DC: American Psychiatric Publishing, 2006.

Greenspan, Stanley, and Serena Wieder. "The Interdisciplinary Council on Developmental and Learning Disorders Diagnostic Manual for Infants and Young Children: An Overview." *Journal of the Canadian Academy of Child and Adolescent Psychiatry* 17, no. 2 (2008): 76–89.

Greenspan, Stanley, Serena Wieder, Robert A. Nover, Alicia F. Lieberman, Reginald S. Lourie, and Mary E. Robinson, eds. *Infants in Multi-Risk Families: Case Studies in Preventive Intervention (Clinical Infant Reports,* No. 3). Madison, CT: International Universities Press, 1987.

Hamlin, Theresa. *Autism and the Stress Effect: A 4-Step Lifestyle Approach to Transform Your Child's Health, Happiness and Vitality*. London: Jessica Kingsley Publishers, 2016.

Hanson, Rick. *Hardwiring Happiness: The New Brain Science of Contentment, Calm and Confidence*. New York: Harmony Books, 2013.

Harris, Nadine Burke. *The Deepest Well: Healing the Long-Term Effects of Childhood Adversity*. New York: Houghton Mifflin Harcourt, 2018.

Hartley Sigan L., Erin T. Barker, Marsha Mailick Seltzer, Frank Floyd, Jan Greenberg, Gael Orsmond, and Daniel Bolt. "The Relative Risk and Timing of Divorce in Families of Children with an Autism Spectrum Disorder." *Journal of Family Psychology* 24, no. 4 (2010): 449–457. doi:10.1037/a0019847.

Harvard University. "Brain architecture." Center on the Developing Child. Accessed August 16, 2018. https://developingchild.harvard.edu/science/key-concepts/brain-architecture/.

Harvard University. "Executive Function & Self-Regulation." Center on the Developing Child. Accessed August 13, 2018. https://developingchild.harvard.edu/science/key-concepts/executive-function/.

Harvard University. "InBrief: The Impact of Early Adversity on Children's Development." Center on the Developing Child. Accessed September 15, 2018. https://developingchild.harvard.edu/resources/inbrief-the-impact-of-early-adversity-on-childrens-development/.

Harvard University. "Resilience." Center on the Developing Child. Accessed August 15, 2018. https://developingchild.harvard.edu/science/key-concepts/resilience/.

Hastings, Richard P., and Helen M. Taunt. "Positive Perceptions in Families of Children with Developmental Disabilities." *American Journal on Mental Retardation* 107, no. 2 (2002): 116–27.

Hatfield, Bridget E., and Amanda P. Williford. "Cortisol Patterns for Young Children Displaying Disruptive Behavior: Links to a Teacher-Child, Relationship-Focused Intervention." *Prevention Science* 18, no. 1 (2017): 40–49. doi:10.1007/s11121-016-0693-9.

Heffron, Mary Claire, and Trudi Murch. *Reflective Supervision and Leadership in Infant and Early Childhood Programs.* Washington, DC: ZERO TO THREE, 2010.

Herring, Sally E., Kylie M. Gray, John Taffe, Bruce Tonge, Deborah J. Sweeney, and Steward L. Einfeld. "Behaviour and Emotional Problems in Toddlers with Pervasive Developmental Disorders and Developmental Delay: Association with Parental Mental Health and Family Functioning." *Journal of Intellectual Disability Research* 50, no. 12 (2006): 874–882. doi:10.1111/j.1365-2788.2006.00904.x.

Higashida, Naoki. *The Reason I Jump.* Translated by Keiko A. Yoshida and David Mitchell. New York: Random House, 2013. First published 2007 in Japan.

Huebner, Dawn, and Bonnie Matthews. *What to Do When You Worry Too Much: A Kid's Guide to Overcoming Anxiety.* Washington, DC: Magination Press, 2006.

Jeans, Laurie M., Rosa Milagros Santos, Daniel J. Laxman, Brent A. McBride, and W. Justin Dyer. "Examining ECLS-B: Maternal Stress and Depressive Symptoms When Raising Children with ASD." *Topics in Early Childhood Special Education* 33, no. 3 (2013): 162–171.

Johanning, Mary Lea. "Premack Principle." In *Encyclopedia of School Psychology*, edited by Steven W. Lee, 365. Thousand Oaks, CA: SAGE Publications, 2005.

Jones, Jessica, and Jennifer Passey. "Family Adaptation, Coping and Resources: Parents of Children with Developmental Disabilities and Behaviour Problems." *Journal of Developmental Disabilities* 11, no. 1 (2004): 25–43.

Jones, Leah, Richard P. Hastings, Vasiliki Totsika, Lisa Keane, and Neisha Rhule. "Child Behavior Problems and Parental Well-Being in Families of Children with Autism: The Mediating Role of Mindfulness and Acceptance." *American Journal on Intellectual and Developmental Disabilities* 119, no. 2 (2014): 171–185.

Kabat-Zinn, Jon. *Full Catastrophe Living: Using the Wisdom of Your Body and Mind to Face Stress, Pain, and Illness.* New York: Random House, 1990.

Karst, Jeffrey S., and Amy Vaughn Van Hecke. "Parent and Family Impact of Autism Spectrum Disorders: A Review and Proposed Model for Intervention Evaluation." *Clinical Child and Family Psychology Review* 15, no. 3 (2012): 247–77. doi:10.1007/s10567-012-0119-6.

Kasari, Connie, Amanda C. Gulsrud, Connie Wong, Susan Kwon, and Jill Locke. "Randomized Controlled Caregiver Mediated Joint Engagement Intervention for Toddlers with Autism." *Journal of Autism and Developmental Disabilities* 40, no. 9 (2010): 1045–1056.

Kasari, Connie, Amanda Gulsrud, Tanya Paparella, Gerhard Hellemann, and Kathleen Berry. "Randomized Comparative Efficacy Study of Parent-Mediated Interventions for Toddlers with Autism." *Journal of Consulting and Clinical Psychology* 83, no. 3 (2015): 554–563.

Kedar, Ido. *Ido in Autismland*. Self-published, 2012.

Keen, Deb, Donna Couzens, Sandy Muspratt, and Sylvia Rodger. "The Effects of a Parent-Focused Intervention for Children with a Recent Diagnosis of Autism Spectrum Disorder on Parenting Stress and Competence." *Research in Autism Spectrum Disorders* 4, no. 2 (2010): 229–241. doi:10.1016/j.rasd.2009.09.009.

Keysers, Christian, and Valeria Gazzola. "Hebbian Learning and Predictive Mirror Neurons for Actions, Sensations and Emotions." *Philosophical Transactions of the Royal Society B: Biological Sciences* 369, no. 1644 (2014): 20130175. http://doi.org/10.1098/rstb.2013.0175.

Kolb, Bryan, Richelle Mychasiuk, Arif Muhammad, Yilin Li, Douglas O. Frost, and Robin Gibb. "Experience and the Developing Prefrontal Cortex." Supplement, *Proceedings of the National Academy of Sciences of the United States of America* 109, no. S2 (2012): 17186–17193. http://doi.org/10.1073/pnas.1121251109.

Koulivand, Peir H., Maryam Khaleghi Ghadiri, and Ali Gorji. "Lavender and the Nervous System." *Evidence-Based Complementary and Alternative Medicine*, no. 2013 (2013): 681304. doi:10.1155/2013/681304.

Kuypers, Leah M. *The Zones of Regulation: A Curriculum Designed to Foster Self-Regulation and Emotional Control*. San Jose, CA: Think Social Publishing, 2011.

Leary, Martha R., and Anne M. Donnellan. *Autism: Sensory-Movement Differences and Diversity*. Cambridge, WI: Cambridge Book Review Press, 2012.

LeDoux, Joseph. "Rethinking the Emotional Brain." *Neuron* 73, no. 4 (2012): 653–676.

LeDoux, Joseph. *Anxious: Using the Brain to Understand and Treat Fear and Anxiety*. New York: Random House, 2015.

Lee, Gloria K. "Parents of Children with High Functioning Autism: How Well Do They Cope and Adjust?" *Journal of Developmental and Physical Disabilities* 21, no. 2 (2009): 93–114. https://doi.org/10.1007/s10882-008-9128-2.

Lickenbrock, Diane M., Naomi Ekas, and Thomas L. Whitman. "Feeling Good, Feeling Bad: Influences of Marital Perceptions of the Child and Marital Adjustment on Well-Being in Mothers of Children with an Autism Spectrum Disorder." *Journal of Autism and Developmental Disorders* 41, no. 7 (2011): 848–858.

Lillas, Connie, and Janiece Turnbull. *Infant/Child Mental Health, Early Intervention, and Relationship-Based Therapies: A Neurorelational Framework for Interdisciplinary Practice*. New York: W.W. Norton, 2009.

Linehan, Marsha M. *DBT® Skills Training Manual*. 2nd ed. New York: Guilford Press, 2014.

Little Flower Yoga. "The School Yoga Project." Accessed August 16, 2018. http://littlefloweryoga.com/programs/the-school-yoga-project.

Lives in the Balance. "About the CPS model." Accessed August 16, 2018. https://www.livesinthebalance.org/about-cps.

Lupien, Sonia J., Maxime Sasseville, Nathe François, Charles-Éduoard Giguère, Janick Boissonneault, Pierrich Plusquellec, Roger Godbout et al. "The *DSM-5*/RDoC Debate on the Future of Mental Health Research: Implication for Studies on Human Stress and Presentation of the Signature Bank." *Stress: The International Journal on the Biology of Stress* 20, no. 1 (2017): 95–111. doi: 10.1080/10253890.2017.1286324.

Malik, Rasheed. "New Data Reveal 250 Preschoolers Are Suspended or Expelled Every Day." *Center for American Progress*, November 6, 2017. https://www.americanprogress.org/issues/early-childhood/news/2017/11/06/442280/new-data-reveal-250-preschoolers-suspended-expelled-every-day/.

McEwen, Bruce S. "Stressed or Stressed Out: What is the Difference?" *Journal of Psychiatry and Neuroscience* 30, no. 5 (2005): 315–318.

McEwen, Bruce S., and Peter J. Gianaros. "Central Role of the Brain in Stress and Adaptation: Links to Socioeconomic Status, Health, and Disease." *Annals of the New York Academy of Sciences* 1186, no. 1 (2010): 190–222. http://doi.org/10.1111/j.1749-6632.2009.05331.x.

McEwen, Bruce S., and Eliot Stellar. "Stress and the Individual. Mechanisms Leading to Disease." *Archives of Internal Medicine* 153, no. 18 (1993): 2093–2101. doi:10.1001/archinte.153.18.2093.

McNerney, Samuel. "A Brief Guide to Embodied Cognition: Why You Are Not Your Brain." *Scientific American*, November 4, 2011. https://blogs.scientificamerican.com/guest-blog/a-brief-guide-to-embodied-cognition-why-you-are-not-your-brain/.

Mehta, Neeta. "Mind/body Dualism: A Critique from a Health Perspective." *Mens Sana Monographs* 9, no. 1 (2011): 202–209. doi:10.4103/0973-1229.77436.

Miller, Lucy Jane. *Sensational Kids: Hope and Help for Children with Sensory Processing Disorder*. New York: Penguin Books, 2007.

Mindsight Institute. "The Mindsight Approach to Well-Being: A Comprehensive Course in Interpersonal Neurobiology." Accessed August 16, 2018. https://www.mindsightinstitute.com/comprehensive-course-in-ipnb.

Miodrag, Nancy, and Robert M. Hodapp. "Chronic Stress and Health Among Parents of Children with Intellectual and Developmental Disabilities." *Current Opinion in Psychiatry* 23, no. 5 (2010): 407–411. doi:10.1097/YCO.0b013e32833a8796.

Moh, Teresa Ailing, and Iliana Magiati. "Factors Associated with Parental Stress and Satisfaction During the Process of Diagnosis of Children with Autism Spectrum Disorders." *Research in Autism Spectrum Disorders* 6, no. 1(2012): 293–303. doi:10.1016/j.rasd.2011.05.011.

National Institute of Mental Health. "PANDAS Questions and Answers." U.S. Department of Health and Human Services. Last modified September 2016. https://www.nimh.nih.gov/health/publications/pandas/index.shtml.

National Institute of Mental Health. "Research Domain Criteria (RDoC)." Accessed July 26, 2018. https://www.nimh.nih.gov/research-priorities/rdoc/index.shtml.

Neff, Kristin. *Self-Compassion: The Proven Power of Being Kind to Yourself*. New York: HarperCollins, 2011.

Neff, Kristin D. "The Self-Compassion Scale is a Valid and Theoretically Coherent Measure of Self-Compassion." *Mindfulness* 7, no. 1 (2016): 264–274.

Neff, Kristin D., and Daniel J. Faso. "Self-Compassion and Well-Being in Parents of Children with Autism." *Mindfulness* 6, no. 4 (2015): 938–947.

Neff, Kristin, and Christopher Germer. *The Mindful Self-Compassion Workbook: A proven way to accept yourself, build inner strength, and thrive*. New York: Guildford Press, 2018.

Nelson, Libby, and Dara Lind. "The School to Prison Pipeline, Explained." *Justice Policy Institute*, February 24, 2015. http://www.justicepolicy.org/news/8775.

Neurorelational Framework Global Communities. "The NRF Manual." Accessed August 16, 2018. https://nrfr2r.com.

Nissenbaum, Michal S., Nona Tollefson, and Matthew Reese. "The Interpretative Conference: Sharing a Diagnosis of Autism with Families." *Focus on Autism and Other Developmental Disabilities* 17, no. 1 (2012): 30-43.

Ogden, Pat. "Polyvagal Theory and Sensorimotor Psychotherapy." In *Clinical Applications of the Polyvagal Theory: The Emergence of Polyvagal-Informed Therapies*, edited by Stephen W. Porges and Deb Dana, 34–49. New York: W.W. Norton, 2018.

Paul, Jeree H., and Maria St. John. *How You Are Is as Important as What You Do*. Washington, DC: ZERO TO THREE: National Center for Infants, Toddlers, and Families, 1998.

Perry, Bruce D. "Maltreatment and the Developing Child: How Early Childhood Experience Shapes Child and Culture." Inaugural lecture presented at the Centre for Children & Families in the Justice System, London, ON, September 23, 2004. http://www.lfcc.on.ca/mccain/perry.pdf.

Perry, Bruce, and Maia Szalavitz. *The Boy Who Was Raised as a Dog: And Other Stories from a Child Psychiatrist's Notebook*. New York: Basic Books, 2017. First published 2006 by Basic Books (New York).

Petcharat, Manika, and Patricia R. Liehr. "Mindfulness Training for Parents of Children with Special Needs: Guidance for Nurses in Mental Health Practice." *Journal of Child and Adolescent Psychiatric Nursing* 30, no. 1 (2017): 35–46. doi:10.1111/jcap.12169.

Picard, Rosalind, and Jonathan Klein. "Computers that Recognise and Respond to User Emotion: Theoretical and Practical Implications." *Interacting with Computers* 14, no. 2 (2002): 89–172.

Pope, Alexander. "An Essay on Criticism: Part II." In *An Essay on Criticism*, lines 215–216. London: W. Lewis, 1711.

Porges, Stephen W. "Articles and Interviews." Accessed July 26, 2018. https://www.stephenporges.com/articles.

Porges, Stephen W. "Neuroception: A Subconscious System for Detecting Threats and Safety." *ZERO TO THREE* 24, no. 5 (2004): 19–24.

Porges, Stephen W. "The Polyvagal Perspective." *Biological Psychology* 74, no. 2 (2007): 116–143. http://doi.org/10.1016/j.biopsycho.2006.06.009.

Porges, Stephen W. "The Polyvagal Theory: New Insights into Adaptive Reactions of the Autonomic Nervous System." Supplement, *Cleveland Clinic Journal of Medicine* 76, no. S2 (2009): S86–S90. doi:10.3949/ccjm.76.s2.17.

Porges, Stephen W. *The Polyvagal Theory: Neurophysiological Foundations of Emotions, Attachment, Communication, and Self-Regulation*. New York: W.W. Norton, 2011.

Porges, Stephen W. "Human Nature and Early Experience." *YouTube* video, 46:38. October 24, 2014. https://www.youtube.com/watch?v=SRTkkYjQ_HU&t=1236s.

Porges, Stephen W. *Associate Manual Safe and Sound Protocol*. Aurora, CO: Integrated Listening Systems, 2018.

Porges, Stephen W. *The Pocket Guide to the Polyvagal Theory: The Transformative Power of Feeling Safe*. New York: W.W. Norton, 2017.

Porges, Stephen W., Olga V. Bazhenova, Elgiz Bal, Nancy Carlson, Yevgeniya Sorokin, Keri J. Heilman, Edwin H. Cook, et al. "Reducing Auditory Hypersensitivities in Autistic Spectrum Disorder: Preliminary Findings Evaluating the Listening Project Protocol." *Frontiers in Pediatrics* 2, no. 80 (2014): 1–10.

Porges, Stephen W., and Deb Dana, eds. *Clinical Applications of the Polyvagal Theory: The Emergence of Polyvagal-Informed Therapies*. New York: W.W. Norton, 2018.

Porges, Stephen W., Matthew Macellaio, Shannon D. Stanfill, Kimberly McCue, Gregory F. Lewis, Emily R. Harden, Mika Handelman, et al. "Respiratory Sinus Arrhythmia and Auditory Processing in Autism: Modifiable Deficits of an Integrated Social Engagement System?" *International Journal of Psychophysiology* 88, no. 3 (2013): 261–270.

Profectum Foundation. "What is DIR and Why Is It Important?" Accessed August 16, 2018. https://profectum.org/about/dir/.

Punwar, Alice J., and Suzannie M. Peloquin. *Occupational Therapy: Principles and Practice*. Philadelphia: Lippincott, 2000.

Quas, Jodi A., Ilona S. Yim, Tim F. Oberlander, David Nordstokke, Marilyn J. Essex, Jeffrey M. Armstrong, Nicole Bush et al. "The Symphonic Structure of Childhood Stress Reactivity: Patterns of Sympathetic, Parasympathetic, and Adrenocortical Responses to Psychological Challenge." *Development and Psychopathology* 26, no. 4 (2014): 963–982. http://dx.doi.org/10.1017/S0954579414000480.

Quintero, Nicole, and Laura Lee McIntyre. "Sibling Adjustment and Maternal Well-Being: An Examination of Families with and Without a Child with an Autism Spectrum Disorder." *Focus on Autism and Other Developmental Disabilities* 25, no. 1 (2010): 37–46.

Robinson, Ricki G. *Autism Solutions: How to Create a Healthy and Meaningful Life for Your Child*. Ontario, Canada: Harlequin, 2011.

Rogers, Sally J., and Geraldine Dawson. *Early Start Denver Model for Young Children with Autism.* New York: Guilford Press, 2010.

Rogers, Stanley J., Laurie A. Vismara, Arnold L. Wagner, Carolyn E. McCormick, Gregory Young, and Sally Ozonoff. "Autism Treatment in the First Year of Life: A Pilot Study of Infant Start, a Parent-Implemented Intervention for Symptomatic Infants." *Journal of Autism and Developmental Disorders* 44, no. 12 (2014): 2981–2995. doi:10.1007/s10803-014-2202-y.

Roggman, Lori, Lisa Boyce, and Mark Innocenti. *Developmental Parenting: A Guide for Early Childhood Practitioners.* Baltimore: Brookes Publishing, 2008.

Rozin, Paul, and Edward B. Royzman. "Negativity Bias, Negativity Dominance, and Contagion." *Personality and Social Psychology Review* 5, no. 4 (2001): 296–320.

Rutter, Michael. *Genes and Behavior: Nature-Nurture Interplay Explained.* Maiden, MA: Blackwell Publishing, 2006.

Satir, V., Banmen, J., Gerber, J., & Gomori, M. *The Satirmodel: Family therapy and Beyond.* Palo Alto, CA: Science and Behavior Books, 1991.

Schore, Allan N. *Affect Dysregulation and Disorders of the Self.* New York: W.W. Norton, 2003.

Selye, Hans. "A Syndrome Produced by Diverse Nocuous Agents." *Nature* 138, no. 3479 (1936): 32.

Sesame Street in Communities. "Breathe." Accessed August 16, 2018. https://sesamestreetincommunities.org/activities/breathe-bundle/.

Shahmoon-Shanok, Rebecca. "Reflective Supervision for an Integrated Model: What, Why and How?" In *Mental Health in Early Intervention: Achieving Unity in Principles and Practice*, edited by Gilbert Foley and Jane Hochman, 343–381. San Francisco: Jossey-Bass, 2006.

Shanker, Stuart. *Self-Reg: How to Help Your Child (and You) Break the Stress Cycle and Successfully Engage with Life.* New York: Penguin Books, 2016.

Shonkoff, Jack P., and Deborah A. Phillips, eds. *From Neurons to Neighborhoods: The Science of Early Childhood Development.* Washington, DC: National Academy Press, 2000.

Siegel, Daniel J. *The Developing Mind: Toward a Neurobiology of Interpersonal Experience.* New York: Guilford Press, 1999.

Siegel, Daniel J., and Tina Payne Bryson. *The Whole Brain Child.* New York: Random House, 2011.

Siegel, Daniel J., and Tina Payne Bryson. *No Drama Discipline.* New York: Random House, 2014.

Silver, Rebecca B., Jeffrey R. Measelle, Jeffrey M. Armstrong, and Marilyn J. Essex. "Trajectories of Classroom Externalizing Behavior: Contributions of Child Characteristics, Family Characteristics, and the Teacher-Child Relationship During The School Transition." *Journal of School Psychology* 43, no. 1 (2005): 39–60.

Solomon, Richard, Laurie A. Van Egeren, Gerald Mahoney, Melissa S. Quon Huber, and Perri Zimmerman. "PLAY Project Home Consultation Intervention Program for Young Children with Autism Spectrum Disorders: A Randomized Controlled Trial." *Journal of Developmental and Behavioral Pediatrics* 35, no. 8 (2014): 475–485.

Sroufe, L. Allen. "Attachment and Development: A Prospective, Longitudinal Study from Birth to Adulthood." *Attachment and Human Development* 7, no. 4 (2005): 349–367.

STAR Institute. "STAR Institute for Sensory Processing Disorder." Accessed August 14, 2018. https://www.spdstar.org.

Substance Abuse and Mental Health Services Administration. "National Center for Trauma-Informed Care and Alternatives to Seclusion and Restraint (NCTIC)." Updated October 26, 2015. https://www.samhsa.gov/nctic/about.

Tarullo, Amanda R., Jelena Obradović, and Megan R. Gunnar. "Self-Control and the Developing Brain." *ZERO TO THREE* 29, no. 3 (2009): 31–37.

Taylor, Ann Gill, Lisa E. Goehler, Daniel I. Galper, Kim E. Innes, and Cheryl Bourguignon. "Top-Down and Bottom-Up Mechanisms in Mind/body Medicine: Development of an Integrative Framework for

Psychophysiological Research." *EXPLORE: The Journal of Science and Healing* 6, no. 1 (2010): 29–41. http://doi.org/10.1016/j.explore.2009.10.004.

Taylor, Renee R., Sun Wook Lee, Gary Kielhofner, and Manali Ketkar. "Therapeutic Use of Self: A Nationwide Survey of Practitioners' Attitudes and Experiences." *American Journal of Occupational Therapy* 63, no. 2 (2009): 198–207.

Thaut, Michael H. "A Music Therapy Treatment Model for Autistic Children." *Music Therapy Perspectives* 1, no. 4 (1984): 7–13. https://doi.org/10.1093/mtp/1.4.7.

The Academy of Neurologic Music Therapy. "Neurologic Music Therapy." Accessed August 17, 2018. https://nmtacademy.co/home/clinic/.

The American Heritage Idioms Dictionary. "Behavior." In *The American Heritage Idioms Dictionary*. Accessed July 26, 2018. http://www.dictionary.com/browse/behavior?s=t.

Torres, Elisabeth B., and Caroline Whyatt, eds. *Autism: The Movement-Sensing Perspective*. Boca Raton, FL: CRC Press, 2018.

Tronick, Ed. *The Neurobehavioral and Social Emotional Behavior of Infants and Children*. New York: W.W. Norton, 2007.

Turner, Lauren M., and Wendy L. Stone. "Variability in Outcome for Children with an ASD Diagnosis at Age 2." *Journal of Child Psychology and Psychiatry* 48, no. 8 (2007): 793–802.

U.S. National Library of Medicine. "What is Precision Medicine?" Genetics Home Reference. Updated September 25, 2018. https://ghr.nlm.nih.gov/primer/precisionmedicine/definition.

van der Helm, Els, and Matthew P. Walker. "Overnight Therapy? The Role of Sleep in Emotional Brain Processing." *Psychological Bulletin* 135, no. 5 (2009): 731–748. doi:10.1037/a0016570.

van der Kolk, Bessel. *The Body Keeps the Score: Brain, Mind, and Body in the Healing of Trauma*. New York: Penguin Books, 2014.

van Steensel, Francisca J. A., and Emma J. Heeman. "Anxiety Levels in Children with Autism Spectrum Disorder: A Meta-Analysis." *Journal of Child and Family Studies* 26, no. 7 (2017): 1753–1767. http://doi.org/10.1007/s10826-017-0687-7.

Vygotsky, Lev S. *Mind in Society: The Development of Higher Psychological Processes*. Edited by Michael Cole, Vera John-Steiner, Sylvia Scribner, and Ellen Souberman. Cambridge, Massachusetts: Harvard University Press, 1978.

Waller, Erika M., and Amanda J. Rose. "Brief Report: Adolescents' Co-Rumination with Mothers, Co-Rumination with Friends, and Internalizing Symptoms." Journal of Adolescence 36, no. 2 (2013): 429–433. doi: 10.1016/j.adolescence.2012.12.006.

White, Nia, and Richard P. Hastings. "Social and Professional Support for Parents of Adolescents with Severe Intellectual Disabilities." *Journal of Applied Research in Intellectual Disabilities* 17, no. 3 (2004): 181–190.

Wieder, Serena. "PLAY: The Window into the Child's Emotional Experiences." Profectum Foundation. Accessed August 16, 2018. https://profectum.org/wp-content/uploads/2015/03/PLAY-HANDOUT.pdf.

Wieder, Serena, and Stanley Greenspan. "Developmental Pathways to Mental Health: The DIR Model for Comprehensive Approaches to Assessment and Intervention." In *The Handbook of Training and Practice in Infant and Preschool Mental Health*, edited by Karen Moran Finello, 377–401. San Francisco: Jossey-Bass, 2005.

Wieder, Serena, and Harry Wachs. *Visual/Spatial Portals to Thinking, Feeling and Movement: Advancing Competencies and Emotional Development in Children with Learning and Autism Spectrum Disorders*. Mendham, NJ: Profectum Foundation, 2012.

Winnicott, Donald W. "The Theory of the Parent-Infant Relationship." In *The Maturational Processes and the Facilitating Environment*, 37–55. New York: International Universities Press, 1960.

Yogman, Michael, Andrew Garner, Jeffrey Hutchinson, Kathy Hirsh-Pasek, and Robert Michnick Golinkoff. "The

Power of Play: A Pediatric Role in Enhancing Development in Young Children." *Pediatrics* 142, no. 3 (2018): e20182058.

Zeltzer, Lonnie K., and Christina Blackett Schlank. *Conquering Your Child's Chronic Pain*. New York: HarperCollins, 2005.

ZERO TO THREE. "National Parent Survey Overview and Key Insights." Updated June 6, 2016. https://www.zerotothree.org/resources/1424-national-parent-survey-overview-and-key-insights.

ZERO TO THREE. *Diagnostic Classification of Mental Health and Developmental Disorders of Infancy and Early Childhood, Revised (DC:0-3R)*. Washington, DC: ZERO TO THREE, 2005.

ZERO TO THREE. "Toddlers and Self-Control: A Survival Guide for Parents." Updated October 3, 2016. https://www.zerotothree.org/resources/1603-toddlers-and-self-control-a-survival-guide-for-parents.

ZERO TO THREE. "Parent Survey Reveals Expectation Gap for Parents of Young Children." Updated October 13, 2016. https://www.zerotothree.org/resources/1612-parent-survey-reveals-expectation-gap-for-parents-of-young-children.

Index